One regrettable gap in Christian theology is the controversial issue of the potential salvific value of the "general self-revelation" of the true God to all peoples. Dr. Jalal's contextual and scholarly study of the work of the Holy Spirit, both within the church and outside the church, gives us a good lead to further exploring this issue. His insights pose before us the challenging imperative to be positive and open-minded to see the work of the Holy Spirit in all humankind.

Christian mission is not us giving Christ to others, but Christ giving us to others to introduce to them the "unknown God," who works in them and clarifies his purposes for them. This book is an indispensable read not only for professional missionaries, but also for all of us who are sent with the gospel of Christ into our world of religious pluralism.

Saphir Athyal, PhD
Former Vice Chairman, Lausanne Committee
Founder-Chairman, Asia Theological Association
Former Principal, Union Biblical Seminary, Pune, India

Dr. Jalal's *The Wider Work of the Holy Spirit: An Indian Theology of Religious Experience* is an essential resource for Christian workers navigating pluralistic societies. It offers invaluable insights into building harmonious relationships in multicultural settings and presents a robust theology of religious experience that remains faithful to biblical revelation while embracing cultural relevance. This work equips us to engage respectfully and effectively with individuals from various faith traditions in an increasingly diverse world. It reminds us of the universal truths that unite us and emphasizes the profound role of the Holy Spirit in diverse religious experiences. I highly recommend this book to all who seek to promote understanding, respect, and harmony in today's complex and pluralistic societies.

George Samuel, PhD
President, Olive Theological Institute, Kerala, India
Director, Value Education Trust, Kerala, India

The Wider Work of the Holy Spirit

An Indian Theology of Religious Experience

Jalal S. L.

© 2024 Jalal S. L.

Published 2024 by Langham Academic
An imprint of Langham Publishing
www.langhampublishing.org

Langham Publishing and its imprints are a ministry of Langham Partnership

Langham Partnership
PO Box 296, Carlisle, Cumbria, CA3 9WZ, UK
www.langham.org

ISBNs:
978-1-83973-938-5 Print
978-1-78641-102-0 ePub
978-1-78641-103-7 PDF

Jalal S. L. has asserted his right under the Copyright, Designs and Patents Act, 1988 to be identified as the Author of this work.

All rights reserved. No part of this publication may be reproduced, stored in a retrieval system or transmitted, in any form or by any means, electronic, mechanical, photocopying, recording or otherwise, without the prior written permission of the publisher or the Copyright Licensing Agency.

Requests to reuse content from Langham Publishing are processed through PLSclear. Please visit www.plsclear.com to complete your request.

Scripture quotations marked (NIV) are taken from the Holy Bible, New International Version®, NIV®. Copyright © 1973, 1978, 1984, 2011 by Biblica, Inc.™ Used by permission of Zondervan.

Scripture quotations marked (NKJV) are taken from the New King James Version. Copyright © 1982 by Thomas Nelson, Inc. Used by permission. All rights reserved.

Scripture quotations marked (NRSV) are taken from the New Revised Standard Version Bible, copyright © 1989 National Council of the Churches of Christ in the United States of America. Used by permission. All rights reserved.

British Library Cataloguing-in-Publication Data
A catalogue record for this book is available from the British Library

ISBN: 978-1-83973-938-5

Cover & Book Design: projectluz.com

Langham Partnership actively supports theological dialogue and an author's right to publish but does not necessarily endorse the views and opinions set forth here or in works referenced within this publication, nor can we guarantee technical and grammatical correctness. Langham Partnership does not accept any responsibility or liability to persons or property as a consequence of the reading, use or interpretation of its published content.

Contents

Acknowledgements ix
Foreword xi
Introduction 1
    Issues of the Spirit in Religious Experience 2
    Objectives of the Study 4
    Scope and Limitation 4
    Method and Procedure 6

Chapter 1 9
    Religious Experience and Its Relevance
    1.1 Religious Experience: An Understanding 9
        1.1.1 Religious Experience in Religion 11
        1.1.2 Religious Experience in Christian Theology 13
    1.2 Religious Experience: An Understanding of Its Nature 14
        1.2.1 Positive Results 14
        1.2.2 Cultural Alliance 15
        1.2.3 Mysterious Nature 17
    1.3 The Spirit and General Revelation 19
    1.4 The Spirit and Religious Experience 21
    1.5 Conclusion 24

Chapter 2 25
    A Biblical Understanding of Religious Experience
    2.1 The Spirit: Breath of God and Inner Knowledge 25
    2.2 Spiritual Experience outside God's Community 28
        2.2.1 The Old Testament 28
        2.2.2 The New Testament 30
    2.3 Means of Spiritual Experience 32
        2.3.1 Culture 33
        2.3.2 Human Philosophy 34
        2.3.3 Religiosity of People 35
        2.3.4 Moral Character 36
    2.4 Role of the Spirit in Spiritual Experience 38
        2.4.1 Mystery 38
        2.4.2 Imperfection 39
        2.4.3 The Value of Human Response 40
    2.5 Conclusion 41

Chapter 3 43
Swami Vivekananda's Understanding of Religious Experience
   3.1 Life of Swami Vivekananda (1863–1902)..............................44
   3.2 Religious Principles of Vivekananda....................................47
   3.3 Religious Experience and the "Ideal Man".........................49
      3.3.1 Knowledge...50
      3.3.2 Self-Realization of Truth 50
      3.3.3 Divine Bliss of Perfection 52
      3.3.4 Union with the Absolute 53
   3.4 Religious Experience and Ideal Society...............................55
      3.4.1 Social Development and Spirituality 56
      3.4.2 Role of Human Effort..59
      3.4.3 Yoga as a Spiritual Discipline.....................................60
      3.4.4 Moral Concept in Perfection 62
   3.5 Exploring Vivekananda's Understanding of the Spirit.....64
   3.6 Summary...68

Chapter 4 73
Religious Experience: The Understanding of Indian Theologians
   4.1 Life of Pandipeddi Chenchiah (1886–1959).........................74
      4.1.1 Indian Heritage and Theology...................................75
      4.1.2 Contextualizing the Holy Spirit in Indian Heritage...........77
      4.1.3 Functions of the Holy Spirit in Religious Experience........81
      4.1.4 Spiritual Discipline and Yoga....................................87
      4.1.5 Ethical Values and Human Beings 89
      4.1.6 Summary 91
   4.2 Life of S. J. Samartha (1920–2001) 94
      4.2.1 Theology in Religious Pluralism................................95
      4.2.2 Unity in a Pluralistic World: A Divine Mystery 98
      4.2.3 The Holy Spirit in Other Religions.........................100
      4.2.4 Religious Experience in Religion 104
      4.2.5 Discerning the Spirit 106
      4.2.6 Interfaith Dialogue 112
      4.2.7 Summary 114
   4.3 Chenchiah and Samartha on Religious Experience: An Evaluation...117
      4.3.1 The Role of the Spirit in Theology...........................117
      4.3.2 Religious Experience and Human Tradition 118
      4.3.3 Transformation 118
      4.3.4 Union 118

Chapter 5 121
   Religious Experience: The Understanding of Western Theologians
      5.1 Jurgen Moltmann (1926–2024) 122
         5.1.1 The Spirit in Human Life..125
         5.1.2 God's Initiative and Spiritual Experience 128
         5.1.3 The Spirit in the Social Life of People..........................129
         5.1.4 Spiritual Experience: God's Revelation.........................135
         5.1.5 Summary 137
      5.2 Kirsteen Kim (1959–) 139
         5.2.1 Spirituality as a Present Priority 139
         5.2.2 Pneumatology in the Indian Context 142
         5.2.3 Terminological Interpretation of the Holy Spirit in
                Hinduism...145
         5.2.4 Functions of the Holy Spirit..148
         5.2.5 Summary 154
      5.3 Moltmann and Kim on Religious Experience: An Evaluation ...156
         5.3.1 Significance of Pneumatology..156
         5.3.2 Need for Transformation 156
         5.3.3 Religious Experience and Hinduism 157
         5.3.4 General Revelation 158

Chapter 6 159
   A Pneumatological Understanding of Hindu Religious Experience
      6.1 Experience 160
      6.2 Culture 164
      6.3 Church 166
      6.4 Tradition 168
      6.5 Two Biblical Qualifiers..172
      6.6 Pneumatology of Religious Experience: Conclusion...................174

Glossary of Hindi/Sanskrit Words 179

Selected Bibliography... 181

Acknowledgements

All glory and honour goes to my God, whose love and grace have inspired and guided me. Without his divine guidance and the empowering work of the Holy Spirit, this book – *The Wider Work of the Holy Spirit: An Indian Theology of Religious Experience* – would not have been possible. I am deeply grateful to a few remarkable individuals who played pivotal roles in the successful completion of this book. First, I extend my heartfelt gratitude and love to my esteemed professor, Dr. Robert K. Johnston, senior professor of theology and culture at Fuller Theological Seminary, California, USA. His captivating lectures sparked multiple questions in my mind during my theological studies and, eventually, formed the foundation of this work. Dr. Johnston later became my PhD mentor, and his profound insights and encouragement have significantly enriched this book's content, and greatly impacted Christian theology in the Indian context. I am indebted to him for graciously contributing a foreword that emphasizes the relevance of the book's topic.

I wish to express my sincere appreciation to Dr. George Samuel, president of Olive Theological Institute (OTI), whose unwavering encouragement and genuine desire for my personal and academic growth motivated me to push forward. His thoughtful comments and support were invaluable in shaping this work. Thanks also to Mrs. Ann Elizabeth Samuel, director of OTI, for her active support, encouragement, and invaluable guidance throughout the writing process. Her dedication to nurturing and fostering scholarly endeavours was instrumental in bringing this book to fruition.

I am so grateful to my beloved wife, Hepsy George, whose sacrificial work and unwavering support stood as a steadfast pillar behind me throughout this project. Her love and understanding made this journey possible. I am deeply grateful to my loving kids – who sometimes had to bear with my absence while I worked tirelessly to complete this book – for their understanding and patience.

Last but not least, I am also indebted to the editorial board of Langham Publishing for recognizing the significance of this work and taking the initiative to publish it, thereby providing a platform for its wider dissemination.

Foreword

In *God's Wider Presence* (2014), I ask this question: What is the inherent value of God's wider revelation, of everyday experiences of the divine presence that prove revelatory? Given my particular interests, I focus in particular on those encounters with God in our everyday lives through the arts. But whether through conscience, creation, or human creativity, such actual experiences of the numinous prove to be transformative moments. While not directly related to our salvation and occurring outside the church and with no direct reference to either Jesus Christ or Scripture, such encounters often prove foundational to life.

As I ended my book, I offered a brief closing case study, a theology of religions. Given our world's shrinking borders, we have a new awareness of our neighbours, including their religions. How are we to account theologically for their spiritual insights, values, and beliefs? Could these be the work of the Spirit? What are we to say about the encounters that others claim to have with God? Are they all bogus? If, as Jesus says, we shall know others by their fruits, the answer would seem to be "No."

Such questions have not often been asked in the history of Christian theology. Historically, few theologians have viewed the insights and experiences of those in other religions as important or have seen them in a positive light. The early church wanted to separate itself from paganism. Aquinas might have used Aristotle, but he had little patience with nonbelievers. Wanting to purify the church, Luther's concerns were elsewhere. Calvin's comments about other religions were christologically centred and soteriologically rooted. It was not until the Enlightenment that things began to change. Towards the end of his life, Wesley, for example, believed that God may have taught those in other religions a measure of true religion by an "inward voice." But, until the last seventy-five years, few have followed up Wesley's inquiries.

Even now, much of a contemporary theology of religions within Protestantism still tends to frame the questions soteriologically. It has been mainly the Roman Catholics who have turned pneumatologically, rather than to soteriology in dealing with questions of revelation. It is they who have typically demonstrated a growing respect for the presence and activity of the Holy Spirit in the religious and spiritual lives of non-Christians. But Protestants are now beginning to join the conversation.

Here is the importance of *The Wider Work of the Holy Spirit: An Indian Theology of Religious Experience*. Jalal, in his book, has not simply written theoretically about a theology of religions. He has, instead, written specifically out of his Indian experience about the Spirit's presence in Hinduism. Such test cases are absolutely crucial for the development of a full-orbed theology of religions.

Jalal is certainly right to anchor his argument in the wider work of the Holy Spirit. For all humanity is blessed with revelation. God's gracious presence is a given in every context, even in the religious life of non-Christians. The Spirit's gracious presence extends towards all humanity for, in the words of the Nicene Creed, he is "the Lord, the giver of life." Unfortunately, even in India, Christians have looked at the Hindu religion and asked, "What the hell is going on? Jalal has helpfully reframed the question, asking instead, "What in heaven's name is happening?" How you frame your question is important!

Robert K. Johnston
Senior Professor of Theology and Culture,
Fuller Theological Seminary, California, USA
August 2023

Introduction

> "It is the glory of God to conceal a matter; to search out a matter is the glory of kings" (Prov 25:2 NIV) – a truth set by God so that people would seek him and perhaps reach out for him and find him (Acts 17:27).

People are ardent about knowing the truth. They search for it and end up with various principles and moral lessons. The aftermath of such a search is the origin of many religions: Hinduism, Buddhism, Jainism, Islam, and Sikhism. Notably, the glory of these religious founders lay in their unusual spiritual experiences and the positive results they experienced. However, people following such religions and traditions do not reach the real God. At this juncture, the genuine heart seeks to ponder the relevance of spiritual experience and how far it reveals the true God that Christians know and love.

Christians typically believe that people's religious experiences are of two types. Some experiences lead people to know the true God, while others only lead adherents to continue their religious rituals and cultural practices. But there are numerous living testimonies that serve as examples of the distinct ways in which human experiences lead people to perceive spiritual truth. The revelatory presence of the invisible God is perceived in a wide variety of ways everywhere in the world, without any discrimination based on human culture, tradition, experience, or religion. But Christians who hold to this binary understanding – mistakenly believing that by doing so they are giving priority to biblical doctrines – often ignore, confuse, or misunderstand the natural work of God in other religions. If all beauty, truth, and goodness come from God through the Spirit – as Christians have claimed for two thousand years – does this not also include aspects of truth, beauty, and goodness found in other religions? How can we understand God's presence within other religions or even within culture, which is a human construct?

Comprehending – in a theological sense – the positive results of various religious experiences will help Christians to move beyond their isolation and will lead to a mutual understanding between Christians and their neighbouring religious people. For instance, Hinduism, one of the Indian religions, is packed with a wealth of spiritual experiences, and its origin, philosophy, moral teachings, visions, and practices all reveal the importance of spiritual activities. Hindus like Swami Vivekananda – who had positive spiritual experiences – authentically contributed valuable religious teachings about Hinduism, and some of these Hindu religious teachings connect well with what is found in the biblical revelation of God. Moreover, the testimony of Hindu converts and Christian theologians supports the claim of God's revelatory presence in Hinduism. Understanding the work of the Spirit outside the church can help Christians to develop a more positive attitude towards their Hindu neighbours and show Christians that they can even learn from their non-Christian neighbours. In addition, recognizing a possible spiritual presence in the religious experience of others can help Christians to find common ground for communicating the gospel to those outside the church.

In their study of God's relationship with other religious traditions, Christians have generally focused on Christology and soteriology. This single focus on matters of salvation has caused them to discuss other religions using terms like exclusivism, inclusivism, pluralism, and syncretism. Such language may have unnecessarily narrowed their theology and been detrimental to the important question of how God's revelation might be found in other religious traditions. Thus, this study focuses on the work of the Spirit in other religious experiences with a view to constructing a theology of religious experience in our multireligious context.

Issues of the Spirit in Religious Experience

In his book *God's Wider Presence*, Robert K. Johnston chronicles how people experience God's general revelation through creation, conscience, and culture (including the religious reflections of non-covenant people). His book helps people to widen their understanding of God's general revelation by seeing this revelation in and through every aspect of human life in which they are engaged. Here, the religious aspects of culture are seen as relevant to the discussion because of their indisputable relationship to human spiritual life. In Christian theology, recognizing and interpreting the positive effects of religious experience in non-Christian religious traditions is an issue that has not been adequately addressed.

Johnston narrates that when people report encountering God, it is not through mountains, or any sense of morality, or a profound musical piece that they receive this revelation but, rather, through God's Spirit, who is there in that moment and in that experience. Only God reveals God, and he chooses to do so through his creation and people. If this is true, then it is not another religion, whether its beliefs or its practices, that functions as a source of truth and goodness but the Spirit who speaks in and through those religions, which leads to a mysterious work of the Spirit in the religious experience of non-Christian people. An understanding of this will enable us to explain more clearly the positive effects of religious experience in Hindu religious traditions from a Christian theological perspective.

General revelation refers to God's revelation to all people everywhere. Many theologians have explored the general revelation of God to people. Some significant theological studies on general revelation are relevant to our topic. Thomas Aquinas discusses general revelation as the knowledge of God that can be attained through the natural world and human reason (*Summa Theologica*, 1485). Augustine of Hippo reflects on faith and recognizing God's presence and truth in the created world (*Confessions*, 397–400 AD). Karl Barth emphasizes the concept of God's revelation in Jesus Christ as the centre of his theology but also acknowledges the importance of general revelation in God's self-disclosure (*Church Dogmatics*, 1969). John Calvin discusses general revelation as the knowledge of God that is evident in creation and available to all people (*Institutes of the Christian Religion*, 1561). Friedrich Schleiermacher explores the idea of God's presence in all aspects of human life and experience (*On Religion: Speeches to Its Cultured Despisers*, 1799). Paul Tillich discusses the concept of God's self-manifestation in both special and general revelation (*Dynamics of Faith*, 1957). Karl Rahner explores the notion of God's revelation as an ongoing and universal process, reaching all people through various means (*Foundations of Christian Faith*, 1982). Reinhold Niebuhr examines general revelation as the manifestation of God's moral law in the conscience of all human beings (*The Nature and Destiny of*

Man, 1996). Jurgen Moltmann discusses the hope and presence of God in the midst of human suffering and suffering in the natural world (*Theology of Hope*, 1993). Wolfhart Pannenberg describes general revelation as the knowledge of God accessible to all people through the natural world and human reason (*Systematic Theology*, 1988). Even though such distinct studies have been done within Christianity in relation to God's general revelation, many Christians misunderstand or are confused about the positive results found in other religious traditions. Therefore, an authentic study of religious experience and its association with God's work needs to be explored to help Christians to appreciate the positive experiences found in other religions and, instead of caricaturing their spirituality, to adopt a new approach to their neighbouring faiths. The question that becomes relevant here is this: How might we, as Christians, understand how Hindu religious experiences might connect with the general revelation of God?

Objectives of the Study

The objectives of this book are:

1. To explain the positive results of the Hindu religious experience from a Christian theological perspective
2. To investigate how God's revelatory presence might be experienced in India within Hinduism
3. To help Christians be more open-minded and effective in their communication with neighbouring faiths
4. To explain how Hindu religious experiences connect with God's general revelation through the work of the Spirit
5. To develop a constructive Christian theology of religious experience in the Indian context in the light of a biblical and theological understanding of Hindu religious experience

Scope and Limitation

This book is designed to expand the theology of religions in the Indian context; people's unique spiritual experiences within their religions. However, the book does not seek to o explore the terms "religious experience" or "spiritual experience"; rather, these terms simply represent human experience beyond the ordinary – that is, something "more" – which people receive through the influence of their religious tradition and faith. Such experiences are represented as "spiritual experiences" because they affect the inner life of a human being and represented as "religious experiences" because they stem from interaction with religion. Accordingly, the focus of this study is on how to understand theologically those spiritual experiences – which are also religious experiences – that happen in and through Hinduism. Therefore, chapter 1 includes a brief explanation about the interchangeable use of the terms "religious experience" and "spiritual experience." The "positive results" of such experiences will include *anything* connected to the divine nature all goodness, beauty, truth, and justice.

To construct a theology of religious experience in the Indian context, we will investigate a selection of appropriate biblical passages, selected aspects of the Hindu religious tradition, and selected contributions by both Indian and Western theologians. The selected portions from the Old and New Testaments that are used for biblical discussion in this study speak clearly to the issue and keep the project manageable and authentic. Similarly, a special focus is given to the concept of Indian religious experience in the thought of Swami Vivekananda even though India adopts different religious traditions and philosophies and even Hinduism includes a wide range of teachings by different adherents, including the insights of different gurus and the beliefs of lower social castes such as Dalits). Explaining Vivekananda's ideology or "theology" in regard to this focus helps us to answer our question. Vivekananda's principles help us to understand Hindu religious experience and his oft quoted philosophical thoughts on Hinduism emphasize his relevance and importance to our learning.

The theological discussion is carried out in conjunction with four Christian theologians: P. Chenchiah, one of the leading classical theologians of India during the twentieth century; S. J. Samartha, a contemporary theologian whose contribution includes relevant dialogue with other religious faiths; Jurgen Moltmann, one of the leading theologians of the last fifty years, who contributed much in the area of pneumatology; and Kirsteen Kim, an evangelical who worked in India and promoted Christian understanding of the Spirit in India. This discussion helps to build a constructive theology by bringing together biblical insight, careful analysis of Hindu thought and practice, and the insights of both Indian theologies and Western understandings of the Spirit. In doing so, this book attempts to describe the contours of the Spirit's work in God's revelation in the Indian context.

Method and Procedure

The book uses qualitative methods to construct a theology of religious experience in the Indian context. Historical-critical methods are used to analyse selected biblical passages. Primary sources have been used wherever possible, along with key secondary writings, in seeking to understand two Indian theologians – P. Chenchiah and S. J. Samartha – two Western theologians – Kirsteen Kim and Jurgen Moltmann – and the Hindu philosopher Swami Vivekananda. The secondary sources used in this study are commentaries, books, and articles published in various periodicals, journals, encyclopedias, websites, and other allied publications. In this study's critical and analytical observations, there has been a focus on the interaction between the insights of the Christian theologians mentioned above and the work of the Spirit in Hinduism. This study of constructive Christian theology focuses on the Hindu religious experience and is designed to be interdisciplinary. The analysis and construction of theology have taken into consideration cultural, biblical, and theological perspectives.

This book consists of six chapters. The first chapter, which deals with the relevance and distinct features of religious experience, is intended to help readers to understand the work of the Spirit in religious experience, especially in Hinduism in India. Claiming the presence of the Spirit in religious experience will be foreign to many readers. So, the book will then explore this reality from a biblical perspective. Hence, the second chapter is an inquiry into the Spirit's connection with people's religious experience based on the Bible. This chapter will discuss several biblical passages to show the Spirit's presence as both the breath of God and the source of inner divine knowledge in all human beings. As such, the Spirit will be viewed as the agent for authentic spiritual experience. Without consideration of cultural differentiation, this work of the Spirit is illustrated biblically through the wide array of God's provision – visions, spiritual wisdom, divine messages, and revelations outside Israel and the church.

If there is biblical support for the revelation of God outside the church and through his Spirit, then it is possible that the Spirit's work might also be found in Indian religion. Thus, the next chapter is a detailed study of Swami Vivekananda, one of the leading Hindu philosophers, and his understanding of religious experience. We consider how Vivekananda understands that a person might be made an ideal (perfect) man through religious experiences. As an outcome of religious experience, he expects men to become perfect, acquire knowledge, realize the truth, achieve the ability to do good works, and achieve self-realization. All these positive results might be filtered through the presence of the Spirit in life.

Vivekananda's teachings on religious experiences resemble those of Christian leaders in both Eastern and Western countries. So, the next two chapters discuss the parallel understandings of religious experience by two Eastern theologians – P. Chenchiah and S. J. Samartha – and two Western Christian theologians – Jurgen Moltmann and Kirsteen Kim. Through presenting these Christian theologians' distinct understandings of spiritual experience, this study argues that the Spirit of God gives a variety of experiences – for example, leading us to obtain new life, establishing harmony among people, bringing reconciliation, and providing a blessed hope – that help people to love God and to love their neighbours. The Holy Spirit functions as an agent for religious experience, and the same Spirit helps people to understand God's will. The goal of this study is to frame an Indian theology of general revelation based on the role of the Holy Spirit in life, including the role of the Spirit in Hindu thought and experience. This enlightens our theological reflections of how the Spirit is present in the Hindu religious experience and what this might mean for Christians.

CHAPTER 1

Religious Experience and Its Relevance

In 1983, the World Council of Churches (WCC), at its sixth assembly in Vancouver, Canada, declared, "While affirming the uniqueness of the birth, life, death and resurrection of Jesus to which we bear witness, we recognize God's creative work in the religious experience of people of other faiths."[1] Here in one of the draft reports to present to all their delegates; the WCC urged the Christian church to consider the work of God in other religious faiths. This statement ignites a hope of reconciliation between different religious faiths through people's religious experiences. This topic is of particular relevance in the Indian context, which is multireligious. Using religious experience as the focal point, we will construct a Christian theology of religion, observing Hindu religious experiences through the spectacles of the Bible and Christian theologians as they describe the Spirit's engagement in human experiences. This study helps to probe new avenues for a Christian theology of religion by focusing on the Holy Spirit in creation, culture, and religion.

1.1 Religious Experience: An Understanding

The term "religious experience" was first used by William James (1842–1907) in his Gifford Lectures on Natural Religion of 1901 and 1902; subsequently, James published a book titled *The Varieties of Religious Experience*,[2] in which he explained more than three thousand types of human experiences.

---

1. WCC draft report, quoted in Johnston, *God's Wider Presence*, 200–201.
2. William James, *The varieties of religious experience: A study in Human Nature* (United States: Longmans Green & Co, 1902).

9

Marianne Rankin, in her remarkable book *Religious and Spiritual Experience*, refines James's work, characterizing thirteen different types of personal experiences: Religious Experience, Spiritual Experience, Transcendental Experience, Paranormal Experience, Exceptional Human Experience (EHE), Peak Experience, Limit Experience, Ecstasy, Cosmic Consciousness, Mystical Experience, Absolute Unitary Being, Out of the Body Experience (OBE), and Near Death Experience (NDE).[3] What is special about all these types of experiences is that some unusual occurrence takes places in a person's life. In relation to religious and spiritual experience, people reach a mystical state of consciousness. According to William James, "Personal religious experience has its root and centre in mystical states of consciousness."[4] His understanding of the mysticism present in spiritual experience, represented as the mystical states of consciousness, points to the relationship between religious experience and people's spiritual experience.

Religious experiences connect with religions; if an experience relates to a person's spiritual life, it is considered a spiritual experience. Religions play a significant role in developing the personality, including a person's spiritual life. Religious experiences are more highly valued than religious principles and rituals. Rankin writes, "A spiritual experience may be thought of as an experience which points beyond normal, everyday life, and which has spiritual or religious significance for the person to whom it happens."[5] People may regard spiritual experiences as proving the existence of God. Conversely Alister Hardy says that religious experience is the sum total of cultural and traditional influences and the growth that happens in a person's life.[6] Ninian Smart considers that "a religious experience involves some kind of 'perception' of the *invisible* world, or involves a perception that some visible person or thing is a manifestation of the invisible world."[7] According to M. M. Thomas, "The core of any religion is the nature of the experience of the people to the pressure of the Ultimate Reality on their spirit. The initiative remains with the transcendent Holy, the Truth that makes itself known at the centre of human

---

3. Rankin, Religious and Spiritual Experience, 11–17.
4. James, Varieties of Religious Experience, 252.
5. Rankin, Religious and Spiritual Experience, 5.
6. Hardy, *Spiritual Nature*, 131.
7. Smart, *Religious Experience*, 15. Emphasis original.

selfhood."[8] These definitions show that religious and spiritual experiences are similar in nature and features.

Gwen Griffith-Dickson says that religious experience refers, in a broad sense, to any experience of the sacred within a religious context – this includes religious feelings, visions, and mystical and numinous experiences.[9] The different terms and phenomena of religious experience demonstrate its wideness and necessity in all religions and human faiths. Religious experiences are indivisible to religions. As people seek refuge in religion when they face problems, the topic of religious experience receives more attention.

Even though there are specific differences between religious experience and spiritual experience, these two terms are used interchangeably to describe human personal experience which people receive through any beliefs and practice related to a particular divine spirit or superhuman power. In India, where many different faiths are practised, people give high priority to religion and religious activities. Moreover, these days, religious experience is a topic that is seriously discussed in Christian circles. Therefore, in Asia, the subject of religious experience is highly relevant in Christian theology.

1.1.1 Religious Experience in Religion

Religious experience cannot be separated from a religion, and a religion's authenticity is based upon its religious experiences. Marianne Rankin says, "Experiences are at the heart of the religious traditions."[10] For H. D. Lewis, "the core of religion is a religious experience."[11] Sarvepalli Radhakrishnan (1888–1975), one of the most recognized and influential Indian thinkers, believed that true religion should be rooted in religious experiences. He says, "It is not true religion unless it ceases to be a traditional view and becomes a personal experience."[12] Speaking specifically about Hinduism, Radhakrishnan says that Hinduism prioritizes religious experience more than all other religions.

Nevertheless, "while the experiential character of religion is emphasized in the Hindu faith, every religion at its best falls back on it."[13] Religious expe-

---

8. Thomas, *Risking Christ*, 8.
9. Griffith-Dickson, "Religious Experience," 682–691.
10. Rankin, Religious and Spiritual Experience, 1.
11. Lewis, "Worship and Idolatry," 266.
12. Radhakrishnan, *Idealistic View*, 88.
13. Radhakrishnan, 90.

rience is undoubtedly present in all religions, whether to a greater or lesser extent, and characterizes its spirituality. We might say that the significance of religious experiences for religion emphasizes its value in the spiritual life of human beings.

In India, many religions originated and prospered because of the spiritual experiences of its founders. For example, Hinduism builds upon the revelations of rishis; Buddhism was formed as a result of the enlightenment of the Buddha; Sikhism was formed around a revelation received by Guru Nanak; and Islam builds on a revelation to Muhammad. Speaking about the religious experience of Gautama Buddha, who founded Buddhism, Harold Coward says that "Gautama rejected a faith acceptance of the Veda and went out in search of a direct personal experience of reality. The words he spoke, which became the Buddhist scriptures, were a description of his experience of striving for and finally achieving the state of nirvana."[14] These religious leaders claim that their spiritual activities and religious experiences are true, and they ask their followers to practise the same values. Thus, religious experience functions as one of the basic sources for the foundation of each of these religions.

Indian religious traditions and practices stem from the religious experience of people. Regarding Hinduism, Radhakrishnan believed that since religion is felt as an inner experience of the entire personality, religious experience is self-certifying in character.[15] M. K. Gandhi, another significant Indian Hindu philosopher, says, "I do not hesitate to freely express to others my opinions based on my inner experience."[16] In addition, other prominent Hindu philosophers – Sankaracharya, Ramanuja, Madhva Swami, Dayanada Saraswati, Ramakrishna Paramahamsa, Rabindranath Tagore, and Swami Vivekananda – give more priority to the inner experiences of human beings than to any other ritual practices in Hinduism. Steven T. Katz comments, "The Hindu mystic says that his experience is one in which his individual self is identical with Brahman or the Universal Self."[17] Katz's study of Hinduism suggests that, for the Hindu, spiritual experiences lead the believer to identify

---

14. Coward, *Sin and Salvation*, 132–133.
15. Reddy, "Critical Analysis," 337.
16. Kher, *Essence of Hinduism*, 30.
17. Katz, "Language," 29.

with the universal spirit and reach ultimate bliss. In India, the Hindu religion gives much priority to religious experiences through which people can achieve the best blessedness.

1.1.2 Religious Experience in Christian Theology

In Christian theology, too, a great deal of attention is paid to religious experiences. The range of such religious experiences were documented years ago by Sir Alister Hardy, an Orthodox Darwinian and zoologist, in *The Spiritual Nature of Man*, a remarkable book on religious experience. In 1969, Hardy also founded the "Religious Experience Research Unit (RERU)" at the University of Wales with the intention of exploring different types of religious experiences.[18] Despite his training in secular disciplines, Hardy gives full weight to religious experience and developed a highly formalized systematic theology that is as notable for its architectonic power as for its adventurous ideas. According to Lalruatkima, an Indian theologian, "experience is the umbrella term used by theologians for the varied encounters with God."[19] Theology rooted in experiences can lead people to know God, and remarkable spiritual experiences of people can impact the history of theology itself.

The different living testimonies of people have led them to understand that spiritual truth demonstrates the relevance of religious experience in theology. In his book *Religious Belief*, C. B. Martin summarizes the importance of religious experience in Christian theology: "I have a direct experience (knowledge, acquaintance, apprehension) of God; therefore, I have a valid reason to believe that God exists."[20] These types of personal experiences are sometimes considered more valuable than doctrines. In his autobiography *Surprised by Joy*, C.S. Lewis recounts several distinct aesthetic experiences where "beauty" led him into the presence of God.[21] Summarizing certain prominent theologians' understandings of religious experience, Johnston states,

> Tillich later labelled his experience of God's wider Presence a "feeling of ultimate concern." Lewis spoke of a "Bright Shadow,"

---

18. Johnston, *God's Wider Presence*, 22.
19. Lalruatkima, *Understanding Christian Faith*, 45.
20. Martin, *Religious Belief*, 66.
21. C. S. Lewis, Surprised by Joy (New York: Harcourt, Brace & World / Harvest Books, 1955), 180–181.

or simply "Joy." ... Friedrich Schleiermacher ... wrote of "a feeling of absolute dependence," and Rudolf Otto ... described such experiences as a "*mysterium tremendum et fascinans*" (a mystery that is awe-filled and yet inviting)."[22]

Speaking of his personal experience, Sadhu Sundar Singh, an Indian Sikh convert, said, "I do not believe in Jesus Christ because I have read about him in the Bible. I saw him and experienced him and know him in my daily experience."[23] Such testimonies affirm the value of religious experience in Christian theology. This study discusses the importance of religious experience in Christian theology from the perspective of four theologians – P. Chenchiah, S. J. Samartha, Jurgen Moltmann, and Kirsteen Kim (see chapters 4 and 5).

1.2 Religious Experience: An Understanding of Its Nature

People's religious experiences from different religious backgrounds appear similar in nature but they create confusion when it comes to discerning the authenticity of each religion. Similarities are found (1) in the outcomes of religious experiences: transformation, morality, ability, and happiness; (2) in the factors that trigger religious experience: human culture, creativity, and traditional faiths; and (3) the mysteries in religious experiences are revealed. If religious experiences produce similar results, why then is there disunity among people? Is the revelation of mystery the same in all religious experiences? Before searching for answers to these questions, let us see how religious experiences confuse people through its positive results, beliefs, practices and revelation of mystery.

1.2.1 Positive Results

A mysterious factor in religious experience is the similar outcome revealed among peoples of many faiths, irrespective of any cultural or religious difference. Religious experience impacts both people's personal and social lives. In our personal life, religious experience enhances our ethical and spiritual

---

22. Johnston, God's Wider Presence., 3.
23. Sumithra, *Christian Theologies*, 99–100.

values, by helping to transform character, achieve divine knowledge, and promote happiness and surprising abilities. In social life, religious experiences motivate people to act for the betterment of society. A significant concern for social justice and equality for the poor and needy can characterize a person who has enjoyed a religious experience. There are numerous examples of spiritual experiences influencing people to initiate social works for the benefit of the community – these include the examples of Mother Teresa, Pandita Ramabai, and Dorothy Day.

Numerous charitable organizations find their origins in spiritual experiences and persist through the unwavering dedication of volunteers who share the same inspiration. These spiritual encounters drive individuals to establish initiatives that serve the community and extend a helping hand to those in need. The profound sense of purpose and compassion derived from these experiences guide the charitable work as like-minded individuals within spiritual communities unite to offer their support, resources, and time to a common cause. Engaging in philanthropy becomes a spiritual practice, allowing individuals to embody their beliefs and translate their faith into impactful action. Through these experiences, there emerges a profound sense of unity among all beings, further fuelling the commitment to uplift and support others in their journey towards a better life. The religious experience provides people with insight, leading them to do positive deeds in society. Similarly, personal transformation and seeking the good of others is a major teaching of the Bible. The book of James teaches that "Every good and perfect gift is from above, coming down from the Father of the heavenly lights, who does not change like shifting shadows." (Jas 1:17 NIV), which means that all kinds of goodness, wisdom, justice, and beauty come from God and enable people to practise such goodness. If religious experiences can strengthen and transform people and motivate them to work for good – for justice and equality – then this indicates that it is possible to accept the authenticity of divine intervention in human experiences.

1.2.2 Cultural Alliance

Not only do religious experiences relate to religious faith but their association with human culture is equally obvious. Distinct human cultural aspects – such as skills, arts, beauty, philosophy, and ethical knowledge – are interconnected with religious experiences. Simon Dein says that no experience can be separated from culture. He notes, "Recent authors have argued that cultural factors construct not only the narration of religious experiences but also the experiences themselves."[24] In the words of Katz, "All mystical experiences are the same, but the mystics' *reports about* their experiences are culturally bound. Thus, they use the available symbols of their cultural-religious milieu to describe their experience."[25] In a sense, religious experiences contribute excellent abilities and valuable thoughts to people, and these then become a part of human culture. The Bible portrays people who receive from God excellent talent to create artwork (Exod 36:1–5; 1 Kings 7), exceptional skills (2 Chron 2:3–16), knowledge and wisdom (Prov 2:6–8), and philosophical thoughts (Acts 17:16–34).

For example, Christian Parker says that the Spirit of God imparts beauty, and therefore, spiritual involvement in culture is essential. Parker comments that Clement of Alexandria, an Ante-Nicene church father, rightly connected the Spirit with cultural beauty: "He (Clement of Alexandria) draws attention to Bezalel, Oholiab and the artists and craftsmen who were filled with the Spirit of God, for the purpose of constructing the tent of meeting and its contents (Exod 31:1–11; 35:30–36:2)."[26] So, Parker says, "The growing interest in the study of aesthetics, not least in the theological community, points to larger shifts in the twentieth century."[27] In relation to human beings, there is interdependence between the contribution of religious experiences to culture and cultural influence in the formation of religious experience. Religious experiences take place in all cultures, and one culture is not to be preferred over another. In every culture, religious experience sharpens the culture and vice versa. But people cannot be expected to blindly follow cultural or religious practices

Religious experiences reveal matters that are hidden. Revelations in religious experience are very common in all religions. Through religious experience, people may receive the revelation of heavenly knowledge to write sacred scripture, to understand human ethical values, and to know God's instructions to people. Revelatory experiences encourage people to write

---

24. Dein, "Religious Experience," 6.
25. Katz, "Language," 24.
26. Parker, "Holy Spirit in the Arts," 212–213.
27. Parker, 207.

down valuable thoughts, leading to texts that are then respected as special teachings or even revered as holy writs. Muslims believe that Muhammad's spiritual experience instructed him to "read" or "recite" – which is what the word Qur'an means. "In Indian philosophy, the narrower sense of the *Sabda pramana* (verbal testimony) looks at *Shruti* (the Vedas as that which is heard) and the *Smriti* (the traditions as that which is remembered) as the corpus of revealed knowledge."[28] Christian understanding also affirms the presence of divine inspiration in the writing and composition of its scripture. In this sense, religious experiences are common to all religions and open the way to know and understand mysterious things.

The exposure of hidden things through religious experiences prompts people to hold on to and value such experiences and to make these part of their faith tradition. This encourages people to follow their religion and religious traditions, which could reinforce the misunderstanding that "all religions are different ways to reach the same goal." Perhaps this is the reason Christians sometimes find it difficult to appreciate the positive results of the religious experience of those of other faiths. How can a Christian appreciate that the spiritual experiences of other religious people have positive results – especially in Hinduism, where polytheism exists? This study investigates answers to this question and tries to explain the positive results of the Hindu religious experience from a Christian theological perspective.

1.2.3 Mysterious Nature

Religious experience reveals mysteries, but the experience itself remains a mystery. The mystery of religious experience is in its source, purpose, and mode. People have different opinions about the source of and reason for religious experience. Some believe that divine intervention is behind it, while others disagree. In this context investigating the source of religious experience and its purpose for human life will help to construct a theology of religious experience in the Indian context.

There is a mysterious power in religious experience, which is revealed through the inner life of human beings and empowers them to do good works and enables them to understand mysterious things. This inexplicable power keeps its source a mystery. Generally, religious factors – worship, festivals,

---

28. Marbaniang, Theology of Revelation, 1.

ceremonies, prayer, *darshana*, pilgrimage, fasting, chanting, and yoga – and non-religious factors – culture, creation, human creativity, ethical knowledge, skills, and arts – help to generate religious experiences. Rankin says, "Many spiritual experiences are not related to any kind of religious practice, but are triggered by glorious music, the beauty of nature or absorption in creativity."[29] But the breadth of these trigger factors makes it more complicated to identify the cause of religious experience. Raimundo Panikkar, an Indian theologian, is correct when he states that many mysteries exist in religions and that spiritual experiences are part of these mysteries.[30]

The presence of an invisible (spiritual) being in religious experience should not be denied its result: transforming power, producing positive results, and revealing mysteries. Religious experiences take place internally, within human beings, and may be caused by certain spiritual beings. The representation of a religious experience as a spiritual experience supports the idea of the Spirit's involvement in such experiences. Since the Spirit is invisible, religious experiences, in all religions, also occur internally. The revelatory presence of the Spirit should be recognized as a source of goodness and enlightenment for all humanity, regardless of their religious beliefs. Christians are called to embrace the belief that every aspect of truth, goodness, beauty, and holiness found in human culture, including within various religions, is bestowed by God's free grace through the Spirit. This understanding encourages Christians to acknowledge and appreciate the common threads of divine inspiration and virtue present in diverse cultures and faiths.

Moreover, the common nature of religious experience in revealing hidden things indicates a common source of mystery, and each revelation happens with a purpose. The invisible God's revelatory presence is inculcated in human beings in various ways everywhere in the world, without any discrimination based on human culture, tradition, experience, or church. Understanding God's different mediums for general revelation can contribute significantly to bringing harmony among different religious faiths. These mediums of revelation are present not only in Christianity but also in all other religions and cultures.

---

29. Rankin, Religious and Spiritual Experience, 78.
30. Panikkar, *Inter-religious Dialogue*, 95.

1.3 The Spirit and General Revelation

In God's general revelation, the active presence of the Spirit is perceptible through different media. Domenic Marbaniang – in his book *Theology of Revelation in the Bible and the Writings of 19th and 20th Century Theologians* – explains that, traditionally, Christian understanding of revelation is divided into two: general revelation (God's communication to all people always) and special revelation (God's communication particularly to particular people on particular occasions). But Marbaniang writes about a third form of revelation introduced by J. Rodman Williams, a charismatic theologian – subordinate revelation, which is God's communication within his community through the continuing ministry of the Holy Spirit.[31] What is labelled general revelation in Marbaniang's list is the continuing presence of the Spirit in creation, culture, conscience, and human experience.

Understanding the work of the Spirit in general revelation through different mediums helps Christians to build good relationships with other religious faiths because God gives revelation to his people and also to people of other religious communities. Clark Pinnock claims that "world religions [also] reflect to some degree general revelation and prevenient grace. just as God Himself is present in the world." He adds, "So too is God's reality and revelation. Since God never leaves himself without witness (Acts 14:16–17), people always have divine light to respond to."[32] According to Johnston, "a better description of 'general' revelation would recognize that God reveals himself not only through Scripture and in the believing community but also through creation, conscience, and culture."[33] Marbaniang says that the main media of revelation is available to people in various ways such as nature (creation), history, and people's inner being, including even their moral and religious natures.[34] Johnston and Marbaniang use slightly different language, but their meaning is identical. If this is so, we ought to think of the presence of God as being visible through various religious experiences that people go through in different cultures and faiths.

---

31. Marbaniang, *Theology of Revelation*, 1.
32. Pinnock, *Wideness in God's Mercy*, 104.
33. Johnston, God's Wider Presence, 9.
34. Marbaniang, Theology of Revelation, 1.

The general revelation of God through distinct mediums, including religious experience, happens as the result of the work of the Spirit. In Johnston's words, "The experience of the wider Presence of God through his Spirit [is] mediated through creation, conscience, and human culture."[35] Amos Yong, writing about the view of Jacques Dupuis, a Jesuit, says that "a pneumatological approach to the religions allows him [Dupuis] to affirm other scriptures as initial revelations of the divine that necessarily precede and prepare the way for the definitive word of God in Jesus Christ."[36] The work of the Spirit represents a way to understand God's revelation and his intention for all human beings. The mysterious presence of the Spirit is apparent in religious experiences through creation, culture, and conscience, and this can lead to the revelation of the truth. "Love of God and neighbour, as, too, the Spirit as Life-giver, are crucial themes around which to orient one's discernment process. So too is the need to 'attend' carefully, listening for the Spirit speaking in and through the religious experiences of others."[37] Compared to other mediums of general revelation, religious experiences are closely associated with religion. So, God's revelation through religious experiences enables Christians to establish unity and open dialogue with other religious people.

Many Christian theologians do not consider the Spirit's role in revealing God's presence in the world. But a theology constructed without understanding the guidance of the Spirit will be a disaster. Maldonado says that divine revelations are essential for leading a successful spiritual life and constructing a right theology.

> Some theologians study God for decades but never know Him because they lack revelation from the Holy Spirit, while others who receive revelation have intimate knowledge of Him, in addition to an understanding of theology. Revelation gives us access to the spiritual world and to elevated realms of faith, and it erases the borders of the impossible.[38]

---

35. Johnston, God's Wider Presence, 128.
36. Yong, *Beyond the Impasse*, 100.
37. Johnston, God's Wider Presence, 213.
38. Maldonado, Glory of God, 53.

The relevance of this fact is emphasized in chapters 4 and 5, which consider how various Christian theologians understand the work of the Spirit in other religions.

1.4 The Spirit and Religious Experience

Hinduism and its traditional faith do not deny the Spirit's work in religious experience and religious revelations. Swami Vivekananda, one of the most influential Hindu philosophers in India, considered spiritual discipline essential for religious experience (see chapter 3). He believed and taught that through Hindu religious experience, people could understand mysteries. This encouraged people to give high priority to religious experience without understanding its reality. For such people, the religious tradition they follow is not wrong in any sense. In the words of Radhakrishnan, "Tradition is able to awaken the spirit in us, it is valid and valuable. While no tradition coincides with experience, every tradition is essentially unique and valuable."[39] Radhakrishnan finds that tradition's significance is central to Hinduism and all religions. He considers that all religious traditions uphold the value of tradition; at the same time, no religious tradition is perfect but is bound to grow as long as its followers are spiritual.[40] The concept of the Spirit's involvement in the Hindu religious tradition opens the way to discuss the matter of the Spirit's involvement in religious experience.

Interestingly, the Hindu understanding of religious experience is not far removed from what we might view as a "common" understanding of the religious experience and its connection with the nature of the revelation of God, "The Spirit is, after all, the meeting point between Christian and non-Christian, and between both and God."[41] Is it enough to continue with religious traditions and spiritual discipline as Vivekananda teaches? What should be the Christian's attitude towards religious experience? Before considering these questions, let us reflect on people's unusual experiences of the Spirit.

R. C. Das (1887–1976), a Hindu convert and one of the key figures of Benares United City Mission (BUCM), experienced Hinduism as an

---

39. Radhakrishnan, Idealistic View, 120.
40. Radhakrishnan, 120.
41. Yong, Beyond the Impasse, 100.

"absorptive force." He observed that Hindu religious practices have the power to lead people to reach higher levels, both spiritual and social. For example, he says that even the Hindu tradition in India represents a Vedic *rishi*, an agnostic Vedantist, or an avatar of Vishnu in the mind of people.[42] He considered that Hindu spiritual teachings understand this truth because they reveal "an essential unity and real growth of certain fundamental truths."[43] His personal experience and understanding of Hindu tradition became brighter when he came to know the full truth in Jesus Christ. But Das does not consider the Hindu traditional faith a hindrance to growing spiritually. He says that he can lead a better Christian life by following Jesus's word and ways in the Indian spiritual atmosphere than in any culture of the Western churches.[44]

Aiyadurai Jesudasen Appasamy (1891–1980), who converted from Shaivism to Christ at the age of twenty-four, became an influential Indian Christian theologian who converted from Shaivism to Christ at the age of twenty-four, experienced a "crude type of fear" through Hinduism. Appasamy later became an influential Indian Christian theologian. Appasamy's inner experience is closely associated with Rudolf Otto's

> qualitative *content* of the numinous experience, to which "the mysterious" stands as *form*, is in one of its aspects the element of daunting "awfulness" and "majesty" . . .; but it is clear that it has at the same time another aspect in which it shows itself as something uniquely attractive and fascinating.[45]

Appasamy explains this crude type of fear from the writings of Otto by describing it as an awareness of the awfulness of God and an essential element present in all religions.[46] Appasamy experienced in Hinduism God's requirement for people to fear God – as something that can lead people to know the truth. This experience in Hinduism helped him to cultivate the *bhakti* system in Indian Christian theology. Appasamy argues that in the *bhakti* system, real devotion comes out of a person's deep and unselfish love for God, which

---

42. Das, *Autobiographical Reflections*, 118–128.
43. Das, "Modern Apologetics," 16.
44. Das, Autobiographical Reflections, 34.
45. Otto, *Idea of the Holy*, 31.
46. Appasamy, "Bhakti in the Bhagavad Gita," 62.

leads to the highest bliss in union with Christ. Here, a disciple's commitment and communion with Christ is equivalent to the Son's unity with the Father.

The experiences of these two Hindu converts show that their past Hindu traditions were not an impediment to understanding God but helped them to know God better. Das's experience of Hinduism's "absorptive force" and Appasamy's experience of "a crude type of fear" (or awe) within Hinduism enabled them to be open to that knowledge of God in Christ Jesus. In both instances, the positive nature of Hinduism – its tolerance and fear of God – functioned as a channel to know God more fully. Such positive results are potentially present in any religion and should not be criticized by Christians. Rather, Christians must appreciate these qualities. Does this mean that Christians can learn something about God from the positive things in Hinduism? Yes! The Hindu convert Pratap Chander Mozoomdar's (1840–1905) helpfully represented the work of the Spirit in Hinduism as an "evolving principle" in the creative process, the source and substance of all things.[47] And P. Chenchiah represents the Spirit as a cosmic energy (see chapter 4). These understandings of the Hindu faith by converts point to the possibility that truth can be revealed through Hindu religious experience.

A final example is the testimony of Christine Mangala Frost, a Hindu convert, which focuses on the significance of yoga practice in Hinduism. Frost grew up learning and practising the Hindu spiritual discipline of yoga. She testifies that she experienced the real yoga and the fullness of its meaning only in Christianity, citing the words of the church fathers and the patriarch Ignatius IV. "The Kingdom of God is nothing other than the glorified Body of the risen Christ, in which each day humanity enters into communion."[48]

Regarding the benefits of yoga, Frost quotes the words of St. Gregory Palamas, who said that the mystical communion with God will provide direct and personal knowledge of God, which happens through the Holy Spirit within a person.[49] Frost also quotes these words of, Déchanet who was her contemporary: "The Christian starts from faith, and reaches a certain experience, in divine charity, of the God of Revelation, experiencing 'Emmanuel,' God with us, God with me. The Hindu has only empirical data

---

47. Sumithra, Christian Theologies. 58.
48. Ignatius IV, *The Resurrection and the Modern Man*, 71
49. Mantzaridis, *Deification*, 114.

to guide him and at the end of his road discovers a sublime but almost savage isolation."[50] Frost's learning about yoga in Hinduism found a similar intention in Christianity, which motivated her to implement such practices in her Christian life. Hindu yoga was not sufficient as a spiritual discipline, but it was a start. Christians do not need to focus on Hindu spiritual exercises like yoga alone. But neither should they despise the openness to the Spirit that can come from Hindu spiritual disciplines, which may be the preliminary work of the Holy Spirit.

However, while some experiences lead people to know the real God, others do not lead beyond religious rituals and cultural practices. But, this can lead to Christians often ignoring, confusing, or misunderstanding God's natural work in other religions. It is necessary to use the concept, of the Spirit's presence in human experience, to construct a theology that can explain the Spirit's work in religious experience, especially in the Indian context.

1.5 Conclusion

An expectation of religious understanding that is based upon religious experience in general revelation will help to clarify our constructive theological proposal. If all beauty and goodness come from God through the Spirit, does this not include aspects of other religions? How can we understand God's presence in other religions and in human cultures? What is the theological position on the Spirit's presence in Hinduism? To put it differently, "How might we as Christians understand how Hindu religious experiences might connect with the general revelation of God?" In the process of responding to this question, we will explore the positive effects of religious experience in Hindu religious traditions from a Christian theological perspective. Such a study, however brief, will serve both to illustrate constructive theology in an Indian context and to integrate, praxeologically, our various theological probings – experiential, cultural, traditional, biblical, and theological.

---

50. Déchanet, *Christian Yoga*, 121.

CHAPTER 2

A Biblical Understanding of Religious Experience

In the biblical understanding, God is Spirit, and his deeds are thus spiritual in nature. The presence of the Spirit is far and wide, encompassing all creation, human beings, and human culture. God, who is spirit, enables people to be born in the Spirit, empowers them to be strong in spirit, gives them spiritual revelations, and guides them to walk in the Spirit and to live by the Spirit. The biblical descriptions of spiritual experiences received by people outside God's community are striking. God conveyed his messages through different media – dreams, visions, nature, traditions, and cultures. The mysterious presence of the Spirit through these various forms resulted in unique experiences for people. Similarly, the Spirit's mysterious presence in religious experience plays a significant role in creating platforms for his mission of drawing people towards God. This chapter will explore the biblical understanding of the Spirit's participation in people's religious experiences.

2.1 The Spirit: Breath of God and Inner Knowledge

As the creator of the universe, God has a special consideration for human beings – who are his creations – which he expressed through imparting the Spirit. The Bible states that God's Spirit is present in all human beings (see Job 32:8; 34:14–15; Eccl 12:7). Through his unique creation of human beings, God fulfils his special plan and accomplishes it through the mysterious presence of the Spirit. The section that follows deals with the presence of the

Spirit in human life as the breath of life and inner knowledge that opens up the possibility of spiritual experiences.

The book of Genesis describes the Spirit of God dwelling in human beings as the breath of life. In the second account of the creation of humanity, God creates Adam (humankind) in his image and breathes into his nostrils the breath of life (Gen 2:7). In the Old Testament, the Hebrew words *ruah* and *neshamah* are used for the Spirit, and the phrase *nishmat chaim* is used for the breath of life. Arnold G. Fruchtenbaum writes, "It is this breath of God, the *neshamah* that produced the life of man . . . God's breath brings animation, causing men to become a living soul."[1] The book of Job says, "The Spirit of God has made me; the breath of the Almighty gives me life" (Job 33:4; see also 34:14–15. When the Spirit of God enters a body, he energizes it – this is the power of life. Correspondingly, when the Spirit leaves a person, this results in death (Ps 104:29–30). In the words of Hans Schwarz, "*Ruah* is the 'wind' which proceeds from Yahweh and which will eventually return to him, constituting the breath of life: 'If he should take back his spirit *(ruah)* to himself, and gather to himself his breath *(neshamah)*, all flesh would perish together.'"[2] Job 34:14–15 (NIV) says, "If it were his intention and he withdrew his spirit and breath, all humanity would perish together and mankind would return to the dust." These biblical passages assert the presence of the Spirit as the breath of life in human beings. Andrew K. Gabriel says, "The Spirit is in every living being. This is a natural conclusion when one considers a doctrine of the Creator Spirit."[3] Walter Brueggemann argues that human beings are a combination of divine presence and matter. He writes, "Combined with the dust or dirt out of which God forms the human (2:7), this gives us an interesting picture of humanity as a peculiar combination of transcendence and materiality. That is how we are physical, earthly beings, but also bear a spark of divinity."[4] God, the creator, imparts the Spirit to all human beings, and the Spirit dwells in them as the breath of life. This presence of the Spirit in human beings makes us "spiritual" beings.

---

1. Fruchtenbaum, *Genesis*, 74.
2. Schwarz, "Work of the Spirit," 197.
3. Gabriel, "Intensity of the Spirit," 369.
4. Brueggemann and Linafelt, *Old Testament*, 58.

However, the Spirit – as the breath of life present in human lives – gives divine knowledge, which can be understood as inner knowledge or the conscience of man. Job 32:8 (NIV) says, "But it is the Spirit in a person, the breath of the Almighty, that gives them understanding." Hans Schwarz interprets this verse as meaning that "it is the spirit *(ruah)* in a man, the breath *(neshamah)* of the Almighty, that makes him understand. Not age or education leads to wisdom, but God himself and his Spirit."[5] In the book of Romans, Paul represents this inner knowledge as conscience through which people who do not know the law are judged. Paul argues,

> When Gentiles, who do not possess the law, do instinctively what the law requires, these, though not having the law, are a law to themselves. They show that what the law requires is written on their hearts, to which their own conscience also bears witness; and their conflicting thoughts will accuse or perhaps excuse them. (Rom 2:14–15 NRSV)

The Spirit who dwells in people allows them to know God's will. Schwarz emphasizes this point, saying, "Human reason, discernment between right and wrong, and culture as self-expression of the humanum are not self-originated results of a natural human faculty. They stem from the work of the Spirit in the world."[6] The Spirit dwells as inner knowledge, enabling people to develop moral capacity and achieve divine knowledge.

The presence of God's Spirit in humankind as the breath of life and as inner knowledge makes our access to God possible. The Spirit motivates people to know God's truth or his will and provides spiritual experiences to people to make such knowing possible. Elizabeth Johnson says, "Every personal encounter of God with human beings occurs in the Spirit, and it is in the Spirit that people make their response. This presence of the Spirit is a power and a joy, an outpouring and a gift."[7] According to Schwarz, the Spirit of God who dwells in human beings enables them to understand God and his intentions. He says, "Humanity's *ruah* (spirit) can only be properly understood out of God's communion with us."[8] The presence of the Spirit

---

5. Schwarz, "Work of the Spirit," 197.
6. Schwarz, 211.
7. Johnson, Quest, 162.
8. Schwarz, "Work of the Spirit," 198.

does not entail controlling or dictating people's actions. Instead, the Spirit functions as a divine reality who interacts with humanity, prompting and inviting responses. Moreover, the Spirit's intimacy and accessibility are evident in human experiences, fostering a deep connection between individuals and the divine. To human beings, the presence of the Spirit imparts divine knowledge of God's will. The presence of the Spirit in human life as the breath of life and conscience gives much space for having spiritual experiences.

2.2 Spiritual Experience outside God's Community

It is a common misconception that God interacts exclusively with specific communities and neglects others. However, the Bible demonstrates that God's spiritual interventions extend universally, without discrimination. His messages, his unveiling of divine mysteries, and his imparting of wisdom are accessible to all. The biblical narratives, spanning both the Old and New Testaments, exemplify God's impartial interactions with people from diverse backgrounds and showcase his all-encompassing care for and guidance of humanity.

2.2.1 The Old Testament

Although the Old Testament is often viewed as being a portrayal of God's dealings with his chosen people, Israel, there are several occasions in the Old Testament where non-Israelites receive special experiences from God. This includes receiving divine decrees, divine messages, and special skills – for example, Proverbs and Chronicles show God granting special abilities to non-covenantal people.

God's all-encompassing presence is evident not only in religious practices but also in culture, tradition, creation, and human creativity. The Bible offers specific evidence of the Spirit's boundless works among both covenant and non-covenant individuals. As an inspired compilation, the Holy Scripture includes writings from within God's community and, occasionally, from outside. For instance, the book of Proverbs comprises collections of wise sayings and teachings, exemplifying the Spirit's influence beyond the confines of a particular group. This includes proverbs collected by Solomon (10:1–22:16); "the words of the wise" (22:17–24:22 NRSV); more proverbs of Solomon compiled by "the officials of King Hezekiah of Judah" (25:1–29:27 NRSV);

the sayings of Agur (30:1–33); the sayings of Lemuel (31:1–9); and a description of "a capable wife" (31:10–31 NRSV). Agur, son of Jakeh, is said to be a non-Israelite, a Massaite, an Arabian wise man, and a foreign prophet. King Lemuel is considered a Massaite, a member of an Arabian tribe.[9] In Proverbs 22:17, "the words of the wise" are taken from thirty sayings of the Egyptian *Instruction of Amenemope*. "Amenemope dates from the period of Egypt's New Kingdom (1558–1085 BCE), most probably in the thirteenth century. The text is the instruction of an official, Amenemope, to his son who is serving in the Egyptian bureaucracy."[10] Here, God's revelation within Egyptian culture also becomes divine instruction for Israel's life.

The book of Proverbs serves as a compelling example of how divine revelation might be manifested even among non-covenantal individuals, showcasing their profound spiritual insights and wisdom. These texts draw from sources outside the covenant community of faith, demonstrating that this "spiritual insight" is a result of the work of the Spirit since every good thing originates from God. This phenomenon highlights the inherent ability of human beings to discern and observe God's revelation in various aspects of life. God's general revelation, accessible to all, is perceived through human observations, conscience, the wonders of creation, and expressions of human creativity. Such spiritual insights are not confined solely to God's chosen community but extend to other communities as well, illustrating the Spirit's inspiring and guiding influence among non-covenantal people. Despite being sinners like everyone else, these individuals display humility and reverence for God, which allows them to receive and understand such profound spiritual insights.

The books of Chronicles also "chronicle" that God's spiritual work is seen in both Israelites and non-Israelites. In telling Israel's story, the chronicler portrays Yahweh as the God of the whole world and the covenanting God of his people. This is confirmed by the mention in Chronicles of different pagan kings (King Neco, King Huram, and King Cyrus), all of whom received special guidance from God. For example, King Neco of Egypt (2 Chron 35:20–27) received from God a revelation that the faithful king, Josiah, had failed to heed. The chronicler emphasizes that the Lord's dominion extends to the

---

9. Johnston, *God's Wider Presence*, 72–74.
10. Johnston, 74–76.

entire world, encompassing Egypt and beyond, as evident in his revelations that were not limited to the covenant community but included others such as King Neco.

Similarly, when King Huram of Tyre (2 Chron 2:3–16 NRSV) was asked by King Solomon to send skilled (wise) men to work with the covenant people, he sent Huram-abi, a skilled artisan, the son of a Danite women and a Tyrian man (2:14). The Spirit does not discriminate when imparting knowledge and wisdom to people in mastering particular skills. God gave wisdom to Solomon to reign over his people. Similarly, God imparted wisdom or "skill" (in Hebrew, this is the same word) to Huram-abi, a man from Tyre, to create works of art (see also Exod 36:1–5). Huram acknowledged Israel's God as the creator of heaven and earth, recognizing that this same God had granted Solomon the wisdom and skill to rule and bestowed on Huram-abi the wisdom and skill for craftsmanship. God's sovereignty extends over the entire world, and he bestows similar gifts on both Israelites and non-Israelites without showing partiality. This revelatory perspective must be firmly grounded in God's Spirit rather than solely relying on the evidence found in the creation footprint.[11] The Spirit's active presence in giving people the ability to understand God's will is in view here, and the Old Testament passages discussed above testify to God's unbiased provision of spiritual insights to non-covenant people.

2.2.2 The New Testament

The New Testament also records instances of the Spirit's works beyond the church. In Luke's writings, one of the best examples of God's impartial provision to people is the outpouring of the Spirit, which is described in the book of Acts. Luke narrates how God takes the initiative to fill Gentiles with the Spirit (Acts 10:44–47). God sent Peter, first to Cornelius and his family to proclaim and prove the impartiality of God. Peter did not criticize Cornelius's past cultural practices but, rather, emphasized God's gracious gift to all. Timothy Johnson notes that validation of Peter's ministry in the house of Cornelius is "evidenced by the fresh outpouring of the Spirit at the 'Gentile Pentecost.'"[12] God considered Cornelius and his household worthy

---

11. Johnston, 211.
12. Johnson, *Scripture and Discernment*, 98.

of the Holy Spirit even though none of them had fully embraced Judaism or received Christian baptism at that point. Not only Cornelius and his family but all who heard Peter's message were filled with the Holy Spirit. Luke included this incident as evidence that in God's eyes, there is no cultural barrier to anointing people with the Spirit.

The traditional faiths of the Athenians became a starting point for Paul to share the gospel. Dunham says that "the cultural flow evidently included a steady procession of foreign deities, for by the time Paul stood in the markets of Athens, a great many religions were co-existent at the centre of the Hellenistic world."[13] Joshua W. Jipp observes that by "the unknown God," Paul describes two biblical truths: God is the singular creator of the world and the one who gives life to everyone. Jipp compares Paul's comments with Isaiah's words – "Thus says God, the LORD, who created the heaven and stretched them out, who spread out the earth and what comes from it, who gives breath to the people upon it and spirit to those who walk in it" (42:5 NRSV).[14] God the creator does not remain distant from his creation but opens ways for people to know him more and receive salvation through his Spirit. DeCelles says that it is the grace of God that flowed upon all people and writes, "The pagan is graced, i.e., alive with the life of the Spirit" (see also 1 John 3:14).[15] Similarly, in various ways, other New Testament passages also point to God's universal saving intent through the work of the Spirit (John 12:47; Acts 10:35; 1 Cor 15:22–23; 1 Tim 2:1–4; 4:10).

Paul presented the message of salvation without condemning other cultures. Lars Dahle comments, "Luke's account describes Paul's proactive approach in Athens as a recommended apologetic in biblically illiterate and pluralistic *agora* contexts."[16] Paul skilfully utilized the forms of Athenian religion and philosophy to articulate people's search for God and identify the ultimate source and destination of that quest. Nevertheless, the Hellenistic religious milieu he confronted was highly pluralistic, making today's multicultural religious diversity appear relatively tame in comparison. This encounter

---

13. Dunham, "Acts 17:16–34," 202.

14. Jipp, "Paul's Areopagus Speech," 579.

15. DeCelles, Charles "The Holy Spirit, Unbound in Her Saving Work." *Journal of Theta Alpha Kappa* 11, no. 2 (Fall 1987), 42.

16. Dahle, "Apologetic Model," 314–315.

offers valuable insights into constructing a theology suitable for a multireligious nation.

However, Paul never compromised with people's the evil practices or accepted their misunderstandings. In his discourse at Athens, Paul tailored his explanation to align with their cultural comprehension. He astutely recognized a spirit of idolatry that hindered them from embracing repentance and yielding to the Holy Spirit of God as revealed in Jesus and his resurrection (Acts 17:16–34). Paul's adept use of Greek thought and language significantly influenced the development of Christian theology, especially in the comprehension of God the Holy Spirit. Understanding the work of the Spirit in other cultures can increase our approachability and acceptability in our dealings with other religious people. The Old and New Testaments provide sufficient information about God's dealings with those outside the church through his provision of wisdom, revelations, the filling of the Spirit, and salvation. If God's spiritual intervention is seen in other religious communities, what should be the Christian's attitude towards it? Christians are often unwilling to search for the source and genuineness of the divine message in the religious experience of people outside the church. Such a rigid system within Christian communities becomes a barrier to fulfilling God's mission in a multireligious nation. In this context, it is relevant to understand the value of the role played by the church in India as it seeks to relate to its Hindu neighbours who have had spiritual experiences.

2.3 Means of Spiritual Experience

Spiritual experience can be mediated through varying forms of revelation such as dreams, visions, moral principles, human culture, and skills. Various media serve as conduits for religious experiences, and the Bible contains numerous instances of individuals receiving divine revelations through dreams and visions. For example, in Genesis 20, Abimelech has a dream concerning Sarah, while Genesis 28 recounts Jacob's dream at Bethel. In Genesis 31, Jacob is warned in a dream to flee, while Laban also receives a warning through a dream. Joseph's early dreams are recorded in Genesis 37, and the cupbearer and baker have dreams in Genesis 40. Pharaoh experiences a significant dream in Genesis 41, and in Genesis 46, Jacob (Israel) is instructed through a dream to go down to Egypt. What is intriguing about this list is the number of individuals outside the believing community of Israel who received divine revelations through dreams. There is also Nebuchadnezzar (Daniel 2 and Daniel 4), Balaam (Numbers 22), Samuel (1 Samuel 3), and Solomon (1 Kgs 3:5–15). The Bible demonstrates that divine messages are not limited to those within the believing community but extend to individuals from diverse backgrounds, emphasizing the universality of divine communication through various mediums, including dreams. God's intervention in the lives of these people through different media gave them the opportunity to know the will of God. The sections that follow explore how culture, philosophical thoughts, religiosity, and ethical values can enhance religious experience, especially for people outside God's community.

2.3.1 Culture

God uses human culture and cultural practices to form religious experiences and reveal his messages. Scripture describes how people of different cultural backgrounds receive God's messages. For example, Balaam, a diviner and non-Israelite, experienced God's presence in his own cultural practices. God used Balaam's own way of "divination" to convey his messages, and Balaam was able to see the angel of the Lord and receive God's message. Johnston finds no obstacle in Balaam's life to prevent him from receiving God's message; in fact, he compares Balaam with Elijah, the great servant of God: "Balaam, like Elijah, looks out across the scorched plains of southern Palestine and, though there is no speech, hears God speak. And though there is no image, he sees the Almighty. He faithfully tells King Balak his experience."[17] Balaam's words imply that he was acknowledging Yahweh as the God who had personally revealed himself to him. In this context, Yahweh was "my God," the deity he had sought answers from through his divination and who had indeed responded to him. Remarkably, Israel's God responded to a prophet's false, religious practices. God intentionally chose to answer this non-Israelite religious practitioner directly, and the Spirit of God descended upon him. As a result, Balaam genuinely heard the Spirit of God speaking to him.

Although explaining God's dealings through other cultural practices is difficult, such revelations remain a reality. The Bible teaches that the Spirit, as creator, may deal with people any time and anywhere. Balaam was ready

---

17. Dahle, 102.

to accept what the Spirit said. Balaam served as the recipient of Yahweh's revelation, just as even his ass received a divine message. The interplay between providence and free will adds a mysterious dimension to the situation, and it is noteworthy that Balaam not only received the revelation but also made the conscious choice to act upon it.

Balaam succeeded in understanding the message of God through his attentiveness to the Spirit. When a person yields to the Spirit, they may receive a divine revelation and a real spiritual experience may take place.

2.3.2 Human Philosophy

Spiritual intervention by God may also take place in people's lives as they consider philosophy and poetry. However, not all people recognize God's truth, which is hidden in these cultural factors. The book of Acts describes how Paul used a spiritual truth that the people of Athens regarded as cultural philosophy to communicate the gospel. Acts 17:16–34 showcases Paul's skill in presenting biblical revelation in a culturally informed and relevant manner to his pagan contemporaries. Regarding Paul's conversation at Athens, Robert E. Dunham says, "Paul begins with the language and tone of the philosophers. He compliments them on their religiosity. He cites their poets. He draws on their insights."[18] Paul unearthed distinct spiritual insights from Athenian culture to lead the people of Athens to the truth and used the thoughts and ideas of pagan poets to get their attention. Fernando says that Paul, in explaining the gospel message at Athens, used non-Christian poets and quoted from these unbelievers. "Yet he saw glimmerings of the truth in these systems that could be used to buttress his case for Christianity. His audience was familiar with these writers and accepted them as their own teachers. Paul used their literature to develop his case for the Christian gospel."[19] In the words of Kim,

> [Paul] affirmed their search for God and the spiritual awareness of their poets, who proclaimed that God is Spirit "in whom we live and move and have our being," and that, as God's "offspring," we are spiritual beings. Paul attempted to use the

---
18. Dunham, "Acts 17:16–34," 203.
19. Fernando, Sharing the Truth, 70.

Athenians' spiritual language to talk about the Creator God and the Christian gospel.[20]

Paul, who understood the boundless work of the Spirit in human cultures, philosophies, and poems, used these to share the gospel with others even though the Greek authors of these philosophies and poems were ignorant of the Spirit who had inspired their insights.

2.3.3 Religiosity of People

The religious nature of human beings is part of human culture and enables humanity to have religious experiences. For example, in the book of Jonah, the sailors experienced God's work and expressed a "fear of God." God had called Jonah to go to Nineveh, a country that was an enemy of Israel. Although Jonah failed to understand the heart of God and his will, the story portrays the sailors on board the ship as having a very different attitude towards God. Despite their ignorance of Yahweh, they were pious people. It was they who prayed to Jonah's God and asked to be spared Jonah's punishment. These sailors become even more fearful when Jonah was thrown overboard and the sea immediately grew calm. The text says that "they offered a sacrifice to the LORD and made vows" (Jonah 1:16 NRSV). The sailors' God-fearing nature enabled them to understand the will of God.

Similarly, in Athens, Paul was able to recognize the Athenians' religious attitude by observing their worship of objects. The altar with the inscription "to an unknown god," revealed the Athenians' intention to know God and their acceptance of their own ignorance. According to Robert E. Dunham, in making particular mention of the inscription on the altar, Luke shows Paul "picking up the inchoate longings of this exceptionally religious people and directing them to their proper object."[21] Paul's message, which interpreted their partial religious concepts, led the Athenians to experience the true God. Paul proclaimed God's truth, which had been uttered by pagan poets even though these poets had failed to understand the reality of their own words: "though indeed he is not far from each one of us. For 'In him we live and move and have our being'; as even some of your own poets have said, 'For we too are his offspring'" (Acts 17:27–28 NRSV).

---

20. Kim, *Holy Spirit in the World*, 177.
21. Dunham, "Acts 17:16–34," 204.

Athenians had the idea of one creator God and, without knowing much about this creator, composed poems about him. The message of Paul led some of the Athenians to know the real God and to deepen their spiritual understanding of God's presence. These converted believers had previously sung about the divine reality without knowing the truth. Later, however, what they recognized became a revelation for them. The hidden reality of their worship of "an unknown god" (17:23 NRSV) was revealed to them because of their willingness to know further. This incident in Paul's ministry shows that the Spirit of God paves ways for people to know God even if their darkened hearts cannot understand him.

Another example is Cornelius, a Gentile who was accepted by God because of his devout religiosity. Cornelius is portrayed as an earnest inquirer and a deeply religious individual. Despite his devotion, it was necessary for one of God's servants to come and make it clear to him that the deity he worshipped was, in fact, the same one revealed through Jesus of Nazareth. Nevertheless, Cornelius was already spiritually prepared to receive a personal visitation from God as well as the promised Holy Spirit.

Such incidents expose the invisible work of the Spirit in human life – guiding people towards the true God through their religiosity. Experiencing the fear of God, aspiring to obtain religious or spiritual knowledge, or receiving a vision can function as a means to draw people near to God.

2.3.4 Moral Character

Regardless of religious and cultural differences, people generally value moral principles and ethical values, which may be expressed by moral actions, a helpful attitude, peace, love, and caring for the poor. These divine affections in people can function as a symbolic presence of the Spirit, leading them to know God. The Old Testament describes Melchizedek as someone who ruled righteously and mediated peace; therefore, he was accepted by God and employed by God for his purpose. The book of Genesis portrays Melchizedek as a mysterious person who was anointed by God to perform priestly work. No details are given about Melchizedek's historical background but, according to the biblical account, he was the king of "righteousness" and the high priest of "Salem" (meaning "peace") (Gen 14:18–20, Heb. 7:1–3). It is interesting to notice that "Melchizedek's name – whether the descriptor for an anonymous priest and king or the actual name of this priest of Salem – would have been heard by Hebrew readers of this text as 'the king of righteousness.'"[22] In Hebrew, "mlch" means "king" and "zdk" means "righteousness." God brought Melchizedek, the high priest of Salem, to bless Abraham, the father of the Israelite people, as there was no elder to ordain him as a leader and prophet. After receiving God's revelation, Melchizedek fulfilled his priestly duty by bestowing a blessing in the name of God, the creator of heaven and earth, who had granted Abram victory over his enemies. The biblical narrative suggests that it was because of Melchizedek's moral standing that God entrusted him with great responsibility. Therefore, it does not seem wrong to conclude that God views the good character of people in a positive light and may choose to bless such people with spiritual experiences of himself.

In the New Testament, Cornelius is represented as a man who demonstrated his love for people by generously giving alms. Cornelius's moral character and good deeds found favour in the sight of God. "The description of him as 'God-fearing' in 10:22 suggests that he was what was called a righteous Gentle, that is, a believer in the Jewish God, but one who had not been circumcised."[23] God is righteous, and those who walk uprightly please him. Scripture regards the righteous response of human beings as the fruit of the Spirit. How do we judge the fruit of the Spirit when seen in other religious faiths? 1 John 2:29 (NIV) says, "If you know that he [God] is righteous, you know that everyone who does what is right has been born of him." Therefore, a person's moral character can function as evidence of the Spirit's intervention in their life. Based on Matthew 25:34–36, DeCelles declares that "love directed to a neighbor is automatically directed to Christ, and from Christ to God."[24] Similarly, the Spirit plays a transformative role, leading to the truth, towards perfection and drawing closer to God. The Spirit resides within humankind, inspiring virtuous actions and fostering a love for others. In the distinction and selflessness of love, God's presence is manifested in all creation.[25] This mysterious presence of human morality undoubtedly functions at times as a spiritual work to bring people closer to God.

---

22. Johnston, God's Wider Presence, 93.
23. Venkataraman, "Acts," 1478.
24. DeCelles, "Holy Spirit," 42.
25. Moltmann, Spirit of Life, 50.

The presence of the Spirit is manifested in diverse ways across cultures, in such areas as human principles, religiosity and morality, but people often fail to identify these functions of the Spirit in their life. Sometimes, the mysterious presence of the Spirit is misunderstood by people and interpreted as merely human intellectual knowledge or human moral principles. Sadly, people are unable to understand the real source and the reason of such good qualities. God, the creator, wants his creation, human beings, to know him more and more. The good characteristics people experience are some of the significant ways God uses to reveal himself.

2.4 Role of the Spirit in Spiritual Experience

It is very difficult to identify the presence of the Spirit in religious experience. The source and messages of religious experience are often marked by a sense of mystery. To understand this revelation and its purpose amid its ongoing mystery, human attitude is important. A positive response to the Spirit's involvement in human life helps to realize the purpose of.

2.4.1 Mystery

God's unbiased spiritual presence among people demonstrates his intention to convey messages. But not everyone understands this divine truth given by the Spirit. Sometimes, divine revelations that come through the Spirit remain a mystery and require the help of a third person, God's servant, to elucidate the truth. In the New Testament, Caiaphas, who was the high priest at the time, uttered a divine prophecy without understanding the reality of his words (see John 11:49–52). When the Jewish people became increasingly unhappy and irritated by the public ministry of Jesus, they approached Caiaphas and the council plotted against Jesus. Caiaphas said, "It is expedient for us that one man should die for the people, and not that the whole nation should perish" (11:50 NKJV). This statement was a divine mystery. Verse 51 says, "Now this he did not say on his own *authority*; but . . . he prophesied that Jesus would die for the nation" (emphasis mine). Caiaphas was not able to understand what he had said. Amazingly, God selected this priest through whom to proclaim a greater truth than he himself understood. For Caiaphas, the truth remained a mystery. It is not necessary that God's people always understand divine mysteries.

Similarly, Pilate, a Roman governor, prepared a notice and fastened it to the cross. The notice read, "JESUS OF NAZARETH, THE KING OF THE JEWS" (John 19:19, NKJV). Pilate was not aware of the truth of his statement, which expressed something that was a divine mystery. To Pilate, his statement was ironic, perhaps even cynical. But the Spirit used Pilate as a channel to proclaim this truth. What is the relevance of these words in Holy Scripture? Surely one conclusion is that it is not required that the speaker understand all the inspiration of the Spirit. Sometimes, such understanding may come through another person. This happened in Athens when Paul interpreted the writings of the Athenians "to an unknown god" (Acts 17). In addition, Scripture narrates many other incidents where a servant of God must interpret God's messages. For example, the meaning of the dreams of the prisoners (the cupbearer and baker) and Pharaoh had to be interpreted by Joseph (Genesis 40–41); King Nebuchadnezzar had to get an explanation of his dreams from Daniel (Daniel 2 and 4), and King Belshazzar's vision was also interpreted by Daniel (Daniel 5); Paul's vision at Damascus was explained by Ananias (Acts 9), and in response to a vision Peter explained the good news of Jesus to Cornelius (Acts 10:1–43). All these incidents reinforce the biblical truth that certain spiritual experiences remain mysteries that are fully revealed only through the interpretation given by a third person.

2.4.2 Imperfection

The Spirit plays a significant role in revealing God's message to people through his active presence in human life, human culture, and human experience. But even here, the Spirit does not reveal his full divine nature and perfection but, rather, functions as an agent who connects human beings with God by providing partial knowledge. Johnston writes, "Surely our knowledge of God through his Spirit remains partial, whether creationally (Eccl 3:1–11), existentially (Rom 11:33–36), or relationally (1 Cor 13:12)."[26] Regarding this partial knowledge, it is not mandatory for all people to be aware or identify the intervention of God in their personal life. Nobody can claim that they are divine or perfect because of the presence of the Spirit in them. Rather, the Spirit prompts and empowers us to know God and his will. Similarly, the presence of the Spirit in culture does not make any culture perfect. Rather,

---

26. Johnston, "Discerning the Spirit," 67.

various cultural artefacts or events function only as signposts that point to the perfect. Regardless of the defective nature of humanity and human cultures, people have the privilege of God's presence through his Spirit.

2.4.3 The Value of Human Response

In religious experiences, a submissive heart and a positive response towards the work of the Spirit are essential for knowing the will of God. People's responses towards the Spirit's action are distinct and produce different results in their lives. The Bible teaches that wickedness and hardness of the heart are barriers to realizing the Spirit's work. At the time of Noah, the wickedness of the people was great, and the Lord said, "My Spirit will not contend with humans forever" (Gen 6:3 NIV). Noah heard and obeyed God while his neighbours did not.

Similarly, Pharaoh hardened his heart to hear the true God even though specific miracles were revealed to him (Exodus 4–14). The Spirit of God dwells in human beings as the breath of life. But the Spirit of God also provides opportunities for men and women to know God. The positive responses of people yield positive results, and their negative responses produce negative results. On the day of Pentecost, when Peter was preaching, some people who heard the message were "pricked in their heart," responded positively towards the message, and became part of the church (Acts 2:37–42 ASV). However, the people who heard the message of Stephen hardened their hearts. Therefore, sadly, they were not able to understand God's will (Acts 7:54–60).

Similarly, at Athens, when Paul explained the truth based on the people's cultural philosophy, a few readily accepted, the good news about Jesus but others did not. The Spirit of God will not usually work in the hearts of people who are arrogant and disobedient. Human beings are given the choice to hear and follow the Spirit (or not). A positive attitude of dependence on God's Spirit is necessary to know the truth.

Above all, Jesus himself is our greatest model of obedience to the Spirit. Paul describes the incarnation of Jesus and the Spirit's work in his life as a great mystery (1 Tim 3:16). But Jesus had a personal relationship with the Spirit, and this strengthened him. Perhaps the need to trust the Spirit is shown most clearly in the prayer life of Jesus, who submitted himself to the Spirit, always ready to obey what the Spirit said. According to Deissmann, Jesus understood and experienced that his prayer was based on his relationship with God.[27] Jesus's prayer was rooted in his understanding of the Father-Son relationship he enjoyed with God. James Dunn is correct in saying that in prayer, Jesus "found God characteristically to be 'Father'; and this sense of God was so real, so loving, so compelling, that whenever he turned to God, it was the cry 'Abba' that came most naturally to his lips."[28] Jesus lived and moved through the Spirit; and this is what God expects from his people. Jesus's understanding of the Father and his relationship with the Father. was revealed throughout his life. Therefore, anyone who prays to God, regardless of their identity or beliefs, is a genuine truth seeker. The act of prayer forms an integral part of the experience of God, a realm we should strive to explore and comprehend. This type of prayer can only be done through the help of the Spirit. Elizabeth Johnson says, "We can indeed maintain that every authentic prayer is called forth by the Holy Spirit, who is mysteriously present in the heart of every person."[29] Jesus, in his human nature, practised trust in the Spirit in every aspect of his life and became a model for us. We must imitate Jesus's willingness to follow the Spirit, his understanding of the weakness of human nature, and his recognition of the need for dependence on God. The Spirit, present in humankind, offers distinct opportunities for us to recognize God. Some use such opportunities, while others do not. Through such religious experiences, the Spirit's presence and work become so powerful that people can know God and understand aspects of his will – though some elements of mystery will always remain.

2.5 Conclusion

As outlined in this study, God created humans as spiritual beings, and his Spirit is present in them as "the breath of God," providing an "inner knowledge." This mysterious presence of the Spirit in all humans makes it possible for them to have spiritual experiences and exercise positive qualities without discrimination. God's intention in every spiritual experience is that people would know him and know his will. Dreams, visions, human culture, tradition, creativity, and even other faiths are distinct means that God uses for

---

27. Deissmann, Religion of Jesus, 63.
28. Dunn, *Jesus and the Spirit*, 26.
29. Johnson, Quest, 171.

spiritual interventions in people's lives. Since all goodness comes from God, any glimpse of truth, beauty, or goodness found in human experience undoubtedly directs them towards perfection. God is the provider of all good things; even to non-covenantal people, and so even works through Indian religious traditions, including Hinduism, in providing opportunities to know him. This is the work of the Spirit in mysteriously leading people towards God. However, this general revelation found in the religious experience of others may not be complete. Sometimes, it requires interpretation by a third party. However, an attentive heart and obedient mind are essential if the revelation is to be received. In a pluralistic world, the biblical evidence of God's presence and spiritual works in other cultures and in human creativity in general point to the relevance of the religious experience even of non-Christians. This is because the religious experience of people of other faiths leads to the possibility of experiencing the Spirit's presence.

CHAPTER 3

Swami Vivekananda's Understanding of Religious Experience

Swami Vivekananda – also known as Karma Yogi or Jnana Yogi – was a leading spokesman for modern Hinduism and neo-Vedanta. He sought to revolutionize the identity of Hinduism with his unrivalled knowledge and wealth of spiritual experience. Swami Vivekananda embraced Vedanta (*advaita*) as his foundation and endeavoured to present Hinduism as a universal religion. Until then, Hinduism had been confined primarily to the Indian populace. However, through the Ramakrishna Mission, Hinduism – contrary to its historical nature – underwent a transformative shift, becoming a missionary and assertive religion.[1] Even as he confronted different Christian leaders and Western missionaries, Vivekananda's principles of Hinduism were constant. M. M. Thomas, a twentieth-century Indian Christian theologian, says, "He [Vivekananda] has a theology of religion, which sees the mystic vision and the experience as the goal and end of all religious experiences, and what he does is to interpret the truths of the religion of the Bible in the light of his faith in the ultimate truth of the Advaitic religion."[2] Thus, understanding Vivekananda's religious principles provides many opportunities to connect Christian theology with the Hindu religious tradition. In particular, Swami Vivekananda's theological concepts centre on the significance of religious experiences. This chapter deals with Vivekananda's understanding of the

---

1. Sumithra, *Christian Theologies*, 17.
2. Thomas, *Acknowledged Christ*, 125.

religious experience and the possibility of spiritual insights into such experiences in order to reconsider a better Christian theology i for our context.

3.1 Life of Swami Vivekananda (1863–1902)

Vivekananda was born on 12 January 1863 in Shimla Pally, Calcutta, into a respectable middle-class Datta family. His father, Vishwanath Datta, was a well-known lawyer, and his mother, Bhuvaneshwari Devi, was a pious, kind-hearted lady, devoted to Hindu traditions. Vivekananda's parents named him Narendranath Datta and called him Narendra, or Naren for short. Vishwanath, a lover of arts and literature, often had scholarly discussions within the family and among his friends on topics such as politics, religion, and society. He used to invite the little boy, Narendra, to join the discussions and even articulate his views on these topics. The life of his parents and the congenial atmosphere of his family helped to mould Narendra, and he grew to be a talented young man with high ideals. He was skilled in every area and possessed a multitude of talents: an impressive singing voice, skill in sports, a quick wit, extensive knowledge of various subjects, a rational mindset, and a deep passion for assisting others.[3] From his childhood, Narendra proved to be a natural leader.

Narendra received a well-rounded British-style education in Calcutta. He passed the entrance examination for the Metropolitan Institution of Ishwar Chandra Vidyasagar and, later, the BA examinations of the General Assembly's Institution, which is now known as the Scottish Church College. During his college days, Narendra learned to play several instruments and became proficient in various languages: Bengali, Urdu, Hindi, English, and Persian. Even though he was a good student of philosophy and Western logic, he also studied history, science, medicine, and English literature. Richard P. Hayes writes that Dr. William Hastie, the principal of Narendra's college, was impressed by his extraordinary skills and considered that "Narendranath Datta was clearly a genius and was without any doubt the most intelligent student he had ever had, including all the students he had known in Germany."[4]

---

3. Lokeswarananda, *Swami Vivekananda*, 1–2.
4. Hayes, "Reflections," 1.

Narendra's religious and spiritual interest began in his childhood. His religious study no doubt started with his mother, who first taught him the *Epics* and *Puranas*. He became interested in questions like, Is there a God? If there is a God, what is he like? What are people's relations with him? Did he create this world, which is so full of irregularities? Such questions disturbed his mind continually. Although Narendra discussed these questions with many, he ended up with unsatisfactory answers. During this time, Brahmo Samaj, a religious organization founded by Raja Ram Mohan Roy in 1828, influenced him, and he became a part of it. This group was strongly critical of religious rituals, idol worship, the hierarchy of priests, and the caste system, all of which were eschewed in favour of the simple worship and adoration of the eternal author and preserver of the universe.

However, Narendra did not find in Brahmo Samaj someone who could talk about God authentically, based on a personal experience with God. However, he found this in Sri Ramakrishna Paramahamsa (1836–1886), a Brahmin priest at Dakshineshwar Kali temple in Bengal. About his meeting with Ramakrishna, Narendra says:

> At first glance, he appeared to be an ordinary man without any notable features. Yet, he spoke in the most straightforward language, leaving me pondering if he could truly be a great teacher. Intrigued, I approached him and asked the same question I had posed to countless others throughout my life: "Do you believe in God, Sir?" Surprisingly, he replied with a confident "Yes." My curiosity prompted another question, "Can you prove it, Sir?" Again, he responded affirmatively, explaining that he sees God just as he sees me, but in a much more profound way.
>
> His words deeply impressed me, and from that moment, I found myself drawn to him day after day. In his presence, I witnessed that religion could be imparted through a single touch or a mere glance, forever transforming one's entire life.[5]

Ramakrishna, who succeeded in removing Narendra's religious doubts, chose Narenda as his favoured disciple. It was under this master's guidance that Narendra first attained the highest Yogic Samadhi at Kashipur. Their

---

5. Vivekananda, *Complete Works*, 4:145.

relationship continued until Ramakrishna died of cancer in 1886. Before his death, Ramakrishna handed over his power and the task of teaching spiritual lessons to Narendra by symbolically giving him the *gerua* cloth. Narendra willingly accepted the mantle of his master. Narendranath was entrusted with the task of comprehending the profound mystical experiences by his master and guiding the other disciples to embody the ideal of renunciation set by their revered teacher.[6] He united the disciples of Ramakrishna to serve the nation of India and instituted the Ramakrishna Mission on 1 May 1897.

Narendranath Datta took vows of celibacy and wandered around the nation of India fulfilling the mission of his master. He was an itinerant pilgrim, and this provided him with a wide knowledge of the people of India. During that time, he received the religious name Swami Vivekananda, which means "the bliss of discriminative knowledge." Vivekananda's knowledge of India was evident in his speech and actions. Rabindranath Tagore once advised Romain Rolland that if he wanted to know India, he should study Vivekananda.[7] Herein lies the significance of studying Vivekananda's ideologies.

On 11 September 1893, at the age of thirty, Swami Vivekananda attended the Parliament of Religions in Chicago as a representative of Hinduism. The message that he delivered at this meeting dominated the minds of world celebrities and brought tribute to the nation of India. It also opened the door for Vivekananda to travel continuously in Europe and Asia to teach, write, lecture, and conduct meetings with prominent religious leaders and intellectuals. For the next nine years, until his death, Vivekananda espoused the principles of "Practical Vedanta," an inclusive form of Hinduism that harmonized active engagement in the world with the pursuit of ultimate union with the One. During Vivekananda's last days, his health issues were aggravated by his work schedule – lecturing engagements, private discussions, and correspondence. He suffered from asthma, diabetes, and other physical illnesses. On 4 July 1902, Vivekananda passed away while he was meditating in the high yogic state of *mahasamadhi*.

---

6. Jones, *Encyclopedia of Religion*, 9629.
7. Lokeswarananda, *Swami Vivekananda*, 7.

3.2 Religious Principles of Vivekananda

Vivekananda gave high priority to spiritual activities and their results. He exalted the glory of Hinduism and spread his teachings around the world. He believed that religions should provide space for individuals to perform spiritual exercises and experience self-realization. Some of Vivekananda's religious principles are explained below.

First, Vivekananda's religious concepts can be distinguished from the common faith and practices that existed in Hinduism: polytheism, idol worship, ritual practices, and superstitions. Vivekananda, among other prominent Hindu philosophers such as Shankaracharya, Ramanuja, Madhava, Swami Dayanada Saraswati, Ramakrishna Paramahamsa, Rabindranath Tagore, and Radhakrishnan, gave priority to spirituality over Hindu ritual practices. This did not mean that Vivekananda underestimated Hindu traditions. Rather, as he said, "Hinduism is a mother of all religion . . . which taught the world both tolerance and universal acceptance."[8] In his eyes, the Hindu understanding of its revelatory origin, its spiritual exercises, and its essentiality, as well as the need for self-realization, were unique. Hindus received their religious ideologies and (scriptures the Vedas) through revelation. Vivekananda found that the spiritual exercises in Hinduism condemned Hindu ritual practices and human intellectual doctrines. He understood that "religion is not in doctrines, in dogmas, nor intellectual argumentation; it is being and becoming, it is realisation."[9] He believed that religious dogmas and books should receive less priority in building a person religiously and spiritually. Vivekananda explains his understanding of the value of religious books in this way: "These books are only the maps, the experiences of past men, as a motive to power us to dare to make the same experiences and discover in the same way, if not better."[10] This belief was not different from his master's understanding that "it is this direct transcendent experience that gives validity to religions, and not books."[11] Vivekananda asserts, "Man must realize God, feel God, see

---

8. Vivekananda, *Complete Works*, 1:4.
9. Vivekananda, 2:45.
10. Vivekananda, 6:13.
11. Bhajanananda, *Harmony of Religions*, 31.

God, talk to God. That is religion."[12] He believed that religions should give priority to spiritual experiences.

Second, Vedanta – the basic principle that both Vivekananda and his master, Sri Ramakrishna Paramahamsa, upheld – understands realization as the essence of religion. "This is the first principle of Vedanta, that realization is religion, and he who realises is the religious man."[13] The relationship of Vivekananda with his master, Ramakrishna, was based on the principle that "spiritual realization is the essence of religion." One of the five doctrines of Ramakrishna's "Harmony of Religions" (*Dharma-Samanvaya*), which Sri Ramakrishna followed in his own life, is that the ultimate aim and meaning of human life lies in the realization of the Ultimate Reality. This profound understanding is not only the core purpose of all religions but also the ultimate goal that humanity seeks. Ramakrishna gave priority to experiencing spiritual powers and live in that spiritual realm.

Ramakrishna not only spent time learning such spiritual truths but also sought to pass on what he taught to others. Swami Gambhirananda, for example, describes Ramakrishna's spiritual thirst like this: "He was a lover of God and wanted to enjoy the bliss of God in different ways. This was what made him follow different spiritual paths."[14] It is no wonder, then, that young Vivekananda, whose mind was unsatisfied and who was searching for a spiritually experienced guru, bonded with this simple, uneducated man, Ramakrishna. Vivekananda acknowledged that a master should have self-experience and the ability to transfer this experience to others. Vivekananda authentically taught and cultivated in his Vedantic principles the transformative religious experience he received from his own master. At its essence, "religion is the pursuit of realization, where we must firmly differentiate between mere words and genuine intuitive experience. True realization emerges from the profound depths of our souls. Interestingly, common sense often appears uncommon when it comes to matters of this nature."[15]

Third, to Vivekananda, having personal experience was more important than learning the truth and understanding others' experiences. He says, "We

---

12. Vivekananda, *Speeches and Writings*, 12.
13. Vivekananda, Complete Works, 6:13.
14. Gambhirananda, *Holy Mother*, 463.
15. Vivekananda, Complete Works, 3:46.

may talk and reason all our lives, but we shall not understand a word of truth until we experience it ourselves."[16] Personal experience alone can provide self-satisfaction. Vivekananda expresses the priority of self-realization and self-satisfaction in these words: "If I do not find bliss in the life of the Spirit, shall I seek satisfaction in the life of the senses?"[17] He found more satisfaction in spiritual experiences than in any kind of worldly pleasure. In other words, giving priority to experiencing spiritual matters enables an individual to recognize reality and experience self-satisfaction. Religious experience is the essence of religion, and such an experience satisfies the human soul. Vivekananda believed that our experience is the only teacher we have to verify and test religious truths. The knowledge and abilities that people achieve through religious experience are of far greater value than human intellectual knowledge. These spiritual outcomes have the power to lead people to self-realization and self-satisfaction. As a monk, Vivekananda not only held fast to these principles but also put his whole effort into achieving these higher positions. He firmly believed that human effort and spiritual discipline were essential for people to reach this goal.

3.3 Religious Experience and the "Ideal Man"

Through having a religious experience, Vivekananda expected a person to become "an ideal man."[18] His expectation of an ideal man meant reaching the highest state of perfection. This was possible through having spiritual experiences, which allowed a person to achieve mysterious knowledge, realize the truth, enjoy the divine bliss of perfection and, finally, be in union with the Absolute. The sections that follow explore the role of religious experiences in achieving these wonderful qualities and making an ideal man.

---

16. Vivekananda, 1:152.
17. Vivekananda, 5:448.
18. For Vivekananda, "ideal man" and "ideal religion" were significant concepts, which he both taught and lived. For him, the ideal man was one in whom all the elements of philosophy, mysticism, emotion and action were equally present in full. In his Neo-Vedantism, Swami Vivekananda combines Jnana, Karma, Bhakti, and Raja yoga. Sooklal, "Neo-Vedanta Philosophy," 42. Vivekananda believed that "work, wisdom, knowledge and mysticism are the different aspects of an individual, together making up a whole." Stephen, *Social Philosophy*, 224. Regarding ideal religion, Vivekananda says, "The attempt to help mankind to become wonderfully balanced in these four directions, is my ideal of religion." Vivekananda, *Speeches and Writings*, 317.

3.3.1 Knowledge

For Vivekananda, attaining real knowledge was deeply connected with religious experience. In Hinduism, many sages and philosophers sacrificed their lives in search of the truth, finding satisfaction in doing so and believing that human happiness depended on such experience. Vivekananda asserts, "The Hindu's view of life is that we are here to learn; the whole happiness of life is to learn; the human soul is here to love learning and get experience."[19] However, Vivekananda believed that real knowledge could not be cultivated in the human intellectual realm of books but could only be awakened in the inner being through experience. The very term "Vedanta," one of Vivekananda's chief principles, means "the end of knowledge." The term is the combination of two Sanskrit words – "Veda," which means "knowledge," and "anta," which means "the end of" or "the goal of." Veda includes all knowledge. It is as infinite as God is and cannot be created by people.[20]

The Vedantic concept of knowledge lies beyond the human intellect and is very close to spiritual experience and the receiving of new revelations. Vivekananda says, "The Hindu word for revelation is 'Veda.' Hence the 'Vedas' are the revelations."[21] Revelation is personal and beyond intellectual knowledge. In Vivekananda's view, all knowledge is derived from direct experience – as in the scientific method – and so, there is no knowledge without experience and a person has to see themselves in their own soul. Thus, religious experience is essential in attaining knowledge, and this experience is the only teacher we have. Religion, like the sciences, requires us to gather facts and to see for ourselves, but this is possible only when we go beyond the knowledge that lies in the region of the five senses. We must have a spiritual experience.

3.3.2 Self-Realization of Truth

In Hinduism, religious knowledge means knowing the truth, which can only be achieved through religious experience. Therefore, discovering a single meaning of truth in Hinduism is very difficult. Different Hindu philosophers and sects have their own varying meanings of truth since they have had different experiences. The seventh-century philosopher Sankaracharya believed

---

19. Vivekananda, *Complete Works*, 2:409.
20. Vivekananda, 8:72.
21. Vivekananda, 9:637.

that truth reveals the only existence of Brahman, the actionless, attribute-free ground of being that can be described as *sat-cit-ananda*, (which means being-consciousness-bliss). According to Nikhilananda, however, truth is divine bliss or perfect happiness. For the Hindu sect ISKCON, the absolute truth is Krishna – a supremely powerful being – whereas to the sect of Veerashaiva the divine truth is Shiva. On the other hand, satyagraha is one of Gandhi's religious principles, which means "holding to truth."

Based on these different concepts, it would not be wrong to say knowing the truth is knowing about ourselves, knowing the real God, and knowing divine happiness. Hindus expect a new age – "the age of truth" (Krita Yuga) – that will replace all the wickedness, strife, and dissension of this era (Kali Yuga) with righteousness.[22] Truth is, of course, a significant concept in all religions and religious movements. The Theosophical Society, one of the contemporary religious movements of India, has the credo "There is no religion higher than truth."[23] Here, again, the priority of truth in religions is asserted. According to Ramakrishna, truth can be found in all the world's religions.[24] As a *sanatana dharma* (eternal religion), Hinduism is best known as a way of searching for the truth, where seekers seek the truth in their own unique ways. In that sense, "the *sanatana dharma* is not merely the religions practised by the inhabitants of India who look upon the VEDAS as the supreme wisdom, but the 'way' of all who seek the highest truth, whatever their religion."[25]

Vivekananda fails to give a specific explanation of truth but says that nothing will satisfy us until we know the truth for ourselves.[26] "By truth," he writes, "we attain fruits of work. Through truth, everything is attained. In truth, everything is established. Relating facts as they are – this is truth."[27] Vivekananda understood that the yearning for truth resides deep within the heart of human beings as they seek to experience it first-hand, embracing it as a profound realization that dispels all uncertainties. According to the Vedas, only when truth is grasped, felt, and known within one's innermost being do all doubts dissipate. The attainment of truth bestows countless blessings upon

---

22. Jones and Ryan, *Encyclopedia of Hinduism*, 223.
23. Jones and Ryan, 243.
24. Jones and Ryan, 482.
25. Jones and Ryan, 380.
26. Vivekananda, Speeches and Writings, 23.
27. Vivekananda, Complete Works, 1:155.

human beings for it illuminates the darkest corners of the mind, purifies the inner realm, and infuses life with newfound strength and purpose.[28] However, removing all kinds of selfishness is essential to attain truth.

Vivekananda says, "Truth will never come into our minds so long as there will remain the faintest shadow of Ahamkâra (egotism)."[29] "As soon as we become aware of this truth, all misery goes, so we must get knowledge of the truth."[30] "He who realises transcendental truth, he who realises the Atman in his own nature, he who comes face to face with God, sees God alone in everything, has become a Rishi."[31] In Hinduism, rishis or seers achieve this truth through their spiritual experiences. Jyotirmaya Sharma writes, "The Vedantic seers had seen the truth. These truths were religious laws as well as the grand truths of spirituality."[32] This spiritual realisation is a continual process which has to be performed as a spiritual discipline. To a Hindu, a person is not travelling from error to truth but from truth to truth, from lower to higher truth.[33] Achieving the knowledge of truth makes a person perfect or ideal.

3.3.3 Divine Bliss of Perfection

To become a perfect being is a spiritual experience through which a person can live with perfect happiness. Nobody can claim to know the truth of perfection without realizing this divine bliss. Vivekananda writes, "And what becomes of man when he becomes perfect? He lives a life of bliss with the infinite. The person who reaches perfection enjoys infinite and perfect bliss, having obtained the only thing in which man ought to have pleased God and enjoys the bliss with God."[34] Vivekananda believed that a real Hindu does not live by words and theories. Rather, if there are existences beyond the ordinary sensual existence, the true Hindu wants to come face to face with such an existence. The Hindu religion does not consist in struggles and attempts to believe a certain doctrine or dogma but in realizing; it is not in believing but

---

28. Vivekananda, 1: 56, 130, ; 2:169.
29. Vivekananda, 5:304.
30. Vivekananda, *Vedanta Philosophy*, 135.
31. Vivekananda, Complete Works, 3:235.
32. Sharma, Restatement of Religion, 221.
33. Vivekananda, Complete Works, 1:17.
34. Vivekananda, Speeches and Writings, 41.

in being and becoming that a religious state is achieved.[35] Vivekananda says that to associate with God and to experience divine bliss, a person needs to be engaged in a constant spiritual struggle. He asserts, "The whole struggle in their [Hindu] system is a constant struggle to become perfect, to become divine, to reach God and see God, and in thus reaching God, seeing God, and becoming perfect, even as the father in Heaven is perfect, consists the religion of the Hindus."[36] Even though the uncertainty of a universal God is made vivid in the writings of Vivekananda, he admits the necessity of God's mercy and consideration to reach perfection. To obliterate all uncertainties, a person must personally witness and experience the presence of God. Hence, the most compelling evidence a Hindu sage offers regarding the soul and God is this: "I have seen the soul; I have seen God." Such profound realization stands as the ultimate attainment of perfection.[37]

3.3.4 Union with the Absolute

The concept of union is an inescapable principle in Hinduism as well as in the teachings of Vivekananda. In Hinduism, union with the Absolute– which is the ultimate goal of human life – is represented by various terms such as *moksha*, *mukti*, and *samadhi*. In a literal sense, union is the release of the soul from the birth and rebirth cycle (*samsara*) to become one with the Absolute Being (Brahman). Regarding *samsara*, Vedanta teaches that all human beings are bounded by three basic desires – endless life, infinite knowledge, and absolute joy. Similarly, "ignorance, inequality, and desire are the three causes of human misery, and each follows the other in inevitable union."[38] Human suffering and the birth-rebirth cycle of human life are considered a bondage that accompanies human beings until they become free of it.

Vivekananda's philosophy of Vedanta implies that people bear full responsibility for their suffering and actions. He says that we can blame neither God nor the devil. Nothing happens to us by the whim of some outside agency, and we are each responsible for what life brings us – all of us are reaping the results of our previous actions in this life or in previous lives. To understand

---

35. Vivekananda, 41.
36. Vivekananda, 41.
37. Vivekananda, 41.
38. Vivekananda, 4:269.

this idea better, we must first understand the law of karma.[39] Whenever we engage in actions or thoughts, they leave an indelible imprint – akin to subtle grooves – on the mind. These imprints are referred to as samskaras – derived from the Sanskrit word *samskri* – signifying refinement. Samskaras are ritual ceremonies that sanctify and mark significant life events. Each samskara involves the presence of a Brahmin priest and incorporates prayers, oblations, offerings, and a fire ritual.[40] When actions and thoughts are repeated, the grooves become deeper. The combination of "grooves" – samskaras – forms our characters and also strongly influences our subsequent thoughts and actions. The effects of karma may come instantly, later in life, or in another life altogether; what is absolutely certain, however, is that these effects will appear at some time or other. Until liberation is achieved, we live and die within the confines of the law of karma – the chain of cause and effect.

Even though every Hindu tradition considers unification with Brahman an ideal principle, different understandings exist within Hinduism based on its diverse nature. Some traditions believe that people can be liberated while they are alive (*jivanmukta*). Some see liberation as merging into a characterless Brahman, while others see liberation as simply becoming one with God or being liberated near God.[41] Vivekananda understood liberation as *jivanmukti* or freedom from bondage while still living in the body. Mukti or liberation signifies complete freedom from the shackles of both good and evil. In the pursuit of liberation, it is essential to recognize that a golden chain is as binding as an iron one. Sri Ramakrishna used to impart the analogy of using a thorn to remove another thorn from the foot – eventually, however, both thorns would be discarded. Similarly, negative tendencies are countered by cultivating positive ones; yet even good inclinations must be transcended in the journey towards ultimate liberation.[42] With regard to a person who experiences a state of real union with Brahman. Vivekananda states that upon

---

39. The word "karma" comes from the Sanskrit verb *kri*, meaning to do. Even though the simple meaning of karma is action, it also holds the meaning of the result of action. Whatever acts we have performed and whatever thoughts we have thought have created an impression, both in our minds and in the universe around us. The universe gives back to us what we have given to it. Good actions and thoughts create good effects, bad ones create bad effects. Vivekananda, *Karma Yoga*, 4.

40. Jones and Ryan, *Encyclopedia of Hinduism*, 114.

41. Jones and Ryan, 292.

42. Vivekananda, Complete Works, 5:361.

attaining the profound realization of oneness, all delusion dissipates. Such a soul remains impervious to deception, comprehending the essence and truth of all existence. Misery holds no sway over them for they have discovered the secret of everything – the lord, the Eternal centre the unity of all. In this state of eternal existence, eternal knowledge, and eternal bliss, there exists no room for death, disease, sorrow, or discontent. Perfect union and perfect bliss prevail. There is no cause for mourning, as reality knows no death or suffering, and there is no one to grieve for or be sorry for. The enlightened one has transcended all boundaries, perceiving the pure one, the formless, the bodiless, and the immaculate.[43]

The human craving for union with the Absolute is achieved through spiritual discipline and having spiritual experiences. Genuine Hindus spend their entire lives achieving the highest state of this union, where they can experience all kinds of eternal bliss and perfection. Vivekananda's religious concept of becoming an ideal man is possible by attaining religious experience. He believed that religious experiences can provide spiritual knowledge to people, helping them move from lower to higher truth, achieving divine bliss in life and union with the Absolute. He himself strived for this, and he asked people to do the same.

3.4 Religious Experience and Ideal Society

Similar to the way religious experience makes someone "an ideal man," Vivekananda believed that religious experience also helps to make society "an ideal society." He put all his efforts into becoming an ideal man and trying to make others do the same with the expectation of building a better India. Vivekananda considered that the spiritual experiences of human beings could transform both their personal and social lives. To reach the concept of ideal man and society, people need not only for spiritual experiences but also for social activities. Unlike many Indian monks, Vivekananda engaged in action rather than spending time only in contemplation and recitation. He considered the earth as a place to work (*Karma Bhumi*). In the personal sphere, human beings are required to work for self-realization and liberation. In the social sphere, they are required to achieve the divine nature by

---

43. Vivekananda, 2:131–132.

helping the poor and needy and establishing social justice. People's religious experience should lead to social development and social uniformity, which can contribute to forming a new India.

Vivekananda considered the social responsibility to help the poor as important as fulfilling the personal responsibility to achieve self-realization. He challenged the people of India to fulfil this duty that is inherent to birth and, once that is accomplished, to embrace the duty that aligns with our position in life and society. His expectation was a bright future for India, which could be attained through helping the poor and uplifting the downtrodden. This is the concept of "Daridra Narayana Seva" – the service of God in and through (poor) human beings. Renouncing worldly pleasures and the possibility of freedom, Vivekananda founded the Ramakrishna Math (mission) on 1 May 1897 in Calcutta. To further these ideas a socioreligious movement was organized to help the poor by providing educational, cultural, medical and relief work. Commenting on Vivekananda's concern for the poor, Swami Prabhananda – a prominent monk in the Ramakrishna Mission and the present head of the Ramakrishna Mission Institute of Culture, Calcutta – says that Vivekananda was a genuine friend of the poor and the weak, particularly the helpless masses of India, and the first Indian leader who sought a solution to their problems through education.[44] Vivekananda believed that educating oneself and helping others were the primary duties of human beings and the way to establish real happiness. He states, "This is a great lesson to learn in life, and when we have learned it fully, we shall never be unhappy; we can go and mix without harm in society anywhere and everywhere."[45] People who have achieved real knowledge will be able to reject their selfish thoughts and begin to think about the benefits to their fellow beings.

3.4.1 Social Development and Spirituality

Vivekananda discovered an inescapable alliance between spirituality and development. People who have undergone transformation and who give priority to spiritual experience bring about progress in society. Vivekananda believed that real spiritual bliss was based on loving others: "It is this Bliss that comes to you through the love of humanity; the shadow of this spiritual Bliss is

---

44. Prabhananda, "Swami Vivekananda," 242.
45. Vivekananda, Complete Works, 1:75.

this human love, but do not confound it with that human bliss."[46] Similarly, giving priority to spirituality over materialism can bring about progress in society. Vivekananda affirms, "That is to say, the mainspring of the strength of every race lies in its spirituality, and the death of that race begins the day that spirituality wanes and materialism gains ground."[47] Vivekananda's answer clearly points towards the question of what a civilized nation is: "The more advanced society or nation is spirituality, the more that society or nation is civilized. No nation can be said to have become civilized only because it has succeeded in increasing the comforts of material life by bringing into use lots of machinery and things of that sort."[48] To Vivekananda, the true development of society depends upon the priority that it gives to spirituality. He viewed social development is a result of spirituality and spirituality as a result of spiritual experience.

"Being of one mind is the secret of society,"[49] says Vivekananda. For him, the last step (*Samadhi*) in reaching the realization of happiness is to realize that "I and my Father are one." This is the transcendent experience of *nirvikalpasamadhi*. This mystical state of a yogi allows him to identify perfectly with the divine self. As a result, the yogi becomes concerned for the well-being of the whole society. Vivekananda believed that the religious experience of self-realization and, thus, union transformed the nature of a man into a divine nature, resulting in equality. Vivekananda understood that the yogi's responsibility included being a part of society by doing good works and reflecting the divine nature through helping the poor. A yogi must refrain from harbouring harmful thoughts, words, or actions towards anyone. Compassion should not only extend to humanity but also encompass the entire world. Similarly, those who are spiritual will not run away from social life or close their eyes and ears to the plight of those in need. Helping others is not about doing the will of an individual but, rather, the will of the divine transforming society through the unselfish actions of individuals. Thus, the yogi is one who gives priority to spirituality and does not hurt anyone but seeks the benefit of everyone

---

46. Vivekananda, 4:169.
47. Vivekananda, 2:60.
48. Vivekananda, 6:519.
49. Vivekananda, 3:248.

equally.[50] And this commitment to everyone happens only as the result of being in union with the Absolute. Abraham Stephen notes, "Vivekananda's treatment of *yogas* sees them as disciplines leading to the *neo-vedantic* ideal where 'oneness' is realized and universal humanity embraced."[51] Vivekananda says, "When a man has come face to face with the one great fact in the universe, then alone will doubts vanish and crooked things become straight. This is seeing God. Our business is to verify, not to swallow."[52] Vivekananda's understanding of how "crooked things become straight" leads us to wonder whether he was influenced by the biblical metaphor "The crooked roads shall become straight" (Luke 3:5 NIV). Here, Vivekananda's moral principles are not very different from Christian teaching. The spiritual experience a yogi craves is the formation of unity and equality in society.

Vivekananda believed that giving importance to religious experience could produce the ideal man and the ideal society. The divine qualities that people develop through religious experience pass into societies. There is a progression from individual transformation to social transformation, which results in forming a better community. What is significant here is Vivekananda's concept of making a better India, which is only possible through producing a generation who are committed to properly fulfilling their social responsibilities. He says that his country's future depends on its people's nature, and this prompted him to seek and build up ideal individuals.[53] Vivekananda wanted to develop a group of people who had a thirst for equality and a spiritual thirst for the progress of the community. This understanding of the importance of societal transformation of our human "spiritual thirst" does not deny the Spirit's involvement in this process. This desire is expressed in Vivekananda's letter to Dr. Nanjunda Rao, who was one of his devotees: "Everything will come right if you are pure and sincere. We want hundreds like you bursting upon society and bringing new life and vigour of the Spirit wherever they go."[54] He is also reported to have said, "Man-making is my mission." Vivekananda longed for a well-advanced society that was free from

---

50. Vivekananda, 1:144.
51. Stephen, Social Philosophy, 224.
52. Vivekananda, Complete Works, 6:130.
53. Lokeswarananda, *My India*, 1–2.
54. Vivekananda, Complete Works, 6:295.

sectarianism, bigotry, fanaticism, and violence.[55] He once said, "There must be equal chance for all – or if greater for some and for some less – the weaker should be given more chance than the strong."[56] His expectation – a spiritual disciplined community accomplished through religious experience – was simple, yet people found it difficult to achieve.

3.4.2 Role of Human Effort

Vivekananda believed that humans had to work hard – practising very strict spiritual disciplines – to attain spiritual experiences and that, through continual efforts, their religious experiences would produce positive results. *Raja-yoga* is one of the significant meditation techniques that Vivekananda taught people who sought religious experiences. Vivekananda believed that spiritual aspirations are common to all human beings and that everyone has a thirst to know eternal bliss and to transcend the sensual world. "It may be observed that since self-consciousness and the desire of self-transcendence always persists in man, therefore religious experience is an inseparable phenomenon of human life from time immemorial."[57] Attaining this goal is not simple but requires a determined effort. Vivekananda says, "However, we may argue, however much we may hear, but one thing will satisfy us, and that is our own realization, and such an experience is possible for every one of us if we will only try."[58] The effort that we put into achieving absolute bliss leads our religious experience towards its realization.

Religious experience find its origin in the innate human instinct to surpass the boundaries of the material world. This is a state in which human beings reach above our common nature. "Man is man so long as he is struggling to rise above nature, and this nature is both internal and external."[59] The internal nature of a human being always thirsts to merge with the Absolute. So, religious experiences occur as a result of human efforts to unite with the Absolute Being. The presence of Absolute in human beings is identified by various names based on the particular understanding of people and their

---

55. Vivekananda, 1:5.
56. Vivekananda, *Letters*, 255.
57. Yitik, "Religious Diversity and Harmony," 2.
58. Vivekananda, Speeches and Writings, 23.
59. Vivekananda, Complete Works, 2:60.

religious beliefs. This "Absolute" expresses a longing for becoming perfect and is seen in all religions. In Vivekananda's view, this establishes a basic commonality in all religions. Vivekananda identifies religion at its core with this transcendental spiritual consciousness and with the human struggle to attain and experience that consciousness.[60] The essentiality of an inner spiritual attitude of knowing or unifying with an Absolute leads us to think that it is a movement from spirit to Spirit. From Vivekananda's perspective, religious experience results from the persistent human effort that springs from humankind's deepest thirst and inner longing.

3.4.3 Yoga as a Spiritual Discipline

In relation to religious experience, Vivekananda taught that the best way to achieve this human craving for being perfect was in the spiritual discipline of yoga or meditation. Through meditation, "the mind itself has a higher state of existence, beyond reason, a superconscious state, and when the mind gets to that higher state, then this knowledge, beyond reasoning, comes to man. Metaphysical and transcendental knowledge comes to that man."[61] There are various such meditations by which Vivekananda taught people to achieve this perfection, the chief among these being *karma-yoga*, *bhakti-yoga*, *jnana-yoga*, and *raja-yoga*. Vivekananda seems to have given priority to *raja-yoga*. The positive results of this type of yoga include knowing the truth and reaching the highest state or perfection. *Raja-yoga* is a psychosomatic exercise that helps people to practise self-control, concentrate, meditate, achieve self-realization, and experience heavenly bliss and perfection. This form of meditation is a "science of yoga" or "psychological yoga," which is a "scientifically worked out a method of reaching this truth" by the concentration of the mind.[62] The ultimate objective of the teachings of *raja-yoga* is to master the art of mental concentration, delve into the depths of our inner consciousness, and synthesize its contents to draw our enlightened conclusions. In its last and highest state, which is Samadhi, in the absence of mental distractions and bodily disturbances, the soul's brilliance will radiate in its complete splendour,

---

60. Vivekananda, 2:41.
61. Vivekananda, 1:150.
62. Vivekananda, 1:105; 2:314.

revealing the yogi's true essence – an immortal, all-pervading being of supreme knowledge.

Raja-yoga has eight significant steps that must be followed to achieve this highest state of self-realization. It is essential to follow these steps to realize the fruits of this practice. The first two steps, Yama and Niyama, have to do with moral training and are essential for the successful practices of yoga. As these steps are followed, the fruits of this practice also begin to be realized. The good deeds of the yogi should pass on to human beings throughout the whole world. The third step, Asana (posture), is a series of physical and mental exercises: a yogi needs to practise these exercises every day until he reaches a higher state. The most significant part of this exercise is to maintain the sitting position so that one may think high thoughts. Vivekananda taught that holding the spinal column upright through sitting erect (holding the chest, neck, and head in a straight line) makes it easier for a person to think higher thoughts.

The fourth step, Pranayama, involves breathing exercises that help to control *prana* (breath). Maintaining a sitting position and repeating a sacred word like "Om" – to awaken the inner power of the spinal cord (kundalini) – is essential for the success of this step. This inner power flows through *sushumna*, helping practitioners to reach a supersensuous and superconscious state. This helps the practitioner to store good thoughts or "Ojas" in the brain, and Vivekananda believed that only a chaste person could do this.

The fifth step is Pratyahara, through which a yogi will know how perception comes. The external instruments and the internal organs acting in the body through the brain centres (mind) could come together around some external object that a yogi perceives. The success of Pratyahara depends upon being able to attach or detach the mind to or from the centres of the mind.

The sixth step is Dharana, which means focusing the mind on a certain point. Through this, the yogi learns to force his mind to feel certain parts of the body to the exclusion of others. The seventh step is Dhyana or meditation. During this stage, a yogi can make power flow towards a particular point. The eighth and last stage of *raja-yoga* is Samadhi, which is called the superconscious state. "When the mind goes beyond this line of self-consciousness," argues Vivekananda, "it is called Samadhi or super consciousness."[63] Attaining

---

63. Vivekananda, 1:148.

this super consciousness is the priority of every human being. In this stage, the yogi intensifies the power of Dhyana, rejecting the external part of perception and meditating only on the internal part.

The last three stages (Dharana, Dhyana, and Samadhi) taken together are known as *Samyama*. Upon reaching the state of Samadhi, the yogi will find himself as he always was; the essence of knowledge – immortal and all-pervading – and the glory of the soul which will be freed from distractions of the mind and body.[64] To reach the last stage of *raja-yoga*, a yogi should practise continuous meditation and spiritual discipline. Thus, *raja-yoga* teaches the truth that Hindu spiritual experiences are rooted in human effort and spiritual discipline.

3.4.4 Moral Concept in Perfection

Vivekananda's spiritual principles of internal cleansing and self-denial for the sake of others give additional meaning to his understanding of being perfect. His conception of ethical teachings goes beyond mere religious practices. Generally, religions consider worldly desires an impediment to human spiritual growth, but Vivekananda regarded selfish thoughts as an impediment to achieving a divine nature. He says that the things attached to the world spring from the selfishness of people. Thus, those who can overcome their selfish thoughts, no matter what material possessions they have, can remove the impediments to spiritual growth.

> What they mean by the world is selfishness. Unselfishness is God. One may live on a throne, in a golden palace, and be perfectly unselfish, and then he is in God. Another may live in a hut, wear rags, and have nothing in the world; yet, if he is selfish, he is intensely merged in the world.[65]

Any action that springs from human selfishness belongs to worldly concerns, whereas the actions that spring from unselfishness belong to God.

Vivekananda was someone who gave priority to spiritual discipline, which enabled him to deny himself and merge with the Absolute. His teachings of *raja-yoga* show that nature exists for the soul's experiential growth, leading

---

64. Vivekananda, 1:154.
65. Vivekananda, 1:73.

to the realization of its eternal detachment from the material world. Through personal encounters with nature, the *raja-yogi* learns the profound lesson of renunciation. Here, evading worldly pleasures and working hard is essential to experience the union. The action of renunciation helps to develop purity and a strong desire for God – that is, to be in union with the Absolute.[66] This teaching of Vivekananda is similar to the biblical concept of the renunciation that is required to inherit the kingdom of God – as Jesus told the young rich ruler, "If you want to be perfect, go, sell your possessions and give to the poor, and you will have treasure in heaven" (Matt 19:21 NIV). Both these renunciation teachings seem similar. Does this mean that Vivekananda was enlightened by heavenly truth? The union of the human soul with the Universal Soul – which is the final stage of spiritual experience in yoga – is possible only for those who dedicate themselves to work towards this goal. Vivekananda says,

> To the worker, it is union between men and the whole of humanity; to the mystic, between his lower and Higher Self; to the lover, union between himself and the God of Love; and to the philosopher; it is the union of all existence. This is what is meant by Yoga.[67]

Having this kind of religious experience, overcoming selfishness, and the union of oneness with the whole help to nullify all human defects.

Vivekananda's understanding was that forming an "ideal man" and an "ideal society" is possible through human efforts and strict spiritual discipline. He taught that *raja-yoga*, with its practice of the meditation technique, could help people to cultivate a nature that renounced selfishness and to purify their hearts. However, Vivekananda was uncertain about a personal God. He also had a specific understanding about the need for human sanctification in order to be perfect. He believed that divine character could be produced within people through greater efforts and affirmed that the spiritual exercises of yoga would enable a yogi to work for the benefit of society, even as he or she was united with the Absolute.

---

66. Vivekananda, 1:245.
67. Vivekananda, 2:313.

3.5 Exploring Vivekananda's Understanding of the Spirit

According to Vivekananda, "Religion is the realisation of spirit as spirit."[68] He viewed humans as spiritual beings and believed that all authentic religious activities should be rooted in spirituality. For Vivekananda, the human soul needs to recognize and comprehend its eternal nature as spirit, not bound by matter, and acknowledge that its connection with the material realm is only temporary. He writes,

> God is spirit and should be worshipped in spirit and faith. Where does the spirit reside? On a tree? On a cloud? What do you mean by God being ours? You are the spirit. That is the first fundamental belief you must never give up. I am a spiritual being. It is there. All this skill of Yoga and this system of meditation and everything is just to find Him there.[69]

Yoga helps adherents understand that religious experiences that happen in human life are "spiritual' experiences."

Concerning spiritual worship, Vivekananda held that "the Spirit alone is infinite. God is Spirit, is infinite; man is Spirit and, therefore, infinite, and the Infinite alone can worship the Infinite. We will worship the Infinite; that is the highest spiritual worship."[70] Here, Christians are reminded of Jesus's teaching that "we must worship [God] in spirit and truth" (John 4:24 NRSV). Vivekananda's recognition that human beings are spirit as God is Spirit is similarly reminiscent of the Christian doctrine of the *imago Dei* – we are created in God's image. He says that people need to understand that they are spirit as God is Spirit. "When you know the Spirit, everything else will vanish. When you see the Spirit itself, you see no matter because that which you called matter is the very thing that is Spirit."[71] This spiritual nature of human beings brings uniformity in connecting them with God. "When His light, His presence, His spirit, shines through the human face, then and then

---

68. Vivekananda, 1:376.
69. Vivekananda, 4:185–186.
70. Vivekananda, 1:277.
71. Vivekananda, 1:407.

alone, can man understand Him."[72] Here, Vivekananda mentions a spirit that shines in human life to give us a real understanding of God.

Consequently, "the spirit of the highest is related to the spirit of the lowest, and the germ of infinite perfection exists in all . . . True religion comes not from the teaching of men or the reading of books; it is the awakening of the spirit within us, consequent upon pure and heroic action."[73] Although Vivekananda fails to give specific teachings on "the Spirit," his concept of "spirit" points outwards to the "Spirit." One is reminded of the "unknown god" whom the Greeks in Paul's day affirmed, even when the concept of an "unknown god" remained a mystery.

However, we do not find in the teachings of Vivekananda the participation of the Spirit as a person in human religious experiences. He never emphasizes the Spirit's work in human life as an aid to humanity in achieving their ultimate goal. Rather, as we have seen earlier, Vivekananda considered human effort and hard work essential for any kind of human achievement. But, regarding the Spirit's work, certain spiritual lessons are related with his religious concepts. For example, in relation to attaining *moksha* or union, he says, "Sitting in august silence, the Yogi, absorbed in deep communion with the Spirit, [has] no other goal in life than Moksha."[74] This statement does not make it clear that there is a Spirit with whom people can enjoy fellowship. Experiencing the Spirit in human life empowers adherents to reach the higher state of *moksha*, which is a spiritual action that can only be facilitated in spirit.[75] While Vivekananda had a certain inner knowledge about spiritual involvement in religious experience, he failed to explain the Spirit as one who assists human beings; nor did he recognize the human need to communicate with the Spirit. We will return to this point in the final chapter. Similarly, in social development, Vivekananda believed that allowing the power of the Spirit to move within us will establish an ideal society. With regard to the development of India, he says, "Bring forth the power of the spirit, and pour it over the length and breadth of India; and all that is necessary will come by

---

72. Vivekananda, 2:44.
73. Vivekananda, 4:153.
74. Vivekananda, 5:476.
75. Vivekananda, 6:139.

itself."⁷⁶ In his concept of the ideal man and the ideal society – while such idealism never rejects a movement of the Spirit – the focus is limited to the human spirit. He does not represent the Spirit as a person from whom we, as human beings or spirits, are supposed to obtain guidance. He says, "Because you are infinite spirit, it does not befit you to be a slave. . . . Arise! Awake! Stand up and fight! Die if you must. There is none to help you. You are all the world. Who can help you?"⁷⁷ He believed that human beings are infinite and that their effort is sufficient to reach the state of perfection. However, Vivekananda was unable to say why this aspiration of knowing the truth is present in human life and why human beings, in every nation and in every society, want to be perfect or ideal. In Hinduism, the answers to these questions remain a mystery. But having said this, we should not overlook or disparage Vivekananda's focus on humankind as being spiritual beings.

Moreover, the entire philosophical teachings of Vivekananda are centred on his concept of the imperfection of human beings, which Christians would call "sin." He believed that the human understanding of liberation from imperfection is a gift of God. He writes, "When we have the three great 'gifts of God' – a human body, intense desire to be free, and the help of a great soul to show us the way – then liberation is certain for us. Mukti is ours."⁷⁸ Vivekananda's statement concerning the three "gifts of God" does not mean that these are a "gift given by God" as Christianity teaches. Rather, it points to the divine nature present in human beings. He asserts, "It was your own heart beating, and you did not know; you were mistaking it for something external. It is the God within your own self that is propelling you to seek for Him, to realise Him."⁷⁹ Although Vivekananda viewed God as the same human soul functioning as a mystery to assist us in our search for the truth, we should not overlook Vivekananda's recognition of the Spirit within. His beliefs, while not Christian truth, are true in part.

Regarding those who squander time searching for God outside themselves, Vivekananda believed that after extensive quests in various places – temples, churches, and earthly and heavenly realms – people eventually return,

---

76. Vivekananda, *Speeches and Writings*, 73, and Vivekananda, *Complete Works*, 4:287–288.

77. Vivekananda, *Complete Works*, 1:371.

78. Vivekananda, 7:107.

79. Vivekananda, 2:74.

completing the circle, to their very own soul. There, they discover that the one whom they sought tirelessly throughout the world, the one for whom they wept and prayed in earnest, the enigmatic mystery veiled in clouds, is none other than the closest of all, their very own self – the true essence of their existence, encompassing their life, body, and soul. This revelation embodies knowledge about their innate nature.[80] Similarly, Vivekananda emphasizes the need for "looking close to the self" through the spiritual disciple of meditation. Here, there is congruence with the Christian faith. The self is connected with some mystery. "Now I know in part" (1 Cor 13:12 NIV), Vivekananda's anticipation of a better future through our mysterious involvement in spiritual experiences might seem to leave us only with some spiritual principles, but these spiritual principles are not without truth. Hold up what is true, good, and beautiful in Hinduism while seeking answers to the mystery in human life. Does this mystery have any relation to the Spirit as the inner breath and consciousness in human life? An investigation of spiritual involvement in spiritual experiences, especially in Hinduism, might provide Christians with a guide to their own spirituality while also constructing a new theological approach to other religious faiths.

To sum up, Vivekananda lays great emphasis on spiritual experience in religion. His life and teachings were focused on personal spiritual experience and its benefits. He believed that the inner experience of human beings could provide self-satisfaction and self-realization. His understanding of the unavoidable human effort and spiritual discipline in religious experience motivated him to prioritize the practice of yoga. He believed that through yoga, a person could attain real knowledge, truth, and perfection and that the ultimate goal of Hinduism, *moksha*, could be achieved through spiritual experiences. His expectation of a yogi as a worker of social development distinguished him from other Hindu monks in India and widens our understanding of what spirituality means. His understanding of religious experience, the concept of the ideal man, union with the Absolute, the role of human effort, the formation of an ideal society, and the role of the Spirit in religious experience are summarized below.

---

80. Vivekananda, 2:74–75.

3.6 Summary

Religious Experience: Vivekananda believed that religious experience was a mandatory activity for religious people because religious experience occurs as a result of our human effort to achieve self-realization. In Vivekananda's view, the inner craving of human beings for perfection is fulfilled through religious experiences. His first principle of Vedanta philosophy emphasizes that "Religion is realization; not talk, not doctrine, nor theories."[81] This principle confirms that true religion connects with religious experience, and the one who realizes spiritual experiences is considered a religious person. Such religious experiences lead people to know the reality of the world – a knowledge that is above all human intellectual thought. Vivekananda's teachings on spiritual exercises, moral principles, and an expectation of a better future display similarities with Christianity. However, his emphasis on human effort as the means to satisfaction, his belief that the movement is from spirit to the Spirit, and his lack of clarity about belief in a personal God require further discussion from a Christian perspective. We must consider what Paul meant when he said, "Work out your own salvation with fear and trembling; for it is God who is at work in you, enabling you both to will and to work for his good pleasure" (Phil 2:12-13 NRSV).

Ideal Man: Religious experience produces people to get with a mysterious knowledge, a knowledge of the truth as it leads them to become perfect, 'an ideal man'. In India, philosophical thoughts originated and developed from – rather than preceded – the spiritual experiences of sages and rishis. India's "philosophers" obtained enormous knowledge and revelation through such experiences. Vivekananda recognized this ordering and gave priority to experience as leading to truth. In Hinduism, the notion of "truth" has been portrayed in various ways. Even though Vivekananda was not able to give the specific meaning of truth, he says that through attaining truth, all darkness in the human mind is dispelled, there is internal purification of the mind, and the person receives new strength and life. He also saw human beings as travelling not from error to truth but from truth to truth, from lower to higher truth. The goal of Vivekananda's teaching was that a person might become an ideal or perfect man, which is accomplished through religious experience.

---

81. Swami Vivekananda, *Practical Vedanta and Other Lectures*, (Culcutta: Advaita Ashrama, 2007), 33.

Vivekananda viewed religious experience as a result of human efforts to unite with the Absolute Being. His understanding of the Absolute Being – known by different names in different religions – does not see Jesus as exclusive. This seems problematic since it regards Hinduism as equal to Christianity. Here, it is important to recognize the distinction between the Hindu concept of the Absolute Being and the Christian understanding of God as personal as well as absolute. Similarly, Vivekananda's recognition of human beings as spirit as God is Spirit surely relates to the Christian theology of *imago Dei*, but his sense of unity with the Absolute both suggests "theosis" and seems distinct from it. Is this monism or monotheism? These differences between Hinduism and Christianity will need to be clarified biblically as we proceed with our discussion; here, however, it is perhaps more relevant to note the importance of the Spirit in both religions.

Union: The Hindu concept of "union" stands as a symbol of oneness in society. The concept of union is an inevitable principle in Hinduism as well as in the teachings of Vivekananda. It is the ultimate goal of a Hindu to merge the *atman* (human soul) with the Brahman (universal being). In Hinduism, this union is described in various ways: *mukti, jivanmukti, moksha*, and liberation from *samsara*. Vivekananda's concept of *jivanmukti* means freedom from bondage, allowing humans to attain a divine nature in their bodies. Selflessness, unity, justice, and equality are divine qualities that flow through the life of a person who is united with the Absolute. This seems similar to certain Christian teachings of "theosis." Do these similarities lead to any meeting point in conveying the truth?

Human Effort: Yoga was the meditation technique that Vivekananda used to attain religious experience. Human effort and hard work are essential if one is to achieve self-realization through spiritual experiences. Vivekananda suggests that distinctive spiritual exercises such as breathing exercises, controlling the mind, casting out egoism, and purifying the mind are essential to have a religious experience. *Raja-yoga*, which Vivekananda advocates for achieving religious experiences, requires practitioners to adopt certain positions, modes of breathing, and spiritual exercises to harmonize and concentrate the mind. Vivekananda believed that through continual spiritual discipline and hard work, human beings can eliminate egoism (*ahamkara*) from their minds. Vivekananda's understanding of human effort is good and essential, but what is missing in his teaching is what is found in Paul's words: "And if by grace, then it is no longer by works" (Rom 11:6 KJ21). Vivekananda failed to understand the Spirit as a helper; instead, he emphasizes human striving alone. It is impossible for human beings to follow the extreme teachings of hard work and effort by themselves. But even though Vivekananda's teaching does not provide the whole truth, we should not reject the good things it contains. Vivekananda's *raja-yoga* is a spiritual exercise; can we find any similarities between the daily striving of *raja-yoga* and the efforts of Christians to discipline themselves to walk daily with the Spirit?

Ideal Society: Vivekananda's understanding was that religious experience enables people to do social work. Doing good work and establishing social justice and equality is humanity's responsibility. The person who achieves self-realization will be motivated to work for the benefit of society. This happens as a result of attaining a divine nature, where the mind is purified through the spiritual discipline of yoga. Vivekananda's concept of "Daridra Narayana Seva" – the service of God in and through (poor) human beings – is an example of such social service. So, it is not wrong to say that social development and spirituality grow in parallel ways within people. Vivekananda's expectation that the inner (spiritual) thirst of human beings will be a driving force that leads them towards social transformation is perhaps too human-centred. The driving force of the Spirit as wind and fire, or as Shekhinah, does not seem to be adequately recognized in his teaching (see chapter 5). But Vivekananda's emphasis on spirits as mysterious and compelling also suggests some congruence between Hinduism and Christianity, and this can function to facilitate dialogue – which may lead to valuable insights – between otherwise different people.

Religious Experience and Mystery: In Vivekananda's teachings, the source of religious experience that causes revelation or realization remains a mystery. Vivekananda considers that such revelations occur as the result of human effort and not by any kind of external forces. But, amazingly, despite his focus on human effort, his understanding of spiritual experience is that it directs people to engage in a new discussion concerning God's intervention in people's lives. He believed that a spiritual work happens in the human soul itself. In addition, he says that God's mercy is necessary for a person to be perfect as God is perfect. Vivekananda's idea that human beings need "God's mercy to reach self-realization" can lead in the direction of accepting a personal God – although Vivekananda himself does not go down that road.

Vivekananda's conceptions of the "gift of God," "God's mercy," and "Spirit" all receive an unusual amount of attention. At the same time, these ideas seem to contradict his teachings about the need for human struggle. Vivekananda's uncertainty about spiritual involvement in religious experience opens a way for us to discuss the possibility of the Spirit's presence in countries like India where multireligious faiths are practiced. His teachings encourage us to ask thought-provoking questions: Are there any external forces at work behind the human religious experience? Why would a person who prioritized human effort also think about life as a gift from God? Where does the internal craving to know the truth come from? Answers to such questions may come by looking at different theologians' views on religious experience, and it is to this that we turn in the next two chapters.

CHAPTER 4

Religious Experience: The Understanding of Indian Theologians

In the nineteenth century, many Christian thinkers who had converted from Hinduism attempted to relate the Christian faith to the Indian context, for example, Krishna Mohan Banerjee, Lal Behari Dey, Nehemiah Goreh, Brahmabandhav Upadhyay, V. Chakkarai, Sadhu Sundar Singh, A. J. Appasamy, and Pandipeddi Chenchiah. Among these Christian theologians, Chenchiah played a significant role in expressing the Christian faith in terms of Indian patterns of thought. Chenchiah, Appasamy, and Chakkarai are sometimes called the "Rethinking Triad" in Madras. As Timothy Tennent writes, "Their encounter with Hinduism enabled them to develop theologies in terms of Hindu thought forms, theological terminology and religious experience."[1] These three theologians took the reality of Indian Christians' affinity with Hindu spirituality and considered how Hindu spirituality could enhance our Christian understanding of Christ.[2] Commenting on Chenchiah's efforts to connect the Christian faith with Hinduism, Robin Boyd says, "As a convert from Hinduism and one who had carved out for himself a successful and honourable career in the secular world of twentieth-century India, he was anxious to retain to the fullest possible extent his Indian, indeed Hindu, cultural heritage."[3]

---

1. Tennent, Building Christianity, 1–2.
2. Manohar, "Spirit Christology," 42.
3. Boyd, *An Introduction to Indian Christian Theology*, 145.

4.1 Life of Pandipeddi Chenchiah (1886–1959)

Pandipeddi Chenchiah was born into an upper-caste Hindu family in Nellore on 8 December 1886. His father, Adinaryanaiah, was a well-known lawyer in Nellore. In 1901, when Chenchiah was a young child, Adinaryanaiah and his family accepted Christ. Chenchiah received his early education at Madras Christian College, South India. He was a brilliant student, with notable abilities in subjects like ethics and philosophy. D. A. Thangasamy comments that Chenchiah had "a high degree of scholarship in various branches of knowledge – chiefly philosophy, history, law and theology."[4] As a well-educated man, Chenchiah was well-versed in both Eastern and Western philosophies and theology. He completed his master's degree in law and taught law at the Law College, Madras. Later, as a distinguished lawyer, he was appointed Chief Justice of the High Court in the Pudukkottai district of Tamil Nadu, South India.

Chenchiah's best-known publication, *Rethinking Christianity in India*, grew out of a spiritual group – later known as the "Rethinking Triad" – in Madras, of which Chenchiah was a key member. "Rethinking Christianity was concerned with redefining Christian faith in Indian terms, thereby relating faith to the cultural traditions of India."[5] In his "rethinking," Chenchiah was influenced by different philosophical and religious scholars of his day, including Sri Aurobindo Ghose, Master Canchupati Venkata Rao Venkatasami Rao, and Henri Bergson. Boyd comments, "Aurobindo's idea of spiritual power, the idea of super-man or Gnostic man and the idea of internal yoga influenced him."[6] C. V. Venkata Sami's philosophical ideas about yoga, which emphasized a spiritual power that descends and transforms human life, and the philosophical thought of "creative evolution" introduced by the French vitalist philosopher Henri Bergson (1859–1941) also influenced Chenchiah's theology.[7]

---

4. Thangasamy, Theology of Chenchiah, ix.
5. Chacko, *Christian Theologies in India*, 130.
6. Boyd, *An Introduction to Indian Christian Theology*, 185–186.
7. Jathanna, *Christ-Event*, 353.

4.1.1 Indian Heritage and Theology

According to Chenchiah, the Indian religious tradition and the religious experience that people adopted for their spiritual satisfaction were indispensable for Christian theology. India's religiosity included people having open minds, thus accommodating different religions and employing different methods when searching for God. At the centre of their spirituality lay the intention to know the truth or reality. This is one of the reasons India has adopted various religions. Chenchiah says that all religions that have either sprung up in India – for example, Hinduism and Buddhism, or have come to India – for example, Islam and Christianity, have had only one intention: "*Satyameya Jayathi,* which means Truth shall triumph."[8]

Compared with other religions, Hinduism allows room for new revolutionary thoughts that are intended to seek answers for questions about human life. Towards this end, Chenchiah noted the revolutionary growth of spirituality that happened in his time, saying, "A stranger to India must remember that Hinduism – religion and culture – for the first time in her history is undergoing a profound revolution."[9] The reasons for this revolution in Hindu tradition, ritual, and philosophy are found in two questions of the soul that Hindus have asked: How I should escape from *samsara* – the endless wheel of births and rebirths? And how shall I ensure my future after death? To find answers to these questions, Chenchiah observed that people in India sought various enlightenments, which they achieved through religious experiences. Contemplation was one of the traditional methods people employed to reach their aspirations. It is evident here that Indian culture and tradition cannot be separated from the people's spirituality, which also suggests that the right approach towards Indian people should be based on their traditional faiths.

Chenchiah believed that Christian theology must build interreligious relationships through accepting the spiritual experiences present in other religions. He was aware of the value and significance of religious traditions that lead people to have specific spiritual experiences. As a convert from Hinduism, Chenchiah did not despise his past beliefs and practices; rather, he praises the positive views of Hindu spirituality, affirming that, as Indians, understanding the faith of our own people groups is necessary to create an

---

8. Chenchiah, "Religion in Contemporary India," 141.
9. Chenchiah, 129.

effective Christian theology. He sought to bring all religious faiths, especially Hinduism, under one umbrella by recognizing the common ideas in different religions. He says, "To us in India, the inter-relations of religions have become a matter of life and death. We can have no peace here or hereafter, and our nation can have no future till we find the key to the mystery."[10] Hinduism proclaims that God will be everything to everyone, encompassing us all. Seeking a multireligious openness, he thus emphasizes, "For this new hope, India renounces the dream of Vivekananda – to preach Advaita to the world."[11] However, Chenchiah believed that building interrelationships between different religious people was essential. To form such a new Christian theology that is cognizant of the traditional beliefs and spiritual experience of people of other religions could play a significant role in helping Christians to share their beliefs.

In saying this, Chenchiah argues that Christians should avoid their traditional ways of approaching people but, rather, seek to contextualize their theologies. He says, "Realization has been the heart and soul of the Indian view of spiritual life."[12] He valued the spiritual experience of Indian tradition and writes, "Religion or religions must escape the bondage of dogma and doctrine, the prison of churches, traditions, rituals and interfuse into each other in spirit."[13] He considered that the reality of Indian spirituality and religious experience should also be the centre of Christianity in India. Consider this statement of Chenchiah: "The sooner we realize that in India the living forces of religion reside in the pew rather pulpit, the better it would be for the growth of Christian life."[14] Chenchiah believed that the advancement of Christianity should be based on its inherent appeal rather than placing reliance on incidental external factors. Christianity should be founded on Christian love, not on exploiting the discontent of Hindus. Christians must cultivate an open mind, embracing other religious traditions. There is no need to sever the umbilical cord; the symbiotic connection between Christianity and Hinduism benefits both Hindus and Christians. This interconnectedness

---

10. Chenchiah, "Christian Message," 144.
11. Chenchiah, 144.
12. Chenchiah, 172.
13. Chenchiah, "Religion in Contemporary India," 142.
14. Chenchiah, "Christian Message," 151.

is made possible by Christianity's integration into Hindu culture. The current crisis necessitates profound introspection, returning to the fundamental roots of our faith to renew and replenish our spiritual reservoirs.[15] Chenchiah believed that building a theology based on the traditional understanding of people from different faiths is the only way to deliver the Christian message effectively.

4.1.2 Contextualizing the Holy Spirit in Indian Heritage

To construct this kind of fruitful Christian theology, the third person of the Trinity, the Holy Spirit, could play a significant role in connecting different religious people. Chenchiah says, "The 'Holy Spirit' – the doctrine and philosophy – if my instincts are sound, will play a decisive role in Indian theology. They may receive a new interpretation and become the cornerstone of the Indian Christian Theology."[16] He believed that the work of the Holy Spirit could easily connect with spiritual nature of Indian tradition with the spiritual work of Christ. Kirsteen Kim supports this understanding of the role of the Holy Spirit in Indian Christian theology, saying, "Indian Christian theology is particularly inclined toward pneumatology because of the Indian heritage of many spiritualities and the Hindu philosophy of the Spirit."[17] Frederick E. Crowe similarly argues that developing an inclusive pneumatology to speak about the Holy Spirit's universal presence would help Christians understand and appreciate those good and holy elements found in diverse contexts.[18] Theologians observe that in Christian theology, the work of the Spirit can fruitfully enlighten the message of the gospel among different religious people. In this context, Chenchiah articulates the work of the Spirit in the life of Jesus and interprets different Hindu terms theologically.

Although Chenchiah does not provide a systematic pneumatology as he writes in scattered fragments about the Spirit, his Christology is interwoven with his doctrine of the Holy Spirit. He examines the role of the Holy Spirit in the life of Jesus, at creation, birth, earthly life, and work. The Gospel of John represents Jesus as the Word of God, active in creation. Chenchiah sees the

---

15. Chenchiah, 152–189.
16. Chenchiah, 152–153.
17. Kim, "Mission Pneumatology," 2.
18. Crowe, "Son of God," 324–343.

Word and the Spirit working together to form creation: "The Spirit of God moved upon the face of the waters. And God said, Let there be light" (Gen 1:2–3 ASV). The Spirit and the Word are connected as vibration and sound. The Word was with God and was the Spirit of God. "Jesus is the manifestation of a new creative effort of God, in which the cosmic energy or sakti is the Holy Spirit."[19] Concerning Jesus's birth, Chenchiah points out that the Jesus was conceived by the Holy Spirit. The biological birth of Jesus was significant because it emphasizes the virgin birth through the work of the Holy Spirit. In the words of Chenchiah, "The Spirit of God overshadowed Mary, and Jesus was born. He is a new creation, the Lord and master of a new creative branch of the cosmos. He is the son of God because the Spirit of God entered in him."[20] Christina Manohar says that Chenchiah understood the incarnation of Jesus, which is mentioned in the Fourth Gospel, as meaning that "the Word became flesh" and "the Spirit became flesh."[21]

Furthermore, at Jesus's baptism, the Spirit descended upon Jesus and dwelled within him. Hence, Chenchiah believed that "what became flesh in Jesus was the Spirit."[22] According to Boyd, Chenchiah thought that "Jesus Christ is the Incarnation or *Avatara* of God; the Holy Spirit is the human experience of the incarnate Jesus Christ."[23] These statements illustrate Chenchiah's desire to create an indivisible amalgamation between Jesus and the Holy Spirit. Similarly, Chenchiah affirms that the Holy Spirit played a significant role in Jesus's earthly life. This is how he describes the relationship between Jesus and Holy Spirit: "The Holy Spirit is the universal Jesus. Jesus was limited in time and space, and His teaching adapted to the age in which, and the people among whom, He lived. Jesus as the Holy Spirit meets India's special needs and demands."[24] Through this explanation of Jesus's life in association with the Holy Spirit, Chenchiah sought to express the essentiality of holistic spiritual experiences.

Chenchiah represents Christ as the supreme Spirit who connects God and humankind by providing new life for human beings. For Indians, the

---

19. Chenchiah, "Jesus and Non-Christian Faiths," 58.
20. Chenchiah, 62.
21. Manohar, *Spirit Christology*, 153.
22. Chenchiah, "Who Is Jesus?," 118.
23. Boyd, *Khristadvaita*, 242.
24. Chenchiah, "Christianity and Hinduism," 217.

world of spirits and, thus, the need for spiritual works is pervasive. Swami Nirmalananda says, "We are spirits within Spirit, in a wondrous way both ourselves and Brahman, both finite and infinite."[25] Chenchiah writes, "Indian Christians should regard Christ as the supreme authority in the realm of the Spirit."[26] He believed that the uniqueness of Christianity and its ability to connect humankind with God lie in the supremacy of Jesus Christ in the spiritual world. In the words of Chenchiah, "As a religion, Christianity is no better or worse than other religions. The supremacy we claim or should claim is not for Christianity but for Christ."[27]

Consequently, "in the company of Jesus we do not feel the gulf that separates God from man. We feel he is the bridge, the hyphen that unites God and man."[28] This union is possible through becoming a transformed person. Jesus accomplished transformation in human life through his spirit – the Holy Spirit. The work of the Spirit in human life is a mystery that transforms and connects people with God. In the same tone, Chenchiah notes, "The Gospel of Jesus operates in a different region. Christianity must engross itself with the Holy Spirit, His place in creation, His methods of operation and with the problems of new birth."[29] In relating and applying the unpredictable work of the Spirit in the world and among persons to Christians, Chenchiah writes, "We do not know what life is, yet we reproduce it. So we may propagate children of God by the aid of the Holy Spirit, though we may not understand what he is and how He operates."[30] Chenchiah's mode of interpretation motivated Christina Manohar to say, "Chenchiah's theology was in many ways innovative. His aim was to rediscover the hidden aspects of Christ's life and make it relevant to both Indian Christians and Hindus."[31]

To present Christian theology in a way that was more relevant to the Indian people, Chenchiah united Christian theological themes with Hindu terms like *Shakti, Mahasakti, Visvakarma and Prajapathi*. In Hinduism, Shakti

---

25. Giri, *Om Yoga*, 7.
26. Chenchiah, "Church and the Indian Christian," 90.
27. Chenchiah, "The Christian Asrama," in *Theology and Church in India*, edited by V. Devasahayam (Christian Literature Society, 1966) 54.
28. Chenchiah, "Christian Message," 168.
29. Chenchiah, "Jesus and Non-Christian Faiths," 62.
30. Chenchiah, 62.
31. Manohar, "Spirit Christology," 197.

is a goddess representing a feminine concept of divine power. "In Hindu religion, Shakti is God's consort or 'female energy,' however, this represents a 'Sanskritization' of an earlier pre-Aryan tradition practised in India from at least 3000 BC, and which underwent a revival in the seventh century."[32] Shakti is a prominent Hindu term that Hindus use to express cosmic energy. Chenchiah viewed the Holy Spirit as this impersonal cosmic Shakti that provides great creative power and energy and saw this cosmic power, the Holy Spirit, as working in the universe to change human life. For Chenchiah, "Hinduism harnesses the *Mahasakti* of nature and man, Christianity brings into evolution the new *Sakti* of the Holy Spirit."[33] He believed that the work of the Spirit is present in all religions, helping them to understand the new creation Christ brings into this world. Thus, Chenchiah frequently presents the Holy Spirit as *Mahasakti* or *Shakti*.

Visvakarma is another Hindu term Chenchiah uses to represent the Holy Spirit. In Hinduism, *Visvakarma* is connected with creative power. In relation to creation, Chenchiah says that Jesus is the *adi purusha* of a new creation, while the Holy Spirit is the *Visvakarma* of a new world.[34] According to Joseph, *Visvakarma* is represented in the Rig Veda "as the personification of the all creative power and the architect of the universe. Sometimes this term is identical with *Prajapathi*. Unlike the cosmic energy, *Visvakarma* refers to a more personalized creative power, the builder of the universe."[35] But despite making these connections, Chenchiah does not attempt to identify or conflate the work of the Holy Spirit with Hindu ways of understanding. Instead, he uses these different terms to express the creative power of the Holy Spirit to Indians in a way relevant to them.

Chenchiah built a pneumatologically based Christology to make Christianity more relevant to Indian Christians and Hindus. His interpretation of Christ's spiritual work in terms of Hindu religious concepts allowed him to relate these two diverse faiths. In particular, he found similarities between various Hindu concepts and the Christian understanding of the works of the Spirit. He saw the Hindu concept of cosmic energy and creative

---

32. Kim, "Mission Pneumatology," 58.
33. Chenchiah, "Christian Message," 185.
34. Chenchiah, "Who is Jesus?," 15.
35. Joseph, Indian Interpretation, 74.

power as being closely associated with the work of the Spirit in the world. As Chenchiah considered Indian Christian theology and mission, he felt that a pneumatological approach was essential.

4.1.3 Functions of the Holy Spirit in Religious Experience

Chenchiah explains that in religious experiences, the Holy Spirit transforms people by providing inner knowledge. Obtaining such knowledge is the great craving of many religions. Chenchiah viewed religious experience as an inner vision closely associated with the *pratyaksa anubhava* of Hinduism. Regarding this inner vision, Mariasusai explains that the inner vision (*avritta caksur*) and the external vision (*paran pasyati*) are two kinds of seeing, typically distinguished in Indian cultural understanding.[36] In the external seeing, the senses open only to the outward and see only external things; in the inner seeing, the eyes turn within and see inward matters. The direct and immediate religious experience or inner vision is *pratyaksa anubhava*, which goes beyond and is much deeper than conceptual knowledge.[37] This inner knowledge or insight has the potential to transform a person entirely. For Chenchiah, the distinctiveness of Christianity lies in people's inner realization that Jesus is supreme over all the world.[38] He says, "Christianity may be conceived, and indeed it is the dominant conception, as the realization of the Christ ideal by the discipline of self just as in other religions." According to Victor Raj, Chenchiah was of the opinion that "Christianity can attract Hindus only if the full potential of Christian spirituality is realized, taking into account the doctrine of the Holy Spirit as the cornerstone of Christian theology."[39]

The Holy Spirit eliminates people's unfulfilled spiritual thirst – something that is the goal of many religions – through revealing Jesus Christ. In India, Hindu tradition adopts the history of searching for reality through discovering an inner realization (*darshana* or vision). Chenchiah says, "Realisation has been the heart and soul of the Indian view of spiritual life."[40] This understanding of the spiritual nature of India has led rishis and sannyasi to

---

36. Dhavamony, *Indian Christian Theology*, 99.
37. Dhavamony, 99.
38. Chenchiah, "Jesus and Non-Christian Faiths," 56.
39. Raj, "Text and Context," 117.
40. Chenchiah, "Christian Message," 172.

achieve a wealth of spiritual experience. But most of these religious experiences have not been able to quench the spiritual thirst of these people. But this failing does not mean that Christians should neglect other religions and religious people merely because their spiritual experiences are fallible. Instead, Chenchiah advises, "If instead of using Christ and Christian experience as a searchlight to discover the defects of Hinduism, we apply Hinduism and Hindu experience to the elucidation of the meaning and purpose of Christ, we are at once rewarded with a two-fold gain."[41] Appreciating Hindu rishis and sadhus who gave priority to spiritual insights, he says to Christians, "You must have a seer or rishi before you can open the mind of a Hindu."[42] In Chenchiah's view, all religious experiences give real insight as a result of the work of the Holy Spirit. Hence Chenchiah believed that a recovery of understanding Hindu heritage might enrich Indian Christian theology and mission.

Chenchiah's teachings focus on various functions of the Spirit in human life and in the world. The role of the Spirit in transforming people into a new creation is well documented in his writings. He presents the unlimited work of the Spirit as cosmic energy, creative power, and a transforming agent for a new world – that is, the kingdom of God. He also explains how traditional Indian methods are adopted to accomplish this mission.

First, Chenchiah observes that the Holy Spirit functions as cosmic energy, bringing transformation and energy to people. His explanation of the Spirit's work in the life of Jesus Christ builds on this idea of a cosmic energy that can establish a new community. Chenchiah's representation of the Holy Spirit as the new creative cosmic energy is similar to the Hindu concept of *sakti* and offers opportunities to bring changes in India. He notes, "Jesus is the manifestation of a new creative effort of God, in which the cosmic energy or sakti is the Holy Spirit."[43] In Hinduism, "Śakti means 'power' and is personified in the Goddess, the Divine Mother, to whom is ascribed all the functions Viṣṇu has for the Vaiṣṇavas, or Śiva, for the Śaivas: creation, the maintenance and destruction of the world, illusion and liberation."[44] In Christianity, this cosmic or creative energy was experienced in the person of

---

41. Chenchiah, "Jesus and Non-Christian Faiths," 56.
42. Chenchiah, "Christian Message," 193.
43. Chenchiah, "Jesus and Non-Christian Faiths," 58.
44. Klostermaier, *Survey of Hinduism*, 114.

Jesus Christ while he was on this earth. Chenchiah regards Jesus's earthly life, which was lived in the power of the Spirit, as an example for people to follow in the new order of life. He writes, "I want to emphasize that we can never get to the heart of Christianity by the way of juridical theology. It is the genetic or creative aspects of Jesus – It is the Holy Spirit as a creative energy that takes the Indian into the new 'given' – in Jesus."[45] The provision of a new order of life for human beings is unique in Christianity, and this is made possible through the power of the Spirit. "For in Hinduism God incarnates when the constitution of the world is threatened and comes not to be with us always, but to restore the mechanism of life to its original condition.... The fact of Christ is the birth of a new order in creation."[46] However, Chenchiah viewed the new creation, the new life, and the new kingdom as originating through the cosmic power of the Holy Spirit: "Christ, however, sought to establish a new universe with a new cosmetic energy – the Holy Spirit."[47]

Second, Chenchiah believed that one distinctive feature of Christianity is that the Holy Spirit empowers people to be transformed into new creations and become a part of the kingdom of God. This new life can be received by anyone willing to accept Christ. Chenchiah says, "It [the relationship of Jesus to other religions] is not the relation of a religion to a religion or of a theology to a theology but of a new creation to the old."[48] However, he also clarifies that, unlike in Hindu religion, "the new creation is not to be realized by man as an ideal."[49] Chenchiah noted that while in Hinduism, God is sought to perfect the old man, in Christianity, God creates a new man in Jesus instead. To put it differently, in Hinduism, a person must become perfect by their own endeavours; but in Christianity, a person is made a new creation.[50] All religions generally embrace an optimistic expectation for a better future and a better human life. Chenchiah compares this human craving to the Hindu concept of "liberation from *samsara*" – freedom from worldly affairs that cannot be attained without Christ. "The supreme longing of the Hindu to escape from *Samsara* Christ does not satisfy and the Lord's gift of rebirth

---

45. Chenchiah, "Christian Message," 165.
46. Chenchiah, 166.
47. Chenchiah, "Jesus and Non-Christian Faiths," 56.
48. Chenchiah, 62.
49. Chenchiah, 56
50. Chenchiah, "Christian Message," 181, 185.

does not appeal to the Hindu. It is by no means easy to discover elements in other faiths which find fulfillment in Jesus."[51] Chenchiah adds, "The facile presumption that in Hinduism we have a search for salvation without satisfaction and that Christianity satisfies the longing is untrue to fact."[52] Also he says, "Jesus is God's answer to man's ambition to become like God, to escape fate and destiny, to become master of life and death. This is an aspiration of all religions for which the answer can only be a new creation."[53]

Third, Chenchiah affirms that the transformative power of the Holy Spirit moulds and reshapes a person's entire life, making them a true child of God. The Spirit's work of transformation of a person into a new creation is visible through their character and attitudes towards others. "In the light of the new life, faith and conduct will change of its own accord and by inner urge as it were rather than by external discipline."[54] Chenchiah writes, "We love our enemies not against the grain of our nature nor from obedience to the extraneous will of God but because that happens to be the natural expression of the new life."[55] Chenchiah believed that character transformation and growth into Christlikeness – which is the outcome of becoming a new creation in Christ – is the core characteristic of a Christian. As Sumithra writes, "The Holy Spirit presides over the new creation and lives in the sons of God as their atman."[56] It is not wrong to call a child of God one who has become part of the kingdom of God.

> To be born again is Christianity, and the new-born is the son of God and the order he evolves – the Kingdom of God. India longs to learn the secret of this new birth, which transcends karma. If we cannot give it, we are offering her sand and ashes calling it loudly, divine food.[57]

But sadly, as Chenchiah says, "The church does not teach us the mystery of new birth. It detracts our attention from the central fact. It substitutes a new

---

51. Chenchiah, 184.
52. Chenchiah, 184.
53. Chenchiah, "Jesus and Non-Christian Faiths," 62–63.
54. Chenchiah, 63–64.
55. Chenchiah, "Christian Message," 175.
56. Sumithra, *Christian Theologies*, 128.
57. Sumithra, 167.

scheme to realize the kingdom of God by a reformation of this world and becoming children of God by repentance and faith."[58] The Holy Spirit plays a crucial role in transforming a person's life and leading them into a new order of existence – the kingdom of God, where Christ embodies the new creation and the new life order.

Chenchiah discerned that the Spirit guides individuals to encounter diverse experiences and attain extraordinary knowledge and abilities. He perceived the Spirit's work as evident in the cosmos, manifested through cosmic energy and creative power, transforming people into a new creation. Every spiritual experience a person undergoes draws them closer to the kingdom of God, aligning with Jesus's incarnation and message. Chenchiah's concept does not criticize the Hindu spiritual discipline of yoga but, instead, supports it to facilitate profound spiritual experiences. He employs various Hindu concepts and ideas to highlight the work of God within the Hindu tradition. According to Chenchiah, the transformative work of the Spirit, as witnessed in the life of Christ, can be replicated in any person, irrespective of their religious background. However, Christ remains pivotal because transformation is not a matter of human effort alone.

Fourth, Chenchiah's understanding of the kingdom of God is that it is a new life that people experience with the help of the Holy Spirit by moulding their life according to the nature of Christ. To be partakers of the kingdom of God in this way, however, is not possible through human efforts but only with the help of the Spirit. Chenchiah asserts that the Holy Spirit alone can transform people. He says,

> The Holy Spirit is the new cosmic energy; the kingdom of God, the new order; the children of God, the new type that Christ has inaugurated. The gospel is that God in Jesus has made a new creation. We are exploiting our will, our reserve energies, our ideals to produce the kingdom of God.[59]

If anyone strives to change without yielding to the work of the Spirit, their efforts will not be successful. "Greater and far reaching in its disastrous effect is the belief that the kingdom of God could be realized by man with

---

58. Chenchiah, "Jesus and Non-Christian Faiths," 57.
59. Chenchiah, 57.

more thorough-going repentance and greater determination of will."[60] Here, Chenchiah does not despise God's compassion towards fallible human beings. He strongly believed that the Holy Spirit alone renews people to grow spiritually and to exercise the blessings of the kingdom of God. In Chenchiah's words, "The Kingdom of God works out the power of the Holy Spirit."[61]

In the kingdom of God, we, as new creations, must undergo a continual character transformation process.

> It [Christianity] does not call us to realize the Kingdom of God by the mechanism of the Kingdom of man. The Christian is not the greatest of the woman born, nor is he a man made perfect. He is not a superman, but a new man. He is a new creation and not a prolongation or perfection of the old creation.[62]

Moreover, renewing our character is reproducing Jesus in human life through the power of the Holy Spirit. Chenchiah says, "If we want to establish the Kingdom of God, we must reproduce Jesus."[63]

> The Kingdom of God is a new world order, expressing a new cosmic power – the Holy Spirit. Still, it recreates man, world and heaven. The Kingdom of God is a continuation of the world, but not merely is a larger edition of it. This is the difference between the Kingdom of God and the Utopias of science. The new world of science is the working out of the energies of the world.[64]

Guided by the Holy Spirit, individuals gain insights into heavenly mysteries; and through the transformative power of the Spirit, human beings, the world, and heaven undergo re-creation. The disclosure of the mysteries of the kingdom of God unfolds under the guidance of the Holy Spirit.

Chenchiah represents the Holy Spirit as a cosmic energy that transforms and leads people towards a new universe – the kingdom of God. He exhorts Christians to prioritize spiritual experience over depending on church traditions or doctrines. Undoubtedly, Chenchiah's contribution to Indian Christian

---

60. Chenchiah, 56.
61. Chenchiah, "Christian Message," 170.
62. Chenchiah, "Jesus and Non-Christian Faiths," 56–57.
63. Chenchiah, 61.
64. Chenchiah, "Christian Message," 170.

theology focused on contextualizing the Christian message according to the Indian way of understanding, and he succeeded in connecting the work of the Spirit with Hindu terms and ideologies. The priority of spiritual experiences in Christianity, which features strongly in his writings, motivated him to stand against many traditional practices of churches and Western-formulated Christian doctrines. Chenchiah saw the Christian life as being formed through spiritual experiences, leading to a new creation and a new social order.

Chenchiah's understanding of the kingdom of God goes beyond Indian liberation theologians' understanding of justice and equality in society. In Chenchiah's view, the function of the Holy Spirit, as a cosmic energy, was to penetrate human life and society to form a new universe – the kingdom of God. He found similarities between Hinduism and Christianity in various aspects – for instance, the meditation experience, the concept of union, and the *antaryamin* (inner working of the Spirit). But he could not tolerate the Hindu concepts of identifying the self with the Absolute or annihilation of the self – a concern sometimes associated with Hindu yoga. He also rejected the idea that we could or should work for our perfection, asserting that such striving will always fail; instead, he believed that a new creation is essential and that our ethical life follows from that new creation.

4.1.4 Spiritual Discipline and Yoga

In Chenchiah's view, it is not wrong for Christians to adopt good traditional practices from other faiths. In the Indian context, this means that "the Christian has to develop the yoga of the Holy Spirit – with a new *sadhana* of eternal life."[65] In Hinduism, yoga and *sadhana* are very common concepts related to spiritual discipline. In Chenchiah's words, "Running through the centre of Hinduism is the stream of life known as yoga. This word literally means union."[66] The ultimate goal of a Hindu yogi is to experience union with the Absolute, and this demands both developing spiritual discipline and experience. According to Chenchiah, yoga, in a broad sense, is a "psycho-physical discipline and technique for attaining the spiritual end of union or

---

65. Chenchiah, "Jesus and Non-Christian Faiths," 62.
66. Chenchiah, "Religion in Contemporary India," 139.

communion with God"⁶⁷ that results in *ananda* and *kaivalya*. He adds, "Yoga, realization, union with God has always been the spiritual ambition of an Indian. But, yoga requires Sadhana, and Sadhana involves ceaseless research and experiment."⁶⁸ In relation to Chenchiah's understanding of Indian spirituality and its role in the yoga of the spirit, J. T. K. Daniel writes,

> Chenchiah, a lay theologian, perceives Christian faith as a spiritual yoga bestowed by the Holy Spirit, with the purpose of unveiling a new humanity that is drawn closer to Christ. Through the yoga of the spirit, one can attain personal experience, the raw encounter with Christ. The Holy Spirit is viewed as the new cosmic energy, and the kingdom of God signifies a new divine order. A proper understanding of the Yoga of the Holy Spirit can serve as the foundation of Indian Christian Theology, which should embrace and address the spiritual quest of the Indian context.⁶⁹

From Chenchiah's perspective, the Hindu understanding of yoga or union can function as a bridge to more easily connect Hindus with Christ. He writes,

> Hinduism always longed for a state in which we could say as Jesus did, 'I and my Father are one' – which was our Lord's affirmation of the Brahma Vakya *Aham Brahmasmi*. . . . This is the message of Christianity that the word has become flesh, and God has become man. To be Christian is to gain this consciousness and this sense of harmonious blend with the divine. The incarnation is as much what man is to become as what God has become.⁷⁰

This is possible in a newborn person's life through the work of the Holy Spirit. "Christian who can see deeper should take to the prayer room and experiment on *rebirth*, harness the Holy Spirit to the creation of new life."⁷¹ So, the Christian life should be one of continual discipline – not by abolishing

---

67. Chenchiah, "Yoga Defined," 263.
68. Chenchiah, "Religion in Contemporary India," 140.
69. Daniel, "Work of the Holy Spirit," 18.
70. Chenchiah, "Christian Message," 169.
71. Chenchiah, 196.

the self but by recognizing that the transforming work of the Holy Spirit is like the sadhana in Hinduism.

Chenchiah connects the ultimate goal of yoga, the union of our soul with the Absolute, with the Christian concept of union with Christ. For him, the Hindu concept of union indicates the importance of spirit, and yogis are the most sensitive souls in India's religious history. He says, "Yogis worship God in spirit and in truth. But the yogi seeks the spirit behind form – the spirit that pervades the variety of forms."[72] Here, it is evident that a sense of spiritual presence exists in the Hindu understanding of yoga.

Similarly, Chenchiah points out, "One noticeable effect of Advaitism is the recognition of *Sayujya* – i.e. absorption into the Godhead. Through this process, man loses his personality and God remains as sovereign. *Sayujya*, the dissolution of man in God, is the reverse of the immanentism of the West which dissolves God in humanity."[73] This understanding is very close to the Orthodox Christian teaching of "theosis." Here, although the Hindu ideas are not equivalent to Jesus's teaching, their closeness cannot be denied. However, Chenchiah warns, "Till the Christian discovers or discloses the Christian yoga of rebirth, we skirmish on the outskirts. Here is the fundamental weakness of the church."[74] For him, Christian salvation makes human beings a new creation through union with Christ by the power of the Holy Spirit, which Chenchiah calls the "*yoga* of the Spirit."[75] Chenchiah also represents the work of the Holy Spirit as "*Parisuddha atma yoga*" (yoga of the Holy Spirit) or "*Amrita yoga*" (yoga of everlasting life).[76]

4.1.5 Ethical Values and Human Beings

Chenchiah attempts to establish that a newborn's distinguishing personality is one that is divinely controlled and spiritually guided, not just a person who lives according to ethical values. Religion places a high value on ethical values. Chenchiah says, "Ethics as God's will may be a theological exaggeration of a religious phenomenon common to Christianity and other faiths."[77] In

---

72. Chenchiah, "Religion in Contemporary India," 139.
73. Chenchiah, "Christian Message," 179.
74. Chenchiah, 195.
75. Chenchiah, "Our Theological Task," 67.
76. Chenchiah, "Yoga of Holy Spirit," 284–285.
77. Chenchiah, "Christian Message," 174.

Hinduism, spirituality is closely intertwined with upholding moral principles and performing good deeds. However, the value of a newborn Christian's experience surpasses any religious encounter that is based solely on ethical values. The distinctive essence of Christian ethics does not arise from a new mode of appreciation or insight but, rather, from the transformative power of creative new life that sets Christianity apart from other religions. To embrace Christianity, the newly born Christian acquires the inherent capacity to discern God's will and overcome challenging situations. The primary challenge lies not in adopting Christian ethics but in discerning God's will within the complexities of everyday life. Moreover, developing a moral character remains significant for the newborn Christian and understanding and living according to God's will is of the utmost importance. This profound understanding serves as the foundation for achieving ethical conduct, thus ensuring that our lives align with God's purpose.

Chenchiah viewed traditional theologies as a stumbling block to the free flow of the Spirit in the deeper realms of the social and personal lives of human beings. He did not want to compromise with the institutionalized church by accepting fundamental Western-formulated Christian doctrines as the traditional categories of Christian thought. He insisted, instead, on the uniqueness of Christianity – not depending on its institutions or doctrines but only on its transcendence over other faiths as the religion of new birth by the Holy Spirit.[78] Chenchiah openly opposed traditional beliefs and practices in church institutions of his time. For him, the troubling reality was that doctrines, institutions, sacraments, priests, and pastors collectively, in the church's name, often overshadow Jesus whom they exalt as God in their teachings. So, Chenchiah argues that "religion and religions must escape the bondage of dogma and doctrine, the prison of churches, traditions, rituals, and interfuse into each other in spirit."[79] His teachings clearly show that people's inner experiences are more important than church-based doctrines. Chenchiah encourages Christians to consider the spiritual and inner experiences of other religious people because they can function as God's general revelation to know his will.

---

78. Chenchiah, "Jesus and Non-Christian Faiths," 58–59.
79. Chenchiah, "Religion in Contemporary India," 142.

Chenchiah's intention to connect Christian theology with Hindu traditions was central to his thinking. He saw the Holy Spirit – the third person of the Trinity – and his work in Jesus and human beings functioning as a bridge to connect with other religions. In relation to Hinduism, here are Sunand Sumithra's five deep convictions about Chenchiah:

(1) The new creation in Jesus lies at the core of the gospel message.

(2) The concept of new creation is so remarkably novel that it sets itself apart from all other religions, which represent the old creation. Regrettably, the true essence of this concept is often scarcely comprehended, even within the Christian religion and the church.

(3) God's divine influence has been at work within all religions, making it feasible to construct bridges from Christ to these diverse faiths.

(4) The spiritual treasures inherent in other religions have the potential to shed light that gives rise to new insights concerning the person of Christ and the Christian way of life and experience.

(5) All religions can realize the new creation in Jesus if they are willing to undergo a profound transformation in their spirit and way of life, facilitated through the Holy Spirit.[80]

4.1.6 Summary

Chenchiah sought to bring different religious faiths under one umbrella by their common ideas. He believed that constructing theologies based on people's faith experiences could resolve various theological issues. In India, it is essential to acknowledge people's traditional and cultural faiths to build better relationships between Hinduism and Christianity. As people prioritize spiritual experiences in Hinduism, in theology also needed to give more priority to inner experience than institutionalized dogmas. Chenchiah demanded that Christianity come out of its bondage to church doctrines, traditions, and rituals because religious experiences are common in Indian tradition and different experiences lead people to know God.

Chenchiah endeavoured to unify diverse religious faiths and by their shared ideas under a common framework. He believed that constructing theologies that were rooted in people's religious experiences could address various theological concerns. In India, acknowledging and respecting people's

---

80. Sumithra, Christian Theologies, 134.

traditional and cultural faiths helps to foster a more robust and harmonious relationship between Hinduism and Christianity. Given the importance of spiritual experiences in Hinduism, Chenchiah emphasized that theology should give prominence to people's inner encounters rather than relying solely on rigid dogmas and institutionalized beliefs. He urged Christians to break free from the confines of church doctrines, traditions, and rituals and to recognize that religious experiences are universal in the Indian tradition and can lead individuals to encounter and understand God in distinct ways.

New Creation: Chenchiah viewed the Holy Spirit as a cosmic power who generates a new new creation, new life, and a new universe. Becoming a new person with the power of the Spirit is one of the significant teachings of Christianity. Christ is the Supreme Spirit who connects God and humankind by giving new life to human beings. As "the new cosmic creative energy," the Holy Spirit, who flowed through Jesus into the world, can transform India. The spiritual experiences of Jesus empowered him to lead a new life, and the same Spirit enables human beings to attain a new life. Chenchiah regarded the exemplary life of Jesus as significant in influencing Indians and providing a new order of life.

Cosmic Energy: Chenchiah's efforts to relate the attributes of the Spirit to aspects of Hinduism resulted from his aspiration to build bridges with other religions. Chenchiah represents the enabling power of the Spirit as the cosmic energy or Shakti. In Hinduism, Shakti is a goddess with divine power – similarly, other Hindu terms such as *Mahasakti*, *Visvakarma*, and *prajapathi* also express cosmic power. Here, *Mahasakti* means cosmic power, great creative power, and the energy of a new world. The Hindu terms *Visvakarma* mean a creative power and *prajapathi* mean the architect of the universe. So, Chenchiah's representation of the Spirit as a cosmic energy opens the door to discussion with Indians who believe in a cosmic power. Such expressions can make Christian theology more relevant to Indian people.

Transformation Power: The work of the Spirit brings transformation in human life and makes men and women a part of the kingdom of God. In Christianity, when people accept Christ with the help of the Spirit, they are born in the Spirit, and the same Spirit empowers them to lead a new life. The new creation becomes part of a new universe – the kingdom of God. For human beings, becoming a new creation is the first step to enter into the kingdom of God. The kingdom of God is an experience that a person receives through the help of the Holy Spirit when they submit themselves to be moulded according to the will of God. The realization of the kingdom of God cannot be achieved by human effort or will but only by the work of the Holy Spirit. Chenchiah's theology of the Holy Spirit as the power of transformation is relevant in India because it accomplishes Vivekananda's intention of bringing transformation among people and society through the power of the Holy Spirit. Becoming new is a continual process through transformation of our character – and this character transformation and growth in Christlikeness must be distinct features of a new creation. The transformed person can produce the fruit of the Spirit and love their neighbour. The Holy Spirit helps them to understand heavenly mysteries. In addition, people with spiritual experiences uphold ethical values and do good works, which is considered part of spirituality in Hinduism. However, Chenchiah warns Christians to challenge the Hindu concepts of self-realization and attempt to progress towards perfection by discipline and striving.

New Creation: In Hinduism, a person tries to become perfect; but in Christianity, a person is transformed into a new creation. The goal of a Hindu is to merge with the absolute, divine being, which is possible through liberation from *samsara*. The ultimate effect of Advaita teachings is sayujya, which means to "absorb one into the Godhead." According to Hinduism, a person loses their personality, while God remains sovereign. To express it in another way, *sayujya* means the dissolution of a person in God. This understanding is very close to the Orthodox Christian teaching of "theosis." But Chenchiah understood salvation in Christianity as making a human being a new creation through union with Christ by the power of the Holy Spirit. Here, a person does not merge with God but, instead, receives the nature of God.

Christlikeness: Religious experience is an inner vision closely associated with Hinduism's *pratyaksa anubhava*. The distinctiveness of Christianity lies in the inner realization of people that Jesus is supreme in the world. The Hindu concept of yoga can be related to Christian spiritual experiences. Chenchiah encourages Christians to develop a new *sadhana* of eternal life through making a yoga of the Holy Spirit. It is a "yoga of the Spirit" – *parisuddha atma yoga* (yoga of the Holy Spirit) or *amrita yoga* (yoga of everlasting life). However, the Christian life should be a life of continual discipline submitted to the Holy Spirit. This practice is like the *sadhana* in Hinduism but rejects the idea of the abolition of self. The outcome that a Hindu yogi expects from yoga – *ananda* and *kaivalya* – is closely connected with the outcome of religious experience. The ultimate goal of yoga – union with the absolute – is also connected with the Christian understanding. While the work of the Spirit in human life to transform a person into a new creation must not be despised in any way, it is not wise to accept the practice of yoga in Christianity. Nevertheless, the human desire to achieve a divine nature that is found in Hinduism can be considered as a guidance from the Spirit which a deeper theological understanding can build on in a more Christian direction and lead to further theological interpretation.

4.2 Life of S. J. Samartha (1920–2001)

Stanley J. Samartha, one of the most influential figures in the World Council of Churches (WCC) from 1968 to 1980, brought to Indian Christian theology. His understanding of Indian philosophy provided a new hermeneutical approach to theology within an Indian framework. His primary goal was to reconcile Christianity and Hinduism. This intention motivated him to relate his Christian faith with the Vedantic context of India. He connected Christian teachings with Indian religious concepts and thoughts. Samartha's theological contributions centred on helping Christians to see God's presence outside the church. His understanding of the work of the Spirit beyond the Christian community provides an authentic study of religious experience. However, as Nimrot Rajagukguk, observes Samartha's contributions are also controversial. His concepts must be tested and critically assessed, especially by Asian theologians.[81]

Stanley J. Samartha was born on 7 October 1920 in Karnataka, South India. He was the son of a pastor in the Basel Evangelical Mission, which originated in the Pietist movement that stressed one's experience with Christ. He grew up in Karnataka's peaceful, multireligious society and obtained his high school education at the Basel Evangelical Mission High School. His life in the Basel Mission cultivated in him an openness and passion towards Indian tradition and godliness, and this prompted him, as he travelled back and forth between India and Geneva, to keep in touch with several of his primary school classmates – including two Hindus and two Muslims – from

---

81. Rajagukguk, "Critical Analysis," 10–11.

the little village of Perdur. Samartha is someone who discovered himself at the crossroads of cultures and religions.

At twenty-one, Samartha started his theological education at United Theological College in Bangalore, continuing as a student from 1941 to 1945 under the guidance of P. D. Devanandan and Marcus Ward. In 1947, Samartha went to the USA for his master's degree and doctoral research and had the opportunity to pursue graduate studies at Union Theological Seminary in New York under Paul Tillich and Reinhold Niebuhr. Before returning to India, he completed his post-graduate research at the Hartford Theological Seminary in 1952 and became the first Indian principal of the Basel Mission's seminary in Mangalore.

While a student, Samartha was active in Christian ministry. During his third year at university, he became the secretary of the local chapter of the Student Christian Movement (SCM) and later became its president. After finishing his theological studies, he was appointed an assistant pastor in Udupi for two years. He served as a professor of history and philosophy of religions at United Theological College, where he enjoyed the opportunity to work closely once again with his teachers, P. D. Devanandan and M. M. Thomas. For a short time, Samartha served as the principal of Serampore College, Calcutta. He moved to Geneva in 1968 and became the associate secretary in the Department of Studies in Mission and Evangelism. He remained in Geneva for twelve years and became the first Asian theologian to be appointed director of the WCC's sub-unit on Dialogue with People of Living Faiths (1971–1980). In 1981, Samartha returned to teaching and writing in his home state of Karnataka, working as a consultant to CISRS and a visiting professor at Union Theological College until his retirement.

4.2.1 Theology in Religious Pluralism

Samartha did not write a systematic theology of religions; instead, his intention was to build new relationships with neighbours of other faiths. His innovative ways of building good relationships with those of different faiths are central throughout his writings. Samartha believed that to develop a comprehensive theology, people must not confine themselves within their own circles but possess a well-informed understanding of other faiths and gain insights through engaging in actual dialogues. Different religions and their religious traditions are significant in interpreting theological concepts. In India, the pluralistic nature of religious beliefs and practices encourages religious unity. The changing perceptions of pluralism encourage Christians to engage in new relationships with people of other faiths, partly due to historical pressures and partly due to theological imperatives.[82] Admitting and appreciating the pluralistic nature of India, Samartha saw the work of the Spirit as playing a significant role in building relationships between these multireligious people. He notes the lack of initiative taken by Christians to discuss their faith with other religious people: "The work of the Holy Spirit in creation and in the lives of our neighbors of other faiths and secular convictions has scarcely entered into the debate so far."[83] As the perception of religious pluralism becomes more prevalent in the contemporary world, emerging Christian theologies or Christian theologies of religion must recognize and acknowledge the significance of these new perspectives.

According to Samartha, India's religious pluralism – which is one of its unique aspects – exposed the reality of a "unity in diversity" within the theological realm. About India, Samartha writes, "Our society has different communities with different visions of life and ways of life, with rituals, symbols and codes of conduct, and a network of relationships that gives an identity and a sense of belonging to particular communities."[84] All these attributes are part of the total heritage of human civilization, including diversity in racial, ethnic, and cultural groups, economic systems, political patterns, and languages. Samartha viewed pluralism as the nature of the world, the very structure of reality. As human beings live in a pluralistic world, their approaches to God are also plural. He writes that "human beings in different cultures, at different times, and in different countries experience and express this tension between the finite and the infinite in different ways cannot be denied."[85]

If this is so, then in India – where multireligious faith is prevalent – it is possible that there are different ways of experiencing God and knowing the truth. Samartha gives various reasons why there is diversity in approaches to God where multireligious traditions exist. First, "since human beings respond to the Ultimate Reality from diverse chronological, geographical, historical,

---

82. Samartha, One Christ – Many Religions, 14.
83. Samartha, 13.
84. Samartha, "Religion, Culture and Power," 68.
85. Samartha, One Christ – Many Religions, 4.

cultural, existential and other conditions, the responses to the Ultimate are also bound to be plural."[86] Human responses to the mystery of the infinite inevitably encompass great diversity. Second, each religious tradition serves as a human expression of our encounter with reality and truth. Given the profound nature of this Mystery, it cannot be confined to a single experience or expressed solely through one set of symbols. Thus, religious plurality becomes a tribute to the inexhaustible nature of the infinite. Third, religious plurality finds its ontological foundation in the inherent pluralistic nature of reality, where diversity resides at the core of existence itself.[87] So, concerning Samartha's thought, Gaikwad Rogers says, "The numerous religious traditions may therefore be understood as varied expressions of the heterogeneous essential characteristics of the nature of reality."[88] In theological terms, a plurality may even be the will of God for all life.[89] Finally, related to this idea, religious pluralism is simply a universal fact present in this pluralistic world, where people try to respond to the ultimate reality or God in different ways. This plurality of nations or societies – including their culture, tradition, and structures – is a design of God. Samartha considers the whole structure of each nation to be significant in constructing its theology.

Religious pluralism is simply a given; it is the world's reality and connected with the nature of God himself. The plurality of Indian culture, tribes, people, symbols, traditions, religions, languages, ethnic groups, and social structures can all embrace God's presence. But this depends on whether all diversities lead to the real God so that unity can be achieved. If this is not so, then all diversity will remain simply as diversity and will only motivate people to continue in their sectarian practices. In such a situation, building relationships between people will remain challenging. From Samartha's theological perspective, relating the common factors of Hinduism and Christianity form a better platform to share the Gospel.

---

86. Samartha, "Dialogue as a Quest," 34–35.
87. Samartha, One Christ – Many Religions, 5.
88. Rogers, "Reconceptualizing Religion," 273.
89. Samartha, One Christ – Many Religions, 4.

4.2.2 Unity in a Pluralistic World: A Divine Mystery

Samartha believed strongly in the mysterious nature of God, understanding that any endeavour to search for God is equally shrouded in mystery. Acknowledging the enigmatic aspect of God's activity in the world is crucial to any attempt to comprehend it. This idea holds significant implications for theology – particularly in India, where people seek God predominantly through mystical practices like prayer and meditation, which lead to distinct spiritual experiences. Such mystical approaches differ from the rational Western perspective on approaching God. Preserving and appreciating the significance of Indian culture and its theological understanding is essential because the mystical dimension and contemplative life play a central role in Eastern contributions to faith. Samartha advocates encouraging and nurturing these traditions in theology. He criticizes the adoption of Western cultural theology in the Indian context, emphasizing that the motives of different denominations in the West are irrelevant to India's historical and cultural context.[90] Thus, Indian theology must focus on an Eastern approach to seeking God, recognizing that rational thinking alone is not the sole method of doing theology and that the mystical and aesthetic dimensions hold their rightful place in theological inquiry. Samartha's stance does not entirely reject rational inquiry; instead, it underscores the value, in theology, of the Indian tradition and its unique ways of seeking God.

Samartha uses mystery as a common factor a common factor within Indian theologies and religions. He remarks, "The knowledge of God has divided and separated Hindus and Christians, but the acknowledgement of their [our] ignorance before the mystery of God brings them together."[91] In his view, "mystery provides the ontological basis for tolerance."[92] The Hindu term *Brahman* represents God, and the Hindu concept of *sat-cit-ananda* – similar to the Christian concept of "Trinity" – remains a mystery. In Samartha's eyes, the term "Brahman" or "God" was culturally-conditioned and remained a term of mystery.[93] Even though different terms might be used to represent

---

90. Samartha, "Vision and Reality," 55.
91. Samartha, "Indian Realities," 315.
92. Samartha, One Christ – Many Religions, 82.
93. Samartha, 95.

the mystical God, Samartha comments that "a sense of Mystery provides a point of unity to all [this] plurality."[94]

Similarly, the Hindu concept *sat-cit-ananda* – which can be translated as truth-consciousness-bliss – might well find its equivalent in the Christian understanding of the Trinity (God the Father, God the Son, and God the Holy Spirit). The Trinity can also be connected with another Hindu term, *Satyam Shivam Sundaram* (Truth, Goodness, Beauty). For Christians, "the Trinity symbolizes and points to the ultimate Mystery of God, the Creator, Redeemer and Sustainer of all creation which includes Christians and people of other faiths."[95] Amos Yong quotes Samartha as saying that Christians, in their theology, should take a "trinitarian approach with *Theos* as the foundation, *Christos* as the historical anchor, and *Pneuma* as the "guiding power for Christian life and witness in a pluralistic world."[96] Yong's understanding of Samartha might seem to distract the relationship of the triune God. But Samartha always tried to bring together the diversified unity of God's life and the internal rhythm of the Trinity, symbolically pointing to its Ultimate Mystery which should be retained for the integrity of Christian theology.[97] Rather than compromising the Mystery of God, a theocentric Christology serves as a foundation for recognizing the uniqueness of Jesus Christ. Additionally, discussing the Spirit extends beyond just the concept of the Trinity to encompass the entirety of Trinitarian life.[98]

Samartha believed that "the power of the Spirit is relating people to people, people to things, and that the whole creation in its relation to God is rooted in the rhythm of Trinitarian life that nurtures and sustains Christians in the world."[99] The theological basis for acknowledging the Spirit in the whole creation lies in the priority of the Spirit. As Kim observes, in a methodological sense, Samartha linked the Spirit and spirituality with interreligious relations, proposing that "training in spirituality" should be incorporated into theological education in India.[100] Implementing Samartha's recommendations

---

94. Samartha, 5.
95. Samartha, "People of Other Faiths," 261.
96. Yong, "Turn to Pneumatology," 446.
97. Samartha, "Revised Christology," 34.
98. Rajagukguk, "Critical Analysis," 104.
99. Samartha, "Promise of the Spirit," 49.
100. Kim, "Mission Pneumatology," 79.

led to his theology of dialogue, which emphasized the work of the Spirit in religions. Samartha's theology and understanding exposed the mystical presence of God in Hindu cultural practices cultural practices and in the broader world outside the church.

Samartha believed that there were distinct ways to know God. Each person has their own unique experiences in knowing and understanding God. These unique experiences do not mean that God is different, but that our experience of God is different. God can function as a mystery, and searching for God can also be mystical. But in Samartha's concept of unity, through the ignorance before the mystery, unity will not happen unless we reach the ultimate God. So, accepting different ways or traditions people use to reach God is not wrong. In Christianity, even the Trinity experiences diversity in the personalities of Father, Son, and Spirit, but the Trinity also has unity since it describes one God.

4.2.3 The Holy Spirit in Other Religions

Samartha wrote various essays about the relevance of the work of the Holy Spirit in connecting the religious experiences of different religious people. His major contribution to interfaith dialogue about the Spirit is found in two papers, written nearly twenty years apart even though their titles are almost identical: "The Holy Spirit and People of Various Faiths, Cultures, and Ideologies" and "The Holy Spirit and People of Other Faiths." The first is a seminal article, based on a lecture delivered in 1971, and the second is a provocative contribution to a pre-Canberra publication. Amos Yong writes,

> In an exploratory essay presented at the Fifth Oxford Institute on Methodist Theological Studies in the summer of 1973, Samartha, the first director of the Dialogue Program of the WCC., acknowledged that, Christian theology has neglected any sustained reflection on the relation of the Holy Spirit to people of other faiths.[101]

Samartha quoted Khodr and spoke sympathetically of the Orthodox vision of divine presence to the Addis Ababa Committee. His concept of the "Unbound Christ" expresses the idea that "Christianity belongs to Christ,

---

101. Yong, "Turn to Pneumatology," 443.

Christ does not belong to Christianity."[102] The work of Samartha up to 1990 has been comprehensively studied by Eeuwout Klootwijk, who characterizes Samartha's approach in interreligious dialogue and the theology of religions as one of "commitment and openness" and includes in his book a chapter dealing with "the wider work of the Spirit as seen by Samartha."[103] Commenting on Samartha's renowned book – *One Christ – Many Religions: Toward a Revised Christology* – Paul Knitter says, "It is the understanding of the Holy Spirit which can open new doors and remove old obstacles in a theology of religions."[104] Samartha says that it is not so much a matter of extending the work of the Spirit "outside the hedges of the Church as a more inclusive doctrine of God himself."[105] Samartha firmly believed that pneumatology holds significant potential for a theology of religions, and he diligently endeavoured to draw the Christian community's attention to this critical aspect. He found the work of the Spirit in religions a significant medium for engaging in interfaith dialogue with different religious people.

While Samartha recognized the reality of the biblical witness in which the Spirit's activities primarily focus on the believing community, he considered that the Spirit's foremost work among believers does not necessarily deny the Spirit's work in a secular world. In particular, this should not be perceived as a negative judgement on Hindus, Buddhists, Muslims, or individuals of other faiths in contemporary times. Samartha claims that this understanding is very close to "Orthodox tradition, which refuses to limit the work of the Holy Spirit in the area of rational beings only but would include all creation within the scope of his presence and activity."[106] He believed that even though the work of the Spirit is primarily focused on Christians, it is also a mystery in other religious faiths. He confesses, however, that "neither the testimony of the scripture nor the tradition of the church gives clear and consistent guidelines to discuss the larger work of the Holy Spirit"[107] in other religious people.

Samartha observes that several complex issues exist in Christianity with regard to the Spirit's relationship to people of other faiths. In his article "The

---

102. Kim, "Mission Pneumatology," 77.
103. Klootwijk, Commitment and Openness, 261–290.
104. Knitter, "Stanley Samartha's *One Christ*," 25–30.
105. Samartha, "People of Various Faiths," 21.
106. Samartha, 22.
107. Samartha, 23.

Holy Spirit and People of Other Faiths," he raises four issues. First, there is "the uncertainty, the vagueness and the haziness about the person of the Spirit within the Trinity."[108] In response, Samartha represents Christian doctrine as understanding that praying to the Spirit is praying to God.[109] He then asks how Christians can accept this doctrine and yet deny the presence of the Spirit in the lives of people of other faiths. There should be theological confidence to affirm the presence of the Spirit in the whole of creation, including all humanity.[110] In Samartha's teachings, while the presence of the Holy Spirit in other religions – including Hinduism – remains a mystery, it is affirmed.

Samartha's second question focuses on the source of the Spirit, "whether the Spirit proceeds from the Father *alone* or the Father *and the Son*."[111] In dealing with this question, Samartha contrasts two views within Christianity: the Orthodox position and that of the Vatican or the Western view. The former says that the Spirit proceeds only from the Father; the latter position is that the Spirit proceeds from both Father and Son.[112] Samartha prefers his understanding of the Orthodox view – that the Spirit proceeds only from the Father – but he understood this to mean that the Holy Spirit is not channelled only through Christianity but is also experienced in other religious faiths.

Samartha's third concern is whether the work of the Spirit began in creation, before Pentecost.[113] Recognizing that God spoke to the prophets through the Spirit, Samartha believed that prophets from other faiths might also find a place within God's *oikoumene* (the place of God's reconciling mission), indicating a potential for openness and inclusivity and suggesting that the Holy Spirit is the Spirit of the Creator as well, and not just the Spirit of Christ.

Samartha's fourth question concerns the relationship between baptism and the gift of the Spirit. He says that "the possibility of the Spirit being present and active among those who are not baptized, and in communities outside the visible boundaries of the institutional church . . . should be left

---

108. Samartha, "People of Other Faiths," 253.
109. Samartha, 254.
110. Samartha, 254.
111. Samartha, 253.
112. Samartha, 255.
113. Samartha, 255.

open rather than closed."[114] For Samartha, the gift of the creator Spirit is not tied to baptism or to some selected people.

Samartha's understanding of the Holy Spirit being active outside the church is expressed vividly in his writings, especially in his discussion of various Christian disputes. He believed that since God seems to be a mystery, the person and work of the Spirit must also remain a mystery. Samartha finds more theological space for the Spirit to work everywhere from the beginning. As the Father and the Son both are from the beginning of creation, the work of the Spirit is also present from the beginning. This view of the presence and work of the Spirit in the world enabled Samartha to posit a unity between Christianity and Hinduism.

Samartha observes that the Spirit who reveals the activities of God is known by different names in Christianity – "the Spirit, the Spirit of God, the Holy Spirit and the Spirit of Christ."[115] The diversity lies in these various descriptions of the Spirit but not in the Spirit's nature. Correspondingly, in Hinduism, different terms – *antaryamin*, *Shakti*, and *ananda* – describe spiritual movements, with each term having distinct features. For Samartha, the term *antaryamin* emphasizes that the works of the Spirit happen in human life. He applies this Hindu term to both God and the Spirit: "It emphasizes that God is not just *the wholly* other but is also the *antaryamin*, the indwelling God." Regarding the work of the Spirit, he writes, "The Spirit as *antaryamin*, the indwelling God, provides anchorage to people to be rooted in the being of God through Christ."[116]

Similarly, he observes, "In India, the Spirit is regarded as *Shakti*, the power of God . . . as 'the giver of life' [*Shakti*] is the source of new life and through baptism, gives birth to new children of God."[117] Samartha did not consider it offensive, as Shakti is a female goddess in Hinduism, to view the Spirit as feminine in this way. He argues, "Since Father and Son are in any case *human* symbols, there is no reason why the Spirit should not be regarded as the Mother and referred to as 'she.'"[118] The perfection of the Trinity lies

---

114. Samartha, 256.
115. Samartha, "People of Various Faiths," 21.
116. Samartha, "Promise of the Spirit," 44.
117. Samartha, 45.
118. Samartha, 45.

in the feminine nature of the Spirit, which Roman Catholic theology has also recognized. Kirsteen Kim notes that Samartha completely agrees with this theological idea "because without a mother, the father-son picture is incomplete and the paternity of the father and the legitimacy of the Son are in jeopardy."[119] Samartha's interpretation of the Spirit as a mother within the Trinity enabled him to find similarities to the Hindu understanding of feminine divinity and its attributes. Finally, the Hindu term *ananda* represents people's happiness when they have spiritual experiences.

Samartha tried to prove an interconnection between Hinduism and Christianity through these terminologies and features. He regarded these Hindu terms as carrying a similar meaning to a Christian understanding of the Spirit. Thus, a theology of the Spirit could be of great assistance in doing theology in an Indian context. Consequently, Samartha recognized the urgent need to discuss the Holy Spirit in our churches. However, his interpretations of Hindu terms should also lead us to this question: Is it the same Spirit who works in all religions, providing good results through different religious experiences?

4.2.4 Religious Experience in Religion

When it comes to religious knowledge, Samartha gave priority to people's personal experiences rather than to intellectual understanding. In Hinduism, the Sanskrit word *anubhava* (or *anubhavah*) denotes experience based on personal knowledge or aesthetic experience. In relation to obtaining knowledge, Samartha believed that there was a vast difference in Eastern and Western thought. In Eastern thought, the emphasis is on knowledge based on experience; in Western thought, reason is considered all-important. Samartha felt that the Indian tradition has an incredible wealth of religious experience – anubhava, dristi, dharsana (vision and intuition) – that enables it to accumulate far greater knowledge than any nation that gives priority to reasoning. He says, "In Hindu tradition, *Jnana* is never the end product of *tarka*. It is the fruit of *anubhava*. It is the result of *dristi*, the vision of God, which in spite of all *sadhana*, we ourselves cannot produce. We can only behold and receive the *darshana*."[120] Samartha believed that the human tendency to search for

---

119. Kim, "Mission Pneumatology," 121.
120. Samartha, "This Is Eternal Life," 15.

the ultimate truth of the world is manifest through religious experience, not through human reasoning or intellectual knowledge. He says, "The knowledge of experience that God is true is a proposition, God becomes true in our life is a witness based on experience."[121] Whatever it may be, for a typical Hindu, true religion is not believed but experienced.[122]

People's religious experiences help them to understand the reality of the world and what ultimate truth is. Samartha confirms that there is only one truth. Kim remarks that Samartha "adopts the Vedic view that 'since truth is one and God is truth, there obviously cannot be a Hindu truth and a Christian truth.'"[123] So, Samartha was of the view that creating a spiritual experience and revealing the truth is the work of the Spirit. To support this idea, he quotes John 16:13 (NIV): "he [the Spirit of truth] will guide you into all the truth." Here, a rational, scripture-based understanding of God is seen as inferior to knowing God through experience. "The perception of Truth through *Anubhava*, inadequately translated as 'intuition' or 'experience', is basic to any knowledge to which the scriptures bear witness."[124] Samartha emphasizes that "*tarka* (logic) must be subordinated to *anubhava* (experience)."[125]

Samartha believed that the unique nature of religious experience is its ability to grant an inward experience that quenches a person's ultimate thirst. The deep desire to relate to the Supreme God is common to all religions, and Samartha believed that this was a reality in every person's life and that any success in knowing this ultimate truth is based upon a person's inward experience. Samartha writes, "Within the core of every religion there lies this powerful *anubhava* (experience) or *dharsana* (vision) that becomes a 'non-negotiable' item in the life of the believing community,"[126] and so, he viewed people's spirituality as resting upon their personal experiences rather than trusting in religious dogmas and practices. Religious experience has the power to transform people and motivate them to live harmoniously with their neighbours. He says, "The Spirit inwardly nourishes the new life in Christ and guides the community of believers in their acts of witness and service in the

---

121. Samartha, 14.
122. Samartha, *Between Two Cultures*, 181.
123. Kim, "Mission Pneumatology," 97.
124. Samartha, One Christ – Many Religions, 69.
125. Samartha, 5, 61, 82–83, 105, 120.
126. Samartha, 113.

world."[127] Samartha was also confident that God's Spirit spreads truth in and through all religions. The work of the Spirit extends beyond the Spirit's relationship to Christ. Samartha disagreed with Bishop Newbigin, who believed that "the Holy Spirit does not lead past, or beyond, or away from Jesus."[128] For Samartha, the ultimate truth is revealed through our personal experience of the Spirit, an experience that is not dependent on Jesus. This may cause us to wonder whether it is possible that the Spirit may reveal truth that is outside the church. However, final and ultimate truth is found in Jesus. I think that both Samartha and Newbigin are partly right. But more on this below.

Samartha believed that the interpretation of the Hindu religious experience could build better relationships between these two religions and that the inward works of the Spirit lead to spiritual experience and real knowledge. Similarly, he agreed with the Hindu understanding that knowledge received through religious experiences is more important than intellectual knowledge. For this reason, Samartha did not hesitate to focus on spiritual experience, which is essential for religious authenticity. Moreover, there are similarities between Hindu concepts and ideologies and biblical teachings. While such similarities cannot be considered as the truth, the similarities found in other religions can lead people towards the truth.

4.2.5 Discerning the Spirit

Discerning the Spirit is essential for Christians to understand the work of the Spirit in other religions and to maintain good relationships with people of other religious faiths. After dealing with whether or not the Spirit is active outside the church, Samartha goes on to ask how this more comprehensive presence and activity of the Spirit is to be discerned: "Christians are called upon to *discern*, not to control the Spirit."[129] But this same ability also allows a person to recognize the fruit of the Spirit in other religious faiths and in their ways of seeking truth. Samartha emphasizes that *viveka*, the ability to discern, is a most excellent quality in a pupil who seeks the knowledge of the Brahman. The pupil should be able to discern between the eternal and the temporal, the heavy and the light, and truth and falsehood. Even when this

---

127. Samartha, "People of Other Faiths," 250.
128. Newbigin, *Light Has Come*, 216–217.
129. Samartha, "People of Other Faiths," 260.

quality of discernment is a gift from above, it has to be acquired through *sadhana* – the way of controlling the body, disciplining the mind, and purifying the heart. This is a spiritual discipline that can also be found in Christianity. Samartha sees discernment as a result of the activities of the Spirit, not as a means of controlling the Spirit.

Samartha believed that wherever the Spirit works, the truth would also be revealed. He viewed discernment as "the passionate concern for relating the promises of God to the facts of contemporary life."[130] He was confident that the Spirit, who gives discernment, will guide us into all truth (John 16:13) and that the recognition of the Spirit is possible through the fruits of the Spirit (Gal 5:22): "This power to discern is exercised not so much to *restrict* the activities of the Spirit as to recognize whether or not it is the Spirit indeed who is really working among people."[131]

Samartha identifies from the Bible some of the significant signs of the work of the Holy Spirit as they apply to the day-to-day life of Christians as they encounter people of other religious faiths. These include (1) the Spirit's mark of freedom, (2) the Spirit's mark of boundlessness, (3) the Spirit's power to bring new relationships, and (4) the Spirit's power to create a new community. It is important that we pay attention to each of these signs. Samartha says that understanding these features of one's encounter with the Holy Spirit would mean that "one may have to be far more sensitive than before to understand what may be the signs of the Spirit in the lives of neighbours of other faiths outside the visible boundaries of the church in the world."[132] This understanding can help to build a new relationship between people of different religions, leading to harmonious living.

Above all, Samartha argues that in the Bible, the Holy Spirit is represented by the marks of freedom, spontaneity, and unpredictability.[133] The Spirit's identification with freedom can be found in delivering, empowering, renewing, and transforming people. It is challenging for a person to predict where the Spirit is and where the Spirit is not. This unpredictable work of the Spirit is especially visible in the public ministry of Jesus Christ as he carried out

---

130. Samartha, "The Holy Spirit", 260.
131. Samartha, People of Other Faiths," 260.
132. Samartha, 258.
133. Samartha, 258.

God's mission. At the time of Jesus's public ministry, no social, cultural, or religious barriers prevented Jesus from extending his work. Noting this idea in Samartha, Kim writes, "In his view, 'Christ is at work wherever people are struggling for freedom and renewal' because these activities are part of 'the same mission of God in the world which we Christians distinctively understand as manifest in Jesus Christ.'"[134] Jesus carried out his ministry in the power of the Holy Spirit. Samartha says, "In the New Testament, where the work of the Spirit is almost entirely connected with the life and work of Jesus Christ, openings are left for the Spirit to move where the Spirit wills."[135] Even after the ascension of Jesus, the Spirit's work continued through the outpouring of the Holy Spirit – the gift of the Spirit being given to people according to God's will (Acts 2:16–21; 1 Cor 12:11). This sovereign feature of the Spirit's freedom is apparent "in the events following the outpouring of the Spirit at Pentecost baptism and the gift of the Holy Spirit."[136] Noting the Spirit's spontaneity, Samartha sought to reform our Christian understanding of how the Spirit relates to our neighbours of other faiths. He asserts that the Spirit cannot be "imprisoned within the steel and concrete structures of Western dogma and a permanent Atlantic Charter."[137] Emancipation is the ultimate result of the work of the Spirit, who reveals himself among people both inside and outside the church.

Second, Samartha expresses the boundless nature of the Spirit. He believed that the Spirit, who knows no limits in accomplishing God's mission, crosses borders, imparts a godly nature, and spreads justice and equality in the world Both the Old and New Testaments describe the Spirit as "wind," which sometimes functions as a gentle breeze and other times as a powerful tempest.[138] The representation of the Holy Spirit as a boundless "storm" was made visible on the day of Pentecost as the Holy Spirit anointed everyone who believed in Christ without any discrimination. Regarding this outpouring of the Spirit on the day of Pentecost, Samartha explains, "The possibility of the Spirit being present and active among those who are not baptized, and

---

134. Kim, "Mission Pneumatology," 90.
135. Samartha, "People of Other Faiths," 258.
136. Samartha, 256.
137. Samartha, Courage for Dialogue, 63–64.
138. Samartha, "People of Other Faiths," 258.

in communities outside the visible boundaries of the institutional church, should be left open rather than closed."[139] For Samartha, "the Holy Spirit's movement is not only in the Church but also in the communities of people outside the visible boundaries of the church."[140] He argues that the doctrine of the Holy Spirit must, therefore, be approached cosmologically as "'the universal Spirit,' for the Spirit is close to God the Father."[141]

Samartha believed that the Holy Spirit – who produces the fruit of the Spirit mentioned in Galatians 5:22–23 (love, joy, peace, patience, kindness, goodness, faithfulness, gentleness, and self-control) – is also present in other religious people. "For Christians, these ethical fruits are rooted in their faith in God through Christ and in the power of the Spirit. They believe that without being in God one cannot produce the fruits of the Spirit of God."[142] If this is so, then moral deeds found in people of other religions affirm the presence of God outside the Christian community as well. Samartha argues, "These are visible and readily recognizable signs which do not need elaborated theological investigations."[143] Samartha never devalued the good works done by other religious people; rather, he considered such deeds a result of the work of the Spirit. Amid religious riots, where demonic forces unleash violence, destruction, and suffering, there are heartening signs of individuals from diverse religious backgrounds spontaneously coming together in acts of friendship, courage, and self-sacrifice.[144] This kind of action is found in all religions. Like them, many Christians are involved in such acts, serving in conflict situations and manifesting the marks of the Spirit in acts of compassion, service, and sacrifice. When similar acts are so obviously performed by our neighbours of other faiths as well, Samartha asks, rhetorically, whether there are serious theological reasons to deny that the presence of the Spirit is among them as well. "For Christians, to be in Christ is indeed to be in God. But in a religiously plural world, to be in Christ is not the only way to be in God."[145]

---

139. Samartha, 256.
140. Rajagukguk, "Critical Analysis," 103.
141. Rajagukguk, 101.
142. Samartha, "People of Other Faiths," 259.
143. Rajagukguk, "Critical Analysis," 103.
144. Samartha, "People of Other Faiths," 259.
145. Rajagukguk, "Critical Analysis," 103.

Third, the Holy Spirit gives the power to build new relationships between people without the bias of any socioreligious or cultural condition. Such relationships are not possible without breaking down old and oppressive structures, both religious and secular. Here, the Holy Spirit functions "as fire" and "destroys all that stands in the way of the emergence of new life – outmoded dogmas, meaningless rituals, obsolete customs, oppressive institutions, barriers that separate people of one community from another."[146] The Spirit makes "koinonia" in Christ a reality for all believers. A person born of the Spirit is empowered to build good relationships with God and human beings. Fellowship on the earth should include accepting as equals people of all castes, colours, cultures, tribes, and nations. But Samartha suspected that the likelihood of such a fellowship among Christians is doubtful. The lack of awareness about the Spirit's relation to people of other faiths might be one of the reasons most Christians, including those residing in multireligious societies, do not contemplate this question. Confessing that this is true in most churches, Samartha admonishes, "If we are serious when we say we believe in the *living* God who is the Lord of history, then the present, the contemporary historical context in which people of various faiths are interdependent and have to live together as neighbours, is equally important."[147] Amos Yong writes that Samartha believed that "it is this presence and activity of the Spirit that empowers people to relate to other people, to creation, and to God."[148] Samartha says, "As the Giver of life it is the Spirit who moves them to demand fullness of life, freedom, self-respect and human dignity."[149] Our moral character and loving spirit towards our neighbour symbolize the flow of the Spirit in our lives.

Fourth, Samartha believed that the Holy Spirit gives power to build a new community that can fight against evil in the world. This is possible only through building harmonious relationships between people without any segregation. The Spirit enables us "to create new communities of people cutting across all barriers of religion, culture, ideology, race and language."[150] Such

---

146. Samartha, "People of Other Faiths," 258.
147. Samartha, "People of Various Faiths," 28.
148. Yong, "Turn to Pneumatology," 446.
149. Samartha, "People of Other Faiths," 258.
150. Samartha, 258.

a community, which is not limited but enhanced by diversity, is formed as a result of the work of the Spirit as the Spirit works to transform personal and social life. This new community attains a new vision and strives forward to achieve it. From Samartha's perspective, "New communities are formed both as tools to fight against injustice and as a result of different people coming together for such common purposes."[151] There will still be diversity, but this does not mean division. Samartha adds that the Spirit provides inspiration, energy, and power to humble folk to rise up in righteous anger against tyranny, oppression, and injustice in society.

Samartha suggests that the four biblical marks of the Spirit – freedom, boundlessness, the power to build new relationships, and the power to create new communities – are each essential if Christians are to discern the presence of the Spirit in other religions. It is relevant here to note Samartha's concluding statements in "The Holy Spirit and the People of Various Faiths, Cultures, and Ideologies," an article regarding the work of the Spirit in people of other faith. First, given that the discussion about the relationship between the Holy Spirit and people of other faiths is in comparison to the Spirit's activity within the context of the life and work of the believing community, this should not be regarded as a negative judgement on Hindus, Buddhists, Muslims, and others today. Second, within the tradition of the church, there are divergent tendencies in the Catholic, Orthodox, and Protestant heritages, and, therefore, Christians may hold different views about the work of the Holy Spirit and people of other religions. Third, living in dialogue, we must always be mindful that true religion is a dialogue between God and us. It is not only a dialogue between persons in sharing our experience and knowledge of the mystery of God in Christ; it is also an inner dialogue within us, with God, in the cave of the heart, at the very source of our consciousness. Fourth, if boundless freedom is of the very essence of the Spirit, then to place any limits on the Spirit's activity is to negate that freedom. Finally, meeting the urgent needs of our neighbours may suddenly become more important than suggested by previous theological discussions.[152] In all Samartha's writings, it is evident that he wished to put the nature of the Spirit as understood in the Bible into dialogue with other religions and, in this way, to justify God's presence and

---

151. Samartha, 258.
152. Samartha, "People of Various Faiths," 30–34.

activities as present everywhere in this world. He concludes by noting that, in a religiously plural world, it might be beneficial to seek the more evident and readily recognizable fruits of the Spirit in people's lives.

Samartha believed that the Spirit cannot be bounded within any boundaries, including human culture, tradition, race, or faith. The work of the Spirit in transforming, renewing, and rebuilding people will continue unstintingly, which means that the Spirit can also work freely in Hindu culture without any distinction based on religion. Wherever character transformation happens in a person's life and new communities are formed with the divine quality of seeking to help others, there the work of the Spirit is evident.

4.2.6 Interfaith Dialogue

Samartha viewed "dialogue" as one of the best ways to bring unity between multireligious people. O. V. Jathanna says this about Samartha's understanding of dialogue: "It is the willingness to see God at work everywhere, without giving up the integrity of the Christian faith and witness."[153] Samartha's understanding of dialogue in a multireligious country is that it helps people to build good relationships, strengthens them to do God's mission, and enables them to grow spiritually. He encourages Christians to enter into fellowship with other religious people through dialogue instead of spending time in debate and says, "Dialogue is between people, not between religions. It is more a matter of relationships than of debates and discussions."[154] Dialogue encompasses more than simply discussing religious ideas with neighbours of other faiths; it also involves collaborating and working together in society.

Dialogue can function as a magnet that draws people closer to Christ. When people are close to one another, the mission of God can be carried out easily. Samartha notes, "In fact, dialogue emerged out of the womb of mission and it has never been easy for missions to cut the umbilical cord and to recognize the independence of the growing child without denying the relationship."[155] He adds, "Depending upon social and cultural situations the experience of Christians in dialogue and the intensity of their involvement

---

153. Jathanna, "Memorial Service," 85.
154. Samartha, "Partners in Community," 78.
155. Samartha, "Guidelines on Dialogue," 155.

obviously vary from country to country."[156] Samartha states that authentic community can only arise when strangers transform into friends and travellers evolve into pilgrims on the journey towards the city of God. Making and keeping relationships is a sign of spiritual maturity. Samartha says, "A Hindu friend, emphasizing that the basis of dialogue was 'a common spirituality,' wondered how dialogue between people of living faiths could also include people who follow certain 'ideologies' (India)." Moreover, the Christian attitude of building good relationships with their neighbours transforms people's personal and social lives. Samartha notes, "Dialogue in the sense of Christian involvement in the religious life of their neighbours leads to new relationships and helps to transform religious values into social virtues."[157] The success of the dialogue depends on acceptability without imposing any limitations based on culture, beliefs, practice, or race.

In summary, Samartha believed that the work of the Spirit in dialogue is essential to establishing harmony among people. The Spirit's work in recognizing and accepting other religious people is vividly expressed in Samartha's writings, which deal with diverse countries and cultural contexts, free from the historical burden of the West. The evolution of dialogue necessitates a renewed comprehension of the role of the Holy Spirit, and such an understanding is pivotal in fostering meaningful relationships between Christians and individuals of various faiths and ideologies.[158]

In his book *One Christ – Many Religions: Toward a Revised Christology*, Samartha discusses dialogue with religions such as Judaism, Islam, Buddhism, and Hinduism. Based on Hindu dialogue models, Samartha examines the views of representative Hindu philosophers: V. A. Devasenapathi, Anantanand Rambachan, K. L. Seshagiri Rao, and K. R. Sundararajan. The views of two of these thinkers are particularly relevant. First, A. Rambachan, who criticized his Hindu tradition by agreeing with Swami Vivekananda's rejection of exclusivism. Second, Sundararajan, who contributed two models in dialogue – "the closed-border model" and "the border-crossing model."[159] Critically aligning the positive aspects of these two models offers a valuable contribution to a

---

156. Samartha, "Dialogue: Significant Issues," 328.
157. Samartha, One Christ – Many Religions, 130.
158. Samartha, "Dialogue: Significant Issues," 335.
159. Samartha, One Christ – Many Religions, 29.

Hindu theology of dialogue in the present day. Samartha states that a compassionate comprehension of the responses of their non-Christian neighbours to Christian-initiated dialogue is valuable for Christians and other faith communities as humanity progresses into the twenty-first century.[160] Engaging in dialogue with people of other faiths fosters connections among communities divided by diverse religions and traditions. Through verbal discussions encompassing all aspects of religion, individuals can share theological ideas and religious experiences. The exchange of personal experiences across religious beliefs helps elucidate the diverse ways in which the Spirit operates. Religious experiences of truth are relational rather than propositional, and the aesthetic dimension provides a bridge for establishing profound relationships between individuals of different faiths.[161] Samartha's understanding of Indian philosophy enabled him to rethink a new hermeneutical approach to Christian theology within an Indian framework. He believed in the necessity of formulating an Indian Christian theology rooted incarnationally in his people's traditional beliefs and practices.

4.2.7 Summary

The Spirit: In developing his theological understanding, Samartha prioritizes the Holy Spirit's nature, role, and functions. He begins by recognizing that since God is a person of mystery, the work of the Spirit remains a mystery. The work of the Spirit happens internally and brings transformation and divine knowledge to people. Samartha believed that any boundaries – including human culture, tradition, race, and faith – cannot restrict the Spirit. The Spirit's nature gives space to accept other religious faiths. Samartha's four marks of the Spirit – freedom, boundlessness, the Spirit's power to build new relationships, and the power to create new community – shows the Spirit as being limitless in accomplishing God's mission. Of course, Samartha agrees that the work of the Spirit focuses primarily on Christians, but he also allows for the mysterious presence of the Spirit in other religious faiths. The nature of the Spirit is shown through crossing borders, revealing God's nature, and bringing about justice and equality in the world.

---

160. Samartha, 35.
161. Samartha, 104.

The Spirit in Hinduism: Samartha finds many similarities between the Hindu tradition and the Bible's description of the features and functions of the Spirit. The Hindu term *antaryamin*, for example, can be used to describe the work of the Spirit in human life. The concept of *antaryamin* deals with the indwelling nature of the Spirit, which connects the internal works of the Spirit with people's spiritual experience. Hindu spirituality has an internal craving for truth and contemplation similar to that of Christian prayer and fellowship with God. Samartha viewed praying to the Spirit as praying to God. He believed that because the Spirit proceeds from the Father, God's Spirit is universally present. Since Samartha's interpretation of the Spirit in the Trinity is feminine – like the Hindu term shakti, or mother – he interrelates Christianity with a Hindu understanding of feminine divinity and its attributes. For Samartha, the Holy Spirit as a mother exposes the feminine nature of caring, relating, and brooding. Through such concepts, Samartha argues that the Holy Spirit is not necessarily channelled only through Christianity but also through other faiths.

Religious Experience: From a theological perspective, Samartha believed that people's religious experience plays a significant role in creating deeper relationship between different religions because spiritual experience establishes religious authenticity. As far as human beings are concerned, only spiritual experiences can quench their ultimate thirst. Samartha believed that a person's spirituality rests upon their personal experience and not in merely trusting religious dogmas and practices. God's Spirit spreads truth in all religions. But Samartha believed that the ultimate truth is revealed through the Spirit's involvement in a person's life (*anubhava*). This is a matter of experience rather than rational thinking. For Samartha, true religion is not only believed but experienced. Samartha's understanding of religious experience with positive results in Hinduism as the results of the Spirit's intervention enables us to accept God's broader revelation in other religious faith.

Discerning the Spirit: Samartha is silent about the distinct spirits in the multireligious nation of India's, but he asks people to discern. He encourages Christians to discern the Spirit and not to restrict the Spirit's presence by any people-made doctrines or institutions. The four marks of the Spirit – freedom, boundlessness, building new relationships, and forming a new community – can help Christians to distinguish the Spirit's work in a world where other spirits are also actively present. If an experience can lead people to know the truth and produce the fruit of the Spirit, then it would be wrong to deny the work of God behind such an experience.

Koinonia: The work of the Spirit in human life will lead to building a new community characterized by a harmonious life. Samartha believed that a community of peace and unity could be formed by being willing to dialogue with all religious people and break the bonds of traditional doctrines. Such peace and unity cannot develop without the help of the Spirit through spiritual experiences. In India, a new theological understanding of "dialogue" can help people build good relationships. To express a willingness to dialogue with others symbolizes spiritual maturity and will lead to carrying out God's mission. The nature of dialogue necessitates accepting all people, regardless of their cultures, beliefs, practices, and religions. The Spirit functions as a fire, destroying all obstacles – whether outmoded dogmas, meaningless rituals, obsolete customs, or oppressive institutions – that separate people from one another. In Christianity, the Spirit makes *koinonia* – a new fellowship with Christ among all believers. The Spirit empowers such a community to fight against evil in this world. The Spirit provides the people with the inspiration, energy, and power to rise in righteous anger against tyranny, oppression, and social injustice. The spiritual experience of people leads them to develop a new relationship with Christ, which in turn breaks all boundaries made by human beings in creating a harmonious community.

Unity: Samartha's concept of unity also emphasizes the equality of all people in their ignorance about the mystery of God. People's false knowledge about God has divided and separated Hindus and Christians, but acknowledging their common ignorance before the mystery of God should bring them together. In his theology of dialogue, Samartha emphasizes the work of the Spirit in all religions to break their ignorance about the divine mystery. This theology recognizes the mystical presence of God outside the church, including in Hindu cultural practices. As plurality is a reality in the world, God's revelation to all people is plural in nature; therefore, people's approaches to God are also plural. And so, spiritual experience may differ from person to person, community to community, and religion to religion. This nature of plurality is perhaps more evident in India, which is multireligious. So, it is better to understand the spiritual experiences of people from other religious faiths as we construct theology in their context

4.3 Chenchiah and Samartha on Religious Experience: An Evaluation

It will be helpful to conclude this section by comparing and contrasting Chenchiah and Samartha. Both these Indian theologians took the initiative to construct new Christian theologies that are particularly relevant to the people of India. While Chenchiah gives priority to considering Indian traditions, Samartha gives priority to developing an open mind to accept the truth of other religions. Both intended to convey the message of the gospel peacefully. Chenchiah believed that until our theology is constructed based on Indian culture and tradition, it will not speak to Indians. Samartha believed that theology should provide a space to freely discuss our spiritual experiences and willingly accept the truth found in other religions. This is a mark of spiritual maturity that will help to bring peace and unity. Religious tradition and the positive outcomes of religious experience undoubtedly support the work of the Spirit. A theology which emphasis the work of the Spirit can establish a harmonious life with peace between people.

4.3.1 The Role of the Spirit in Theology

Chenchiah developed a pneumatologically based Christology that exposes the Holy Spirit's work within other religious traditions. In his theology, Chenchiah represents the Holy Spirit as a "cosmic creative energy" that can transform a person into a new creation. As with Jesus, this new creation grows through the continual intervention of the Spirit. Samartha believed that the Holy Spirit is a mystery, working in the inner life of human beings. He connects this with the Hindu concept of *antaryamin*, an inner working of the Spirit which he saw as present not only among Christians but also outside the church. Concerning the cosmic power of the Spirit in Indian tradition, Chenchiah and Samartha use the Hindu term *shakti*, which refers to a Hindu goddess. In addition, Chenchiah uses other Hindu terms such as *Mahasakti*, *visvakarma*, and *prajapathi*. But Samartha asks people to discern – *viveka* is the Hindu term he uses – the Spirit because there is polytheism in Hinduism; thus, many spirits exist. These two theologians' theological understandings of the Spirit help to construct a pneumatological-based theology in the Indian context effortlessly and to build relationships between various religious people. Constructing such a theology is particularly relevant in India, where people prioritize spiritual experiences.

4.3.2 Religious Experience and Human Tradition

Both these theologians prioritize religious experience for the spiritual growth and transformation of Christians. The faith is not first about doctrines. For Samartha, the authenticity of religion is based upon authentic spiritual experiences. In Hinduism, he considers the term *anubhava* – an inner experience – equal to religious experience. Chenchiah similarly believed that a person's inner experience is more important than institutionalized dogmas, and he connected people's spiritual experience with yoga – a spiritual exercise in Hinduism – with the positive results of Christian discipline. Chenchiah found the *ananda* and *kaivalya* a Hindu yogi expects from yoga similar to the outcome of a Christian's spiritual experience. Both experiences provide bliss and happiness. The nature of religious experience as an inner occurrence and the reality of positive outcomes in religious experience undoubtedly provide an opportunity to connect with other religious faiths.

4.3.3 Transformation

Chenchiah and Samartha believed that religious experiences take place with the help of the Spirit and bring positive transformation both in people and in society. For Chenchiah, from a Christian perspective, spiritual experiences transform people into new persons and enable them to adopt the character of Jesus. Such a new person becomes part of the kingdom of God. Their spiritual experience helps them grow in Christlikeness and develop ethical values. For Samartha, spiritual experiences help people to engage in peaceful dialogue with different religious people and lead a harmonious life. Together, these "new creations" form a new community, a *koinonia* – "the fellowship" or "the church of God." People who belong to the kingdom of God become part of a new community. Like Christ, the transformed person becomes more open to love and accept all people. Samartha says that such fellowship expresses spiritual maturity, enabling Christians to dialogue harmoniously with neighbouring faiths.

4.3.4 Union

Both these theologians deal with the concept of "union," which is closely connected with people's spiritual experience. Chenchiah uses the Hindu term *sayujya* to explain union and sees Christianity as making human beings a new creation through union with Christ by the power of the Holy Spirit. He does not view it as wrong for Christians to adopt the Hindu spiritual exercise of yoga as a spiritual discipline. In fact, he encourages Christians to develop a new *sadhana* of eternal life by making "yoga of the Holy Spirit," which he represents as *parisuddha atma yoga* (yoga of the Holy Spirit) or *amrita yoga* (yoga of everlasting life). Samartha's explanation of unity also connects easily with Indian contextual understandings, particularly *advaita,* ignorance, and pluralism. The unity that Samartha finds in these concepts can bring unity between religions. For him, *advaita* means "holding together God-self-world in one continuum." He also acknowledges people's ignorance about the mystery of God, a shared ignorance that should bring them together. However, since God's revelations to people are plural and, thus, people's approaches to God are plural, unity can only be found in plurality. Christians need not deny in their theology the reality of plurality in our search for God and in God's dealings with people. But this also does not preclude an even more basic unity. We are one in the Spirit. A common ground for connecting theology in the Hindu tradition can be found in Chenchiah's concept of "yoga of the Holy Spirit" and Samartha's notion of "unity in pluralism."

CHAPTER 5

Religious Experience: The Understanding of Western Theologians

In the previous chapter, we considered the insights of two leading Indian theologians who recognized the theological importance of religious experience and located their inquiry in an expanded pneumatology that was in dialogue with the Indian multireligious context. In this chapter, we turn to two Western theologians – Jurgen Moltmann and Kirsteen Kim – and their understanding of religious experience. These two contemporary theologians – one male, the other female – are widely respected in Christian circles. The reason for selecting these two theologians is the emphasis in their writings on the work of the Spirit in human life, culture, and the world. Adding the thoughts of Western theologians to our study can widen our perspective on the topic we are dealing with. These two theologians also have somewhat different agendas. Moltmann focuses more on public theology, while Kim highlights mission theology. We will deal with each theologian's understanding of the Spirit in human experiences and then make some general observations about the Holy Spirit from an Indian perspective. First, we will look at Moltmann; then, we will consider Kim, who lived in India for a time and contributed greatly to the Indian context.

5.1 Jurgen Moltmann (1926–2024)

Jurgen Moltmann, a theologian from the Lutheran tradition, was born in Hamburg, Germany, on 8 April 1926. He was influenced by distinguished theologians like Dietrich Bonhoeffer, Ernst Wolf, and Hans Joachim Iwand, whose input led Moltmann to reflect deeply on the church's involvement in social ethics. In 1952, Moltmann received his doctorate in theology, under the supervision of Otto Weber, from the University of Göttingen. After his theological studies, he served as a pastor in the Evangelical Church of Bremen for the next five years. He then became a theological professor at Kirchliche Hochschule Academy in Wuppertal. In 1963, he came in contact with Wolfhart Pannenberg and joined the theological faculty at Bonn University. Then, from 1967 until his retirement in 1994, he served as a professor of systematic theology at University of Tübingen. He continued to be active as a speaker and writer until his death in June 2024.

Moltmann's theological contributions are considered an outstanding and unparalleled endowment to Christianity. His major works can be categorized into the early trilogy (1964–1977) and continuing systematic contributions to theology (1978–). The early trilogy includes his widely praised *Theology of Hope* (1964), which centres on God the Father and shaped his Trinitarian theology. This book presented a doctrine of hope for the oppressed and suffering in Christian eschatology. Next in the early trilogy is *The Crucified God* (1972), which centres on Christology and describes the solidarity of a loving God with the world in its suffering. Finally, *The Church in the Power of the Spirit* (1975) focuses on themes of ecclesiology and pneumatology. Having defined the Trinitarian shape of his theology in this way, Moltmann turned to other more particular topics. His systematic contributions to theology include the following works: *The Trinity and the Kingdom: The Doctrine of God* (1980), which deals with the Trinity from a theological and anthropological perspective based on Scripture; *God in Creation: An Ecological Doctrine of Creation* (1985), which is focused on the theological and ethical implications of the doctrine of God through eschatological and Trinitarian perspectives; *The Way of Jesus Christ* (1989), which focuses on the personality of Jesus; *The Spirit of Life: A Universal Affirmation* (1991), which develops a holistic doctrine of the person and work of the Holy Spirit in relation to Moltmann's Trinitarian doctrine; *The Coming of God: Christian Eschatology* (1995), which deals with the theme of a new beginning with the coming of

God and the cosmic Shekhinah of God; and *Experiences in Theology* (2000), which deals with a theological method. In all these writings, it is noticeable that Moltmann's focus is on hope, on the expectation of a blessed future for humanity. In sum, Moltmann is well-known as an advocate of Trinitarian theology, in which he could cultivate liberation theology on the one hand and Trinitarian pneumatology on the other, always focusing on the public relevance of theology. His theology of hope expresses the love of God that provides a future that changes the present.

Moltmann's writings provide readers with a better understanding of the person of the Holy Spirit and the work of the Spirit among human beings. He says, "If we talk in Hebrew about Yahweh's *ruach*, we are saying: God is a tempest, a storm, a force in body and soul, humanity and nature."[1] The Holy Spirit is a creative power inherent in every living creature. The transcendent aspect of the *ruach* lies in God's creative power. Contemplating the *ruach* leads us to recognize that God exists in all things and that all things exist within God without equating God with everything else. Building upon his understanding of the Spirit as *ruach*, Moltmann contends that the Holy Spirit can illuminate individuals with divine knowledge. Metaphors portraying the divine Spirit incorporate the concepts of light and power. The luminous aspect of the Spirit can be perceived indirectly through the illumination and reflection. This light is akin to the hope that shines brightly in our hearts which Paul perceived as emanating from "the knowledge of the glory of God in the face of Jesus Christ" (2 Cor 4:6 KJV).[2]

Concerning the function and nature of the Holy Spirit, Moltmann uses both masculine and feminine expressions and explains this with the analogy of God's breath and voice in creation. The masculine "word" (*dabar*) and the feminine "life force" (*ruach*) naturally go together.[3] Moreover, in all creation, the Spirit is seen as being a creating and enlightening power, the power of the divine presence. This divine nature brings transformation in human lives. Moltmann says, "To start from the experience of the Spirit [means] finding largely non-personal words and phrases to describe it: the Spirit is a divine energy, it is wind and fire, light and a wide space, inward assurance and

---

1. Moltmann, *Spirit of Life*, 40.
2. Moltmann, 66–67.
3. Moltmann, 42.

mutual love."[4] The true spiritual experience of people expresses the divine nature of love and care for their fellow beings, because there is no specific mode for the Spirit to work in human life. Moltmann says, "To experience the *ruach* is to experience what is divine not only as a person, and not merely as a force, but also as *space* – as the space of freedom in which the living being can unfold."[5] God's universal provision for everyone is that the Spirit can be experienced as person, force, and space.

Moltmann gives a detailed account of the third person of the Trinity and the work of the Spirit in his book *The Spirit of Life: A Universal Affirmation* (1992). He does so from a distinct position that seeks to blend Protestant, Catholic, Western, and Eastern traditions. He says, "This work on the doctrine of the Trinity is dedicated especially to an overcoming of the schism between the Eastern and Western churches, which has so tragically burdened the whole life of the Christian faith ever since 1054."[6] Moltmann, along with many Eastern and Western theologians, noted the insufficiency of teaching on the work of the Holy Spirit in the creed of 381 and later creeds. This understanding motivated him to attempt a new formulation of Christian theology. Convinced that it was essential for Christian theology to develop a holistic doctrine of God the Holy Spirit, Moltmann writes, "The objective grounds are to be found in the logic of trinitarian thinking. I began this series in 1980 with *The Trinity and the Kingdom: The Doctrine of God*, and the social doctrine of the Trinity."[7] Not rejecting his own work in Christology, Moltmann nevertheless believed that the fundamental understanding of Christ must be based upon the work of the Spirit and states, "My starting point is that the efficacy of Christ is not without the efficacy of the Spirit."[8] With this thought, he began to formulate a Trinitarian pneumatology that emphasized the work of the Spirit in the spiritual experiences of human life. Moltmann tried to develop a Trinitarian pneumatology out of the experience and theology of the Holy Spirit. He considered that "to assert the personhood of the Spirit in the theology of the Trinity can lead in a different direction from statements

---

4. Moltmann, 10.
5. Moltmann, 43.
6. Moltmann, *Trinity and the Kingdom*, xv.
7. Moltmann, Spirit of Life, x.
8. Moltmann, xi.

based on the experience of the Spirit."[9] In addition to the relationship within the Trinity, Moltmann connects the history of the second person, the Son, with the Spirit. He argues that in the history of the Son, the Trinity means that the Father sends the Son through the Spirit, the Son comes from the Father in the power of the Spirit, and the Spirit brings people into the fellowship of the Son with the Father.[10]

5.1.1 The Spirit in Human Life

Moltmann's terminologically based discussion of the Spirit as *ruach* focuses on the Spirit as a divine force for transformation. Moltmann explains that this transforming power, the Spirit, is active in the personal and social lives of human beings. His theology, rooted both in Trinitarian pneumatology and in the public relevance of theology, focuses on the work of the Spirit in humanity. The next section elucidates how this transforming power of the Spirit establishes a "blessed hope" in the lives of individuals and in society. The work of the Spirit in the personal life of human beings is vividly described in the writings of Moltmann. His Trinitarian pneumatology centres on the presence of the Spirit in Jesus's life as an example for human beings to follow.

Jesus's spiritual experiences during his earthly life demonstrate the necessity of the work of the Spirit in human life. In his own life, Jesus experienced the invisible presence of the Spirit ceaselessly. The baptism, call, proclamation, and ministry of Jesus were all carried out in and through the Spirit. According to Moltmann,

> It is in the special relationship to God in this Spirit that Jesus experiences himself as the messianic 'child,' and experiences Israel's God as 'my beloved Father.' In the Spirit, Jesus prays, 'Abba, dear Father.' In the Spirit, he knows himself to be the beloved Son. So the Spirit is the real determining subject of this special relationship of Jesus to God and God to Jesus.[11]

Even amid Jesus's suffering, the divine presence of God, revealed through the Spirit, strengthened and empowered him. Moltmann says, "The Spirit

---

9. Moltmann, 11.
10. Moltmann, *Trinity and the Kingdom*, 75.
11. Moltmann, *Spirit of Life*, 61.

himself was involved in Jesus' suffering, because he rested on the Son and accompanied him in to his passion. We have assumed a kenosis of the Spirit, which is to be seen in his Shekhinah in the suffering, assailed and dying Jesus."[12]

Moltmann also points out that Christ is a perfect covenant partner in the work of the Spirit and the sending of the Spirit into the world. He appeals to Berkhof to support this point, saying that for Berkhof, "God the Father is the One God, who is Person. The Holy Spirit is the mode of efficacy of the one God, who creates his human partner to the covenant in the Spirit imbued Christ, and through Christ's mediation draws human beings into this divine covenant."[13] Regarding the resurrection of Jesus, Moltmann similarly emphasizes the Spirit, noting that the Father raised the Son from the dead through the activity of the Holy Spirit. Jesus was raised through the creative Spirit (Rom 1:4; 8:11; 1 Pet 3:18; 1 Tim 3:16), through the glory of the Father (Rom 6:4), and through the power of God (1 Cor 6:14). For Moltmann, God's power, glory, and creative Spirit are synonymously at work in the resurrection of Jesus.[14] The understanding that it was the Spirit who was at work motivated Moltmann to claim that Christ's resurrection power, revealed through the creative Spirit, works in all flesh. "With Jesus' resurrection, transfiguration, transformation and glorification, the general outpouring of the Holy Spirit 'on all flesh' begins. This experience was, and is, interpreted eschatologically by Christians."[15] In sum, the same Spirit, whose active presence was observable throughout Jesus's life, is present to empower and spiritually guide all human beings.

Moltmann describes the invisible works of the Spirit as being evident in all human beings irrespective of human effort. As in Chenchiah's theology, Moltmann explains that the presence of the Spirit in all human beings remains a mystery. Moltmann says, "It is characteristic of these divine in-dwellings to be hidden, secret and silent. In everyday life, they are perceived as God's inexpressible closeness."[16] Moltmann regards the presence of the Spirit in

---

12. Moltmann, 67.
13. Moltmann, 13.
14. Moltmann, 88.
15. Moltmann, 124.
16. Moltmann, 19.

human life as an expression of God's love towards his creation and says that God's love is a creative force that leads him to dwell empathetically within every created being, intimately connecting with them through the power of his love.[17] Moltmann emphasizes God's love for people – a love made evident by giving his Spirit – by saying that God's eternal Spirit is in all things as their vital force. Moltmann considers that the Spirit mediates in all people through various experience so that they might know the creator. This experience is the presence of the infinite in the finite, the eternal in the temporal, and the enduring in the transitory.[18] But Moltmann suggests that "though we may call *ruach* the confronting event of the personal presence of God, and the life force immanent in all the living, this is still not enough to exhaust the full meaning of the word."[19] Again, Moltmann's theology emphasizes the mysterious work of the Spirit in human life.

In his presentation on natural theology, Moltmann describes the mysterious presence of God in human life as a significant fact that could bring unity between people of different religious faiths. He writes,

> If we are to have co-operation with other religious communities and philosophies, but above all with the sciences and technologies, we need the framework of natural theology; for it is through a natural theology that others can be brought to the mystery of God's presence in all things and in all the complexes of life.[20]

Today, theologians interpret the presence of the divine Spirit in human beings differently. Moltmann says that this divine presence in life is "often identified with human beings' special position in the cosmos – their openness to the world (Max Scheler's phrase), their self-transcendence (Karl Rahner's description), their ecstatic self-transcendence (Wolfhart Pannenberg) or their excentric position (Helmuth Plessner)."[21] The mysterious presence of the Spirit in human life is understood differently by each person. So, in understanding the presence of the Spirit in human life, it is possible that mystery will remain.

---

17. Moltmann, 50.
18. Moltmann, 35.
19. Moltmann, 42.
20. Moltmann, "Natural Theology," 80.
21. Moltmann, Spirit of Life, 32.

5.1.2 God's Initiative and Spiritual Experience

Moltmann believed that all blessings that flow from experiencing God's presence come solely from God's love so that human beings cannot boast in their own works or efforts. He believed that true spiritual experiences do not result from any psychological effect but only from the inspiration of the Spirit, who works inwardly in human life. In making this claim, Moltmann opposes the view of J. P. Jossua, who says, "Experience is constituted by consciousness and reason . . . we acquire most of our experiences neither through our consciousness, nor through our reason, nor as the result of any deliberate intention."[22] Moltmann regarded this inward work as authentic – even for a child of God who experiences Christian fellowship. The encounter with the Holy Spirit extends beyond the confines of the church community. People experience the Holy Spirit profoundly and intimately within themselves as the realization that "God's love has been poured into our hearts through the Holy Spirit" (Rom 5:5 NRSV).

In saying this, however, Moltmann was not claiming that spiritual experiences contradict human intellectual knowledge. He says, "It is only in the narrow concepts of modern philosophy that 'revelation' and 'experience' are antitheses."[23] The experience of God can still be present as the transcendental foundation of human self-consciousness. Human self-consciousness is intricately connected to the divine and to the world where humans exist. Therefore, every genuine experience of the self becomes an encounter with the divine Spirit of life within the human being. It is undeniable that people's spiritual experiences are sometimes guided by a divine presence.

Moltmann recognizes that external factors or influences help people to have internal experiences. "Experience has an outward reference, in the perception of the happening, and an inward reference, in the perception of the change in the self."[24] He believed that the formation of personality depends on people's culture, faith, and social values. He writes, "Our culture moulds our personal lifestyle."[25] At all events, the experience of the self is greatly influ-

---

22. Moltmann, 20.
23. Moltmann, 6.
24. Moltmann, 23.
25. Moltmann, *Coming of God*, 54.

enced by outward experiences. Human thoughts and understanding also play a significant role in getting spiritual experiences. According to Moltmann,

> there are no elemental experiences in life without receptivity – that is to say, without the preparedness for inward change and the risk that involves. Without the pain of this change, we shall hardly experience life at all; nor shall we arrive at any new experiences.[26]

He says, "Every experience of life thrusts towards its expression in the people affected, whether it be expression through their Gestalt, their attitude to life, or through their thoughts, words and deeds, images, symbols and rituals."[27] From this perspective, Moltmann contends that consciousness, reason, and understanding are integral components of experience and its processing. But he concludes,

> The final dimension of experiences goes beyond things, events and people. It is in this dimension that we find 'the basic trust' with which people commit themselves to this life, the expectation with which they lay themselves open for the experiences that come to meet them.[28]

Moltmann considered this final dimension of our spiritual experience is to be the living with the presence of the Spirit who dwells in us as a mystery. It is the provision of the Creator for his creation to express his nature. In describing spiritual experiences, Moltmann did not limit his reflection to human effort or psychological effect; rather, he believed that spiritual experiences are, first and foremost, outcomes of the work of the Spirit. At the same time, Moltmann does not deny the role of human culture and creativity in moulding a person's spiritual experience – and here, we find some resonance with Samartha's ideas.

5.1.3 The Spirit in the Social Life of People

Moltmann believed that the Spirit, parallel to his work in the personal lives of human beings, is also present and active in their social lives. Moltmann's

---

26. Moltmann, 54.
27. Moltmann, 19.
28. Moltmann, 27.

writings on public theology deal mainly with people's social development, represented in four distinct dimensions: an experience of Shekhinah, establishing social justice, a new beginning, and bringing eschatological hope. We will now consider how, in Moltmann's view, the spiritual experiences of people can bring a positive transformation in society.

Moltmann's theological contributions make readers aware of their responsibilities in society. Moltmann believed that theology should also exist for society. His contributions to public theology deal with Christian responsibilities concerning social inequalities, uplifting the poor, and establishing an eschatological hope for the hopeless. Relating theology to social concern, Moltmann says, "The practical act which is necessary for today's misery is the liberation of the oppressed. Theology is hence the critical reflection about this essential practice in the light of the gospel."[29] He asserts that "there is no Christian identity without public relevance and no public relevance without theology's Christian identity."[30] According to Moltmann, the work of the Spirit among people may be understood on different levels: establishing harmonious living and equality and bringing new life and hope to the hopeless.

An Experience of Shekhinah: Moltmann believed that his theology of love is a theology of the Shekhinah, which might also be considered a theology of the Holy Spirit. He says that the love and presence of God can be revealed through the work of the Spirit: "The theology of love is a theology of the Shekinah, a theology of the Holy Spirit."[31] His explanation of experiencing Shekhinah is not complicated. He uses three points to explain the Shekhinah experience. First, in the doctrine of the Shekhinah, the Spirit is represented as the productive presence of God. Here, the Spirit is God's empathy, whereby he identifies with that which he loves. Second, the concept of the Shekhinah draws attention to the sensibility of God the Spirit. The Spirit enables people to connect with God and become new creations. Third, the idea of the Shekhinah points out the kenosis of the Spirit, as one who indwells in created beings.[32] This nature of God is seen in the presence, work, and fellowship of the Spirit in human life. "A new divine presence is experienced in the experience of the

---

29. Moltmann, Trinity and the Kingdom, 7.
30. Moltmann, God for a Secular Society, 1.
31. Moltmann, Trinity and the Kingdom, 57.
32. Moltmann, Spirit of Life, 51.

Spirit. God does not simply confront his creation as creator. The experience of the Spirit is therefore the experience of the Shekinah, the divine indwelling."[33]

Such a theology prioritizes the work of the Spirit, who can lead people to produce the fruit of the Spirit. Here, Moltmann's ideas are similar to those of Chenchiah and Samartha. People with spiritual experiences will be guided to implement God's intention for the earth. God's love for the whole world is thus revealed through the work of the Holy Spirit. As Kirsteen Kim writes, "Moltmann himself began to articulate in *God in Creation* and *The Spirit of Life*, a theology of the Spirit's work in the world beyond the boundaries of Christian confession. Another way of describing this approach is 'mission pneumatology.'"[34] In theology, the significance of the Spirit and the spiritual experience can contribute much to accomplish the mission. Moltmann summarizes it succinctly: "If the Spirit is a modality of our own experience, then the human experience of God is the foundation of human theology."[35] For Moltmann, the concept of God's indwelling in Christian theology is discussed in the doctrine of the Holy Spirit.

Establishing Social Justice: God's concern for the whole world is central to Moltmann's theological teachings. He understood people's spiritual experience as strengthening them to work for social improvement. Establishing equality in society is one of the outcomes of people's encounters with the Spirit. "Without equality there is no free world. It is in the spirit of early Christianity that we call the truth that all human beings are created free and equal 'self-evident.'"[36] As a social concept, human equality means justice; as a humanitarian concept, it promotes solidarity. Kim writes of Moltmann,

> He advocates a spiritual struggle to overcome the forces of violence and oppression in society and to bring about justice. According to him, the Spirit is the 'breath' or yeast of new life that invigorates the 'bread,' which is the earth, and in so doing, brings about a redistribution of its resources to the benefit of all.[37]

Moltmann says,

---

33. Moltmann, Trinity and the Kingdom, 104.
34. Kim, *The Holy Spirit in the World*, 177.
35. Moltmann, Spirit of Life, 5.
36. Moltmann, God for a Secular Society, 69.
37. Kim, "Holy Spirit in Mission," 137.

> As a Christian concept, equality means *love*. Either we shall create a world of social justice, human solidarity and Christian love, or this world will perish through the oppression of people by people, through asocial egotism, and through the destruction of the future in the interests of short-term, present-day profits.[38]

The nature of love towards our fellow beings can only be cultivated through an experience of the Spirit. "By experience of the Spirit, I mean an awareness of God in, with and beneath the experience of life, which gives us assurance of God's fellowship, friendship and love."[39] Thus, our spiritual experience should motivate people to work for the growth of society.

A New Beginning: According to Moltmann, spiritual experiences can enable people to make a new beginning in their lives, in society, and even in their life after death. A person who accepts Jesus as their Saviour starts a new life with Christ. Moltmann comments,

> With the coming of Christ into this world, his death and resurrection, and the outpouring of the divine Spirit, the spring of eternal life begins for human beings, all living beings, and the earth. Mortal and earthly life is taken up into the divine, eternal and heavenly life.[40]

Similarly, he writes, "The Spirit actually brings men and women to the beginning of a new life, and makes them the determining subjects of that new life in the fellowship of Christ."[41] This joyous and cheerful experience through the work of the Spirit endures forever:

> It becomes lastingly and permanently present, and in its way abolishes the transience of time, for – as Nietzsche said – 'all delight longs for eternity, for deep, deep eternity.' The events with which love begins mold the present, because they are the beginning of a new life story.[42]

---

38. Moltmann, God for a Secular Society, 69.
39. Moltmann, Spirit of Life, 17.
40. Moltmann "Religion of Joy," 8.
41. Moltmann, Spirit of Life, 2–3.
42. Moltmann, 21

Elsewhere he writes, "the presence of God's Word and Spirit in Christ's church is the advance radiance and beginning of the presence of God's Word and Spirit in the new creation of all things."[43] For Moltmann, the cosmological spiritual experiences provide eternal hope to people.

> That is why experience of the Spirit is described as a rebirth to true life, a personal rebirth which anticipates the rebirth of the whole cosmos. These are the images of hope with which the present experience of the Spirit is described as the experience of life's new beginning: it is the springtime of life, a new birth and a new start.[44]

> So when humans wake to new Life, the Spirit links this awakening with the expectation of 'sighing' nature. 'Community' seems to be the particular nature of the Holy Spirit and his creative energies, just as 'grace' determines the nature and specific action of the Son, and 'love' the nature and efficacy of the Father.[45]

An Eschatological Hope: Moltmann's Christian theology has public relevance as it enhances anticipation of a better future for people. Its foundation in eschatology – the "theology of hope" – provides the foundation for a better future for all people. It is the expectation of the coming kingdom of God, which happens through the work of the Spirit. Moltmann says that his theology is a "kingdom-of-God theology which has a long connection with the experience of the Spirit."[46] For Moltmann, this new beginning through an experience of the Spirit is connected with the eschatological future of human life. He considers that experiencing the Spirit includes a remembered past and an expected future. For Christians, "The experience of the Spirit is never without the remembrance of Christ, and never without the expectation of his future."[47] A person's new life in Christ is always encouraged and strengthened by their eschatological hope. The blessed hope of a better future satisfies the present life. The experience, life, and fellowship of God's

---

43. Moltmann, God for a Secular Society, 105.
44. Moltmann, Spirit of Life, 74.
45. Moltmann, "Natural Theology," 326.
46. Moltmann, God for a Secular Society, 1.
47. Moltmann, "Natural Theology," 326.

Spirit that is manifest when Christ is made present and the anticipation of the new creation of all things emerges. These aspects resonate with Christ and serve as a prelude to the kingdom of God. In perfect harmony with this expectation and remembrance, the experience of the Spirit assumes a unique and irreplaceable significance, aptly referred to as an experience of God. In this context, pneumatology presupposes Christology and paves the path for eschatology.[48]

For Moltmann, the significance of eschatological hope drives Christian theology. He understood that spiritual experiences provide a blessed hope to people. He writes, "The third form of the kingdom is the kingdom of the Spirit. It is the rebirth of men and women through the energies of the Spirit. It brings the *intelligentia spiritualis*. In this kingdom, God rules through direct revelation and knowledge."[49] These works of the Spirit, although invisible, have a blessed future. "Seen christologically, faith is a response, but seen eschatologically it is a beginning. If this faith is experienced 'in the Spirit,' then here the Spirit itself is indirectly experienced."[50] Here, Moltmann explicitly mentions the Spirit's role and comments,

> It is pneumatology that brings Christology and eschatology together. There is no mediation between Christ and the kingdom of God except the present experience of the Spirit, for the Spirit is the Spirit of Christ and the living energy of the new creation of all things. In the present of the Spirit are both origin and consummation.[51]

He also adds,

> In the experience of God's Spirit, there is already here the experience of the rebirth to eternal life in the midst of a life that has to die.[52]

The new beginning that commences with a spiritual experience is for eternity. We know this because the resurrected life of Christ is a signpost.

---

48. Moltmann 17–18, 326.
49. Moltmann, Trinity and the Kingdom, 205.
50. Moltmann, Spirit of Life, 68.
51. Moltmann, 69.
52. Moltmann, Coming of God, 231.

Moltmann says, "Like the raising of the dead Christ by God through his life-giving Spirit, the resurrection of the dead is also expected as a physical happening touching the whole person, namely as a 'giving life to mortal bodies' (Rom 8:11)."[53] In finding a connection between the nature of eternal presence and eternal future in people's spiritual experience, Moltmann notes a similarity with the Hindu understanding of eternity. He writes that in Hinduism, the doctrine of the immortality of the soul goes beyond merely addressing life after death and affirms that the human being possesses a divine identity that transcends both birth and death. That which remains unaffected by the body's death was never born with the body either and has never experienced the life of the body; only that which has never lived the life of the body can escape the fate of dying with it. Echoing a similar sentiment about the divine spirit within the human being, the Bhagavad Gita states, "Never is it born nor dies; never did it come to be nor will it ever come to be again: unborn, everlasting."[54]

In relation to the eternal life of human beings, Hindus do not have faith in life after death, but their expectation of immortal life is obvious. Even though their notion of an immortal soul does not attribute any value to the body, their cravings for eternal bliss and divine identity are fascinating, leading us to think that this understanding of eternal hope and the presence of a life beyond life and death in them is the work of the Spirit who lives in all human beings as a mystery.

5.1.4 Spiritual Experience: God's Revelation

Spiritual experiences are God's revelation to people and one of his modes of communicating with people. Moltmann believed that God's dealings with people could only be understood through the Spirit. He says, "There are no words of God without human experiences of God's Spirit."[55] Moltmann summarizes, in a nutshell, the experience of God that takes place through the coming of the Spirit. First, this experience is "universal," which means that it is no longer particular but applies to "all flesh" and spans the breadth of all creation. Second, it is "total," which means that it is no longer fully effective

---

53. Moltmann, 69.
54. Moltmann, 59–60.
55. Moltmann, *Spirit of Life*, 3.

in the human heart, in the depths of human existence. Third, it is "enduring," which means that it is no longer temporary but is conceived of as the resting or dwelling of the Spirit. Fourth, it is "no longer mediated through revelation and tradition" but is grounded in the contemplation of God and his glory.[56] After recounting these four points, Moltmann emphasizes that God's eternal presence serves as the focal point to which historical experiences of God direct us.

God's Spirit is present in human beings, the human spirit is self-transcendently aligned towards God.[57] In this sense, God's intimate presence among men and women and his intention to reveal himself as transcendent to all humankind can connect easily through the Spirit. In God's Spirit, there is revealed an immanent transcendence.

In Moltmann's view, Christians are responsible for expressing the results of their experience with the Spirit to others. He says,

> Christian faith is response to the word of the messianic gospel, and the resonance of that word in the hearts and lives of men and women. But, in this very way, Christian faith is the experience of the quickening Spirit – experience of the beginning of the new creation of the world.[58]

God's presence can be understood through reading the Bible and church fellowship, but only through the help of the Spirit can the presence of God be felt in the world. Hence, the words of proclamation from the Bible and the church must resonate with the experiences of people today, ensuring that they are not just passive hearers of the word but also become active advocates, proclaimers and doers of the word. The Spirit's experience transforms Christians, enabling them to receive new life and share this new life everywhere, with everyone, as God expects them to do.

Concerning the person and work of the Spirit, Moltmann has made valuable contributions to Christian theology. His Trinitarian pneumatology focuses on the peculiarities of the Holy Spirit in this present generation. The public relevance of this theology focuses on the Christian responsibility to

---

56. Moltmann, 57.
57. Moltmann, 7.
58. Moltmann, 68.

work towards social justice. The personal relevance of Moltmann's theology of love centres on the divine presence in human life and provides a blessed hope to people. Moltmann explains these spiritual experiences by describing the Spirit's work in the life of Jesus as Shekhinah. His explanation of God's intention in giving spiritual experiences to all can transform people, enabling them to make a new beginning with eschatological hope. Moltmann intended that Christians who receive this blessed hope through the Spirit should communicate this hope to the whole world.

5.1.5 Summary

The Holy Spirit in Jesus's Life: Moltmann's theological descriptions focus on the work of the Spirit, who is present mysteriously and works uniquely in human life. The Spirit has the power to create, enlighten, and transform people, but his dealings with them are indirect and inexplicable. In his Trinitarian pneumatology, Moltmann describes the indwelling Spirit in human lives as the breath of life, as a mystery, and as one who worked powerfully in Jesus's life. He explores the work of the Spirit in the life of Jesus and holds this up as an example for how human beings are to acknowledge their need to trust the Spirit. In Jesus's life, the Spirit strengthened, empowered, resurrected, and glorified him. Moltmann refers to the fellowship of the Trinity to articulate the attitude that human beings need to cultivate in their lives. He highlights the interconnectedness within the Trinity, illustrating that the Father sends the Son through the Spirit and the Son comes from the Father in the power of the Spirit. Similarly, the Spirit empowers individuals to engage in communion with God. The enigmatic presence of the Spirit in Jesus's life serves as a lesson, emphasizing the significance of obedience and trust in the Spirit. As in Jesus's life, experiencing the Spirit can guide individuals in understanding God's perfect will and living in accordance with that will. The same Spirit who empowered Jesus to fulfil God's purpose enables people to gain divine knowledge, experience transformation, embrace the divine nature of love, and care for others.

The Holy Spirit in Human Culture: Moltmann represents the Spirit as both masculine – "word" (*dabar*) – and feminine – "life force" (*ruach*) – which describes the nature of the Spirit. He also narrates the Spirit's are visible in distinct human creativities. The mysterious presence of the Spirit in human culture, faith, moral teachings, and social values is regarded by Moltmann as the external force that triggers spiritual experiences. Moltmann believed that it was possible to unearth the Spirit's presence in cultures – which are typically the product of human creativity and moral principles. In this way, people can receive spiritual knowledge and understanding from other faiths. There is a relationship between the action of the Spirit on the one hand and human creativity and the religious and ethical values of human culture on the other. Since spiritual experiences exist as a mode of God's revelation, his revelation of himself to people happens through human culture, religious expressions, and social values.

The Holy Spirit: An Agent of Transformation: God does not hesitate to reveal the importance of social equality through the work of the Spirit. Through spiritual experiences, God expects people to know him, adopt his nature, and love their neighbour. Moltmann's public theology reveals his concern for the social relationships in human life. His theology of love – the Shekhinah of God that people experience – leads people to establish social justice by offering both a new beginning and an eschatological hope. Regarding social justice, Moltmann believed that the Spirit desires satisfactory living conditions and equal opportunities for all people. God's intention to establish equality is visible through the Spirit, who is imparted to all without discrimination. Concern for the person – which begins with new life in Christ through the Spirit – enables Christians to effect changes in their personal and social lives. In personal life, the Spirit strengthens a person's relationship with Christ, while in social life, the Spirit strengthens a person's relationship with their fellow beings. By the work of the Spirit, people are enabled to produce the fruit of the Spirit and to establish equality in society. Spiritual experiences make people more selfless and motivate control them to engage in the work of social deliverance. A person's inner experience should overflow into practical action to liberate the oppressed. Understanding this reality provides a new beginning and a new hope for humankind.

The Holy Spirit: A Guide to the Kingdom of God: Moltmann's writings emphasize the role of the Spirit in impartially bestowing new life and hope upon those who respond positively and welcoming them into the kingdom of God. The diffusion of spiritual influence extends this blessed (eschatological) hope from individuals to society. According to Moltmann, the Spirit is a transformative force who instils this "blessed hope" within both individuals and society, establishing the kingdom of God. This new beginning in the Spirit initiates a fresh life for the recipients and forges new connections with their fellow human beings and with God. It marks the starting point of a journey towards the kingdom of God. Through the experience of God's Spirit, the rebirth into eternal life becomes a present reality. As children of God, individuals are continually encouraged and strengthened by the eschatological hope of the present and future kingdom of God.

The Holy Spirit in Spiritual Experience: Moltmann observes that the initiative for our spiritual experiences comes not from us but from God. Spiritual experiences are one of the means that God – the Creator – uses to communicate with people – his creation. These experiences occur due to the work of the Spirit, who is already present in all human beings. Such experiences cannot be cultivated by any kind of psychological effect. Sometimes, these Spirit-induced spiritual experiences may contradict human intellectual knowledge. Perhaps it is better to say that spiritual experiences are different occasions by which people receive knowledge about God. Experiences of the Spirit are God's provision for human beings. This conviction motivated Moltmann to develop a holistic doctrine of God the Holy Spirit. Spirit-given spiritual experiences help people to recognize the Creator and his creation but also go beyond mere recognition. Real spiritual experiences happen when a person responds positively towards the Spirit in obedience. Such spiritual experiences will bring positive results and the transformation of life.

5.2 Kirsteen Kim (1959–)

Kirsteen Kim – a well-known contemporary teacher, writer, and researcher of Christian theology – has contributed valuable insights into pneumatology. She served as the vice moderator of the Commission on World Mission and Evangelism (CWME) in the World Council of Churches (WCC) and was the research coordinator of Edinburgh 2010. She is a professor in the School of Intercultural Studies at Fuller Theological Seminary in Pasadena, California.

5.2.1 Spirituality as a Present Priority

In this modern period, without consideration of any religious tradition, people give high priority to spirituality. Kim, in her article "Mission's Changing Landscape: Global Flows and Christian Movements," comments, "In the 21st century, what is recognized as religion has also changed. Most of those who have become Christians more recently have come from indigenous religions or spiritualities."[59] This reveals the significance and presence of spiritual experience in all religions. Kim notes that one of the reasons behind this change is the contemporary trend of people's disinterest in philosophical thoughts. People seem more concerned with the practical questions of how and where the Spirit is to be discerned and believe that spiritual experiences have potentiality beyond individual fulfilment and temporal satisfaction.[60] Even in multireligious contexts, there is a common belief that spiritual experiencesIn this scenario, Kim does not hesitate to express her concern for considering the work of the Spirit in the Christian community. She says, "What is needed is a new paradigm of the Holy Spirit in the context of globalization and postmodernity."[61] Kim says that this is because "the Spirit in the church is not some general spirit of the age or life principle, nor is the Spirit just one of the many spiritual forces at work in the world."[62] The church needs to know the Spirit and the work of the Spirit in the world. Oleska comments, "The church ... knows where the Holy Spirit is, but can never be sure where the Holy Spirit is not."[63] An understanding of the work of the Spirit, from Kim's writings, enlightens people and enables them to recognize the invisible act of the Spirit in different religious faiths, facilitating reconciliation and dialogue.

The need to reconsider the work of the Spirit in Christianity has motivated some theologians like Kim to construct a theology of pneumatology. Kim notes that this rediscovery of the truth of the creedal statements in relation to God the Spirit was initiated late in the twentieth century by some in the Western churches.[64] By 1991, at the World Council of Churches in Canberra, Australia, this new emphasis on the work of the Holy Spirit in the world was chosen as the conference's theme: "Come Holy Spirit: Renew the Whole Creation." Kim writes, "The Canberra documents frequently stress the free and unbound nature of the Spirit (often alluding to John 3:8), which may suggest that a pneumatology for the twenty-first century needs to begin from the experience of spirits below rather than from the assertion of one Spirit from

---

59. Kim, "Mission's Changing Landscape," 251.
60. Kim, *Holy Spirit in the World*, 2.
61. Kim, 1.
62. Kim, "Mission Theology," 52.
63. Oleska, "Holy Spirit's Action," 331.
64. Kim, "Holy Spirit in Mission," 1.

above."65 Jesus's promise of the Holy Spirit moving in the world and guiding people to know the will of God, who is in heaven, might be a helpful starting point. This understanding encouraged Kim to prioritize the work of the Holy Spirit in theology. Giving priority to the Holy Spirit does not mean that she degraded the work of Jesus. In her article *The Potential of Pneumatology for Mission in Contemporary Europe*, Kim confesses, "Though my paper is concerned with the Holy Spirit, this should not be taken to mean a lack of interest in Jesus Christ or a denial of traditional doctrines about the person and work of Christ."66 Her pneumatological teachings are Christ-centred, with the expectation of reaching people with the gospel but beginning with the spiritual experiences of people.

Kim's research on the work of the Holy Spirit in Asian contexts, particularly India and Korea, lends authenticity to her understanding of this subject. Her study explores a Christian understanding of the Holy Spirit that is influenced by meanings associated with "spirit" in broader society. She observes that the concept of "spirit" in other cultures can be a way to understand the Holy Spirit better,67 and this knowledge encouraged her to prioritize "Spirit Christology," in which she emphasizes Christ's life through the Spirit's work. Kim says, "Spirit Christology emphasizes that Jesus is the receiver as well as the giver of the Spirit."68 "Spirit Christology conceives of the Holy Spirit as the indweller. The Holy Spirit rested on Jesus or indwelt in Jesus. When we speak about the union between the Spirit and Jesus, the mediation between God and the man Jesus happens in the Holy Spirit."69 Spirit Christology widens the outlook of Christians as they realize the work of the Spirit in the life of Christ, in the church, and in the broader community. Kim states that Spirit Christology embodies an inclusive approach towards people of other faiths, acknowledging and affirming the goodness and truth in their beliefs. This openness is rooted in the understanding that the mission of the Spirit extends beyond and precedes the incarnation, embracing all humanity.70 This understanding can encourage religious harmony in India – where

---

65. Kim, "Post-Modern Mission," 176.
66. Kim, "Potential of Pneumatology," 334.
67. Kim, "Discerning the Spirit," 12.
68. Kim, "Potential of Pneumatology," 339.
69. Manohar, "Spirit Christology," 145.
70. Kim, "Holy Spirit in Mission," 7.

multireligious faith is practised – and can function as a theology of liberation for the poor, where the spirituality of the Hindu caste system is a major cause of their poverty. Kim writes, "Taken together they [Spirit Christology] imply that the Spirit of mission is a way of peace with justice in the knowledge that the Spirit of Jesus Christ both inspires whatever is good and true and empowers challenge and change."[71] She says that the Asian theologians we have studied share a vision of the Spirit's work that transcends doctrines and institutional boundaries, encompassing the entirety of creation beyond the confines of the Christian community.[72]

5.2.2 Pneumatology in the Indian Context

Due to a complicated spiritual understanding, theologians have found it difficult to construct theologies of spiritual experience in nations like India. Kim says, "India – a land where there is deep awareness of one universal Spirit and there are also many spiritualities – offers outstanding examples of creative thinking on the Spirit from Christian theologians."[73] She acknowledges that a contemporary theology of the Spirit must consider the presence of other spirits encountered in our evermore diverse and pluralistic world, where we encounter a multitude of spirits – religious and secular, natural and supernatural, political powers and authorities, as well as personal spirits and demons.[74] So, a theology of the Holy Spirit can offer new theological approaches in this nation where a plurality of faiths and practices exist. As Robin Boyd affirms, "Pneumatology has arguably become the 'cornerstone' of Indian Christian theology because of a shared perception, due to the dominant Hindu culture, of a cosmic Spirit universally present and the background of fascination with spiritualities of all kinds."[75]

According to Kim, a presentation centred on the Spirit and spiritual works is more readily accepted by Indians in places where there is a misconception of Christianity as a religion of the West. Many native philosophers like Swami Vivekananda, S. Radhakrishnan, and Mahatma Gandhi

---

71. Kim, 8.
72. Kim, *Holy Spirit in the World*, 141.
73. Kim, "Holy Spirit in Mission," 1.
74. Kim, "Discerning the Spirit," 18.
75. Boyd, *Introduction to Indian Christian Theology*, 241–242.

questioned and rejected the practice of establishing a Western civilization in India through Christianity. These Indian leaders were not ready to accept truths introduced by foreigners. Instead, they encouraged the development of pluralist philosophies[76] and embraced India's tolerant nature. Kim writes, "Swami Vivekananda's address to the World's Parliament of Religions in Chicago in 1893, in which he presented Hinduism as a more tolerant faith than Christianity, was a watershed in inter-religious and intercultural relations."[77] The Hindu nature of tolerance of other religious faiths opens the door for Indians to interact with people's spiritual affairs. Kim observes that popularizing the teachings of the Holy Spirit can foster reconciliation between the people of India. She says, "This pneumatological approach also raises the issue of whether concepts and experiences of spirit in other faiths can provide a starting point for interfaith discussions."[78]

Kim observes that taking into consideration the spiritual experiences of different religious faiths not only brings reconciliation but also leads to harmonious living. She notes, for example, how liberation theology in India has functioned as a spiritual encouragement to work towards justice and peace. Regarding liberation theologians of India, she says, "They argue that Christian mission involves co-operating in the Spirit with movements of nation-building, justice and peace."[79] According to Samuel Rayan, spiritual revolution can bring unity and justice to society, and Kim comments that "he advocates 'spiritual struggle' to overcome the forces of violence and oppression in society and bring about justice."[80] For Kim, liberation theology postulates spiritual struggles. She says, "As we have seen, other liberation theologians, including Samuel Rayan and Suh Nam-Dong, see the Spirit as the divine agent of social liberation."[81] Experiencing equality, justice, and liberation among people brings nothing but peace and harmony.

Kim's study of spirits in Indian and Korean contexts encouraged her to distinguish the Spirit from spirits. In her article "Discerning the Spirit: The First Act of Mission," attempting to interpret the Holy Spirit and other spirits,

---

76. Kim, "Missiology as Global Conversation," 44.
77. Kim, 44.
78. Kim, *Holy Spirit in the World*, 156.
79. Kim, 179.
80. Kim, "Holy Spirit in Mission," 5.
81. Kim, *Holy Spirit in the World*, 155.

Kim considers two different cosmologies of spirit: "One-Spirit" cosmology and "many-spirits" cosmology.

> One-Spirit" cosmology is present in Hinduism, where there is a universal "Spirit" and no real consideration of "spirits" (plural). However, "many-spirits" cosmology – mainly found in Korean shamanism and other local religious beliefs – envisages a complex universe in which the Holy Spirit is one among many others.[82]

In differentiating the Holy Spirit from other spirits of the world, Kim says, "In much discussion of pneumatology, the Spirit of God is simply described as 'the Spirit' (with a capital S) or even just 'Spirit' (with no article attached). But, in the context of many spirits, the adjective 'holy' is important to distinguish the one from the many spirits."[83] Consequently, it is complicated to explain the Spirit in India due to the multiple cosmologies that exist among people.

In India's complex situation of distinct spiritualities, discerning the Spirit is essential to recognize the truth. Kim considers the need for people to use their own criteria in discerning the Spirit based on their particular spiritual understanding. She writes, "Different faith and ideological communities have their criteria for deciding what is right and wrong."[84] Kim says that "people have different criteria for discerning the spirits according to their spiritual context."[85] But people who have a spiritual vision and are close to God can discern the spirits. In the words of Kim, "The question of whose spiritual vision is most closely in touch with God or Ultimate Reality or the universe can only be answered at the end."[86] It is the real spirituality of people that enables them to think like God and to discern the spirits appropriately. Kim writes, "Discernment requires wide horizons, in view of the breadth of the Spirit's mission; openness, because of the unpredictability of the Spirit's movements; and humility, since the Spirit is the Spirit of Almighty God."[87]

---

82. Kim, "Discerning the Spirit," 13.
83. Kim, 13.
84. Kim, 18.
85. Kim, *Holy Spirit in the World*, 167.
86. Kim, "Discerning the Spirit," 18.
87. Kim, 18.

Kim writes that for the Christian, discernment of the Spirit should be Christ-centred.[88] For Christians, Jesus Christ serves as the ultimate standard for discerning the Spirit, acting as the key to unlocking the mysteries of the universe. Kim also proposes four biblical criteria for discernment of the Spirit:

(1) the ecclesial, to understand the confession of Jesus as Lord, through the Holy Spirit;
(2) the ethical, through the evidence of the fruit of the Spirit;
(3) the charismatic, through the practice of the gifts of the Spirit; and
(4) the liberational, through giving preferential option for the poor.[89]

These distinct works of the Spirit, which Kim sees as ways to discern the Spirit, indicate the presence of the Spirit in other religions and brings opportunities for dialogue, spiritual growth, and reconciliation.

5.2.3 Terminological Interpretation of the Holy Spirit in Hinduism

To understand the Holy Spirit in Hinduism, Kim describes three Hindu terms that Boyd mentions in his book on the Spirit. She writes, "Boyd pointed out that the concept of the Holy Spirit may be rendered in Sanskrit by several different words – *atman, antaryamin* and *shakti* – each reflecting a different tradition and carrying different connotations."[90] Using these three terms, Kim explains that the Spirit functions internally and brings unity between religious people.

First, Kim says that "the word *atman* (spirit, soul, self) and its cognates – including *Paramatman* (Supreme Spirit) and *antaratman* (inner spirit) – come from *advaitic* or classical Hinduism."[91] *Advaita* is a significant philosophical teaching in Hinduism. "Advaita means 'oneness' or more literally 'not two-ness' or 'nonduality.'"[92]

> The atman is the self or soul. The word is derived either from the root *at* (to move) or the root *a* (to breathe). It is used both

---

88. Kim, 12, 18.
89. Kim, *Holy Spirit in the World*, 168; Kim, "Discerning the Spirit," 17.
90. Boyd, *Introduction to Indian Christian Theology*, 241.
91. Kim, "Holy Spirit in Mission," 3.
92. Kim, 3.

for the individual self or soul and for the transcendent 'Self' or 'All-soul,' which is all reality.[93]

George Gispert-Sauch finds the expression "ground of being" a better translation of the concept of *atman* than "soul" or "self."[94] Hindus believe that *atman* is the small particle of Brahman, the Supreme Being, and dwells in human beings. Thus, the internal soul is given priority in Hinduism. "In the context of India, advaitic Hinduism allows little room for a spirit world since spiritual life is more an internal matter of the heart than, engagement with external forces."[95]

Kim's description of the Spirit as *atman* draws attention to the unifying nature of the Spirit. To explain this, she turns to the theologian Abhishiktananda – a Catholic ascetic – who portrays the Holy Spirit as "the *advaita* of God, the mystery of the non-duality of the Father and the Son"[96] – and to Vandana Mataji – a prominent leader of the Catholic ashram movement – who represents *ashramic* spirituality that flows from a realization of oneness with the One Spirit and hence a connectedness with the universe and with the "spiritual" in people regardless of gender, caste, or religion.

Stanley Samartha (see chapter 4) – another Indian theologian – developed a "theology of dialogue," claiming that the universal or "unbound" Spirit or *advaita* provides the "unitive vision" that holds Indian communities together and allows for a "traffic across the borders" that is dialogue. Samartha describes such dialogue not as a method or technique but as "a mood, a spirit, an attitude of love and respect" for "our neighbours of other faiths."[97] Thus, the Spirit may be recognized in a world of many faiths. In this way, Samartha laid a pneumatological foundation for interfaith dialogue for the World Council of Churches. This approach to people can reduce the gap between different religious people.

Second, the Hindu term *antaryamin* is used to represent the Holy Spirit as an "Indwelling One." In Hinduism, this term is drawn from the *bhakti*

---

93. Jones and Ryan, *Encyclopedia of Hinduism*, 51.
94. Kim, "Holy Spirit in Mission," 3.
95. Kim, *Holy Spirit in the World*, 151.
96. Kim, "Holy Spirit in Mission," 3.
97. Kim, 7.

tradition of devotion to a personal deity.[98] Kim understands that Samartha's theology of dialogue functions as an inner attitude rather than an action. According to Appasamy – an Indian Christian theologian – the Holy Spirit abides in the believer's inner life, particularly in its moral dimensions. Appasamy says, "Just as the soul is within the body, controlling it and directing it, so God is within the world of nature and human beings, ruling over it from the inner depths."[99] In his book *Christianity as Bhakti Marga*, Appasamy tries to relate the inner spirit of Christianity and the inner spirit of Indian religious thought through the *bhakti* type of religious thought.[100] He connects the Johannine idea of *logos* and the Hindu idea of an immanent God – the *antaryamin*, who is the indweller. As Chakkarai says, the Holy Spirit is Jesus himself as he takes his abode within us.[101]

Third, the Hindu term Shakti has been used to explain the Spirit. Kim writes, "The *shakti* tradition derives from the pre-Aryan concept of primal energy, the feminine power of the creation."[102] To support this idea she cites theologians like Chenchiah (see chapter 4), who say that the Universal Spirit or Brahman is manifested in the power of Shaki or the Spirit. She also notes that Chakkarai[103] even sees this energy as working in Hindu mantras. Chakkarai says, "Each letter of the mantra is charged with energy and creates vibrations in the inner consciousness. Sound vibrations are said to be the manifestation of the Sakti and consequently are sound equivalents of the deities."[104] Chakkarai's understanding of the Hindu term Shakti reveals his intention to relate Hinduism and Christianity.

With reference to these three terms – *atman*, *antaryamin*, and *Shakti* – Kim describes the nature of the Spirit as the unifying, indwelling, and primal power for creation. "However, use of *atman* and *antaryamin*, which lead to theologies of the Spirit of peace who promotes cooperation and mutual

---

98. Kim, 3.
99. Appasamy, "Christological Reconstruction," 173.
100. Appasamy, *Bhakti Marga*, 21.
101. Kim, "Holy Spirit in Mission," 4–5.
102. Kim, 5.
103. Vengal Chakkarai Chettiar (1880–1958) – a Hindu convert and member of the "rethinking triad" – placed much emphasis on a personal experience of Christ. He tried to relate Christology to pneumatology, explaining the Holy Spirit as the continuation of the incarnation – that is, as the living Christ.
104. Chakkarai, *Jesus the Avatar*, 121.

respect and who brings personal and religious harmony, contrast in India with theologies of non-Brahminic *shakti*, the Spirit of fire who refines and humanises society."[105] The nature and functions of the Spirit as the indweller in human life, and the one who unifies men with God irrespective of any religious barrier can function as the central point to construct a better theology in Indian context.

Kim believed that constructive theologies related to other faiths could bring harmony between religions, but she also reminds readers of their dangers. She writes that *advaidic* philosophers assert that the perceived differentiated world is an illusion and seek to transcend it and unite with the Real beyond the distinctions of various religions. According to this perspective, all individuals are interconnected and share the same Spirit within the greater whole. Christian theologians who draw upon Hindu nondualism to inform their pneumatology often share such aspiration for pan-religious unity. In some cases, however, this approach may lead to tendencies towards monism and pantheism when discussing the Holy Spirit.[106] Here, Kim emphasizes a monotheistic view, to distinguish God and man as creator and creation.

5.2.4 Functions of the Holy Spirit

According to Kim, the works of the Spirit are unpredictable. When it comes to people's spiritual experiences, the Spirit's work is also essential. Kim's contribution to building a theology about the Spirit's role among people can significantly assist our study. The next section deals with how human spiritual experiences related to the nature and functions of the Spirit can help us in constructing a theology of religious experience. This section includes the distinct ways in which the Spirit functions: crossing boundaries, being a symbol of peace and reconciliation, serving as a mediator of God's revelation, and becoming an agent of mission.

Kim observes multiple biblical passages that indicate that the work of the Spirit overflows beyond the church or Christian community – for example, the outpouring of the Holy Spirit among Gentiles at the day of Pentecost. She writes, "In the book of Acts, the fact that the power of the Spirit was shown in Gentiles in the same way as it was in Jews, was the evidence that there

---

105. Kim, "Holy Spirit in Mission," 7–8.
106. Karkkainen, Kim, and Yong, *Spirit-Filled World*, 248.

should be 'no distinction' between Jew and Gentile (Acts 10:44–48; 15:8–9)."[107] This should prompt Christians to give more attention to considering other religions. Kim explores this unlimited work of the Spirit by presenting the ideas of different theologians.

First, the Spirit's infinite work is connected with the creation story. Jurgen Moltmann and others say that the Spirit is active in the whole created world and point out that the Spirit of God moved over the waters at creation. In connection with this idea, Kim turns to John V. Taylor, who stresses creation and creativity in the mission where the Spirit is presented as a healer of life. Kim adds, "So, Christian mission now engages with ecological issues and takes a holistic approach because the Holy Spirit is acknowledged as 'the giver of life' (Nicene-Constantinopolitan creed)."[108] As a creator, the Spirit is a lifegiver to all human beings.

Second, based on the teachings of Karl Rahner and Paul Tillich, Kim presents the possibility of experiencing the Spirit in human cultures. She encourages "Christians to affirm human cultures, and to think of mission as the inculturation of the gospel."[109]

Third, the work of the Spirit can be observed in social movements. To illustrate this, Kim presents the work of Samuel Rayan, an Asian liberation theologian who worked for the deliverance of the poor. She recognizes that the Spirit is active in social movements that empower the poor and the marginalized.

Fourth, the Spirit can be acknowledged in a world of many faiths. Kim believed that Stanley Samartha laid a pneumatological foundation for interfaith dialogue in the World Council of Churches when he asked people to be in dialogue about the work of the Spirit as the one who leads people into all truth (John 16:13). In 2003, Kim was herself involved in two events in Britain that discussed "the Holy Spirit in a world of many faiths."

Finally, Kim says that the Spirit functions to reconcile our diversity. She notes that Amos Yong, a Pentecostal pastor from the United States, dared to relate to other religions positively.[110] Yong presents the Pentecost event as a new way of being together. Kim quotes Yong as saying, "It is no longer a case

---

107. Kim, "Potential of Pneumatology," 335.
108. Kim, 336.
109. Kim, 336.
110. Kim, 336–337.

of Jews being alone or Gentiles being alone but of Jew and Gentile together in the Spirit. This is a model of reconciled diversity."[111]

Together, these five insights concerning the Spirit prompted Kim to say,

> When we appreciate the history of the Spirit and the freedom of the Spirit, we realize there are wide possibilities of discovering the presence and activity of the Spirit outside the boundaries of the church or Christian society, and so we can ungrudgingly and whole-heartedly affirm many aspects of our world today.[112]

Christians should have an open mind to accept the work of the Spirit because of this varied understanding of the Spirit's nature, and effects. Kim writes,

> The Spirit may be encountered in silent meditation or in charismatic worship, in movements of liberation or in interfaith dialogue. The Spirit may simply be perceived as a presence, or seen as an event or activity. I suggest that we should keep an open mind on the issue of the identification of where the Spirit is and how the Spirit works.[113]

In conclusion, Kim says that to remain relevant in contemporary society, pneumatology must acknowledge the Spirit's work extending beyond the confines of the church or the Christian heart.[114]

In her article "The Reconciling Spirit: The Dove with Colour and Strength," Kirsteen Kim notes, "The dove is used as a symbol of the Holy Spirit, and also of peace and reconciliation."[115] To illustrate this, she turns to the biblical concept of reconciliation through the fellowship of Jews and Gentiles: "For Paul, reconciliation meant the communion of Jew with Gentile in the one Spirit (Eph 2:11–22): that is, life in community, fellowship in the Holy Spirit, working cooperatively, and, most significantly, eating together (Gal 2)."[116] Kim explains that because we are one in the Spirit, there is no slave or free, male and female in Christ (Gal 3:28). Similarly, Indian Christian

---

111. Kim, 337.
112. Kim, "Discerning the Spirit," 8.
113. Kim, 14.
114. Kim, *Holy Spirit in the World*, 3.
115. Kim, "Reconciling Spirit," 20.
116. Kim, 22.

theologians who promote the work of the Spirit seek reconciliation among India's different religious communities. Kim observes that in classical Hinduism, God is perceived as Spirit and all life is seen as one with this Universal Spirit. This philosophical foundation, combined with the diverse spiritual paths present in the Indian context, has fostered the growth of Indian pneumatology.[117]

Kim also explores the ideology of Vandana Mataji, who tried to reconcile Christianity and Hinduism by comparing the spiritual practices of Hindu ashrams (religious communities) with Christian spirituality. Kim describes how Mataji presented Jesus Christ as a supreme guru to Hindus. Samuel Rayan describes the Spirit as a "breath of fire" and as the refiner's fire that brings repentance and release from bondage. Kim writes, "For Rayan, the reconciliation of the Spirit is the peace with justice that results in liberation and a redistribution of the fruit of the earth so that all can share bread and wine in abundance (Luke 3:10–17; 4:18–19)."[118] Understanding the Spirit's presence in the world, as their universal guide and provider, will help to reconcile people.

Kim observes that there are certain external factors by which the Spirit can help people to be receptive to revelation. She says, "If the Holy Spirit is understood as a person with whom it is possible to have relationship, it is reasonable to suppose that it involves emotion and intuition, as well as intelligence."[119] To explain this idea, Kim uses an analogy from a New Testament passage that narrates the story of the two disciples who travelled on the road to Emmaus after the crucifixion of Jesus Christ (Luke 24:13–32). This text states that it was only much later in their encounter with Jesus that the eyes of the two disciples were opened and they were able to recognize Jesus. Concentrating on verses 15 and 32, Kim says that the disciples' recognition of Jesus Christ involved their hearts (verse 15 says that they were talking and discussing) and their minds (verse 32 says that their hearts were burning within them). The recognition of their Lord by his disciples also involved knowledge of the Scriptures and their personal relationship with Jesus Christ. Here, the

---

117. Kim, 24.
118. Kim, 25.
119. Kim, *Holy Spirit in the World*, 169.

presence of Jesus Christ was seen in a place where the disciples least expected to encounter him.

Using this account as an analogy, Kim suggests that the Holy Spirit – like Jesus who appeared to the disciples as an unrecognized fellow traveller – may initially be indistinguishable from many other spirits. It is challenging to understand the transcendent or eternal nature of the Spirit in a plural world. But Kim regards this encounter on the road to Emmaus as an occasion of revelation because "he was made known to them" (24:35 NABRE). Could this be similar to the surprise of the Spirit? Kim writes, "Many commentators are cautious of using philosophies of spirit, whether Indian or modern, to express the Holy Spirit's revelation in the world because they tend to impose a human construct on God's revelation."[120] She says, "Theologically, the emphasis on the incarnational nature of revelation necessary for contextual theology has been accompanied by an interest in the immanence of God in creation and the person and work of the Holy Spirit."[121]

One notable contribution of Kim to Christian theology is her presentation about the role of the Spirit in furthering a holistic mission. Kim describes the Spirit as providing all kinds of deliverance to all people. She believed that the success of Christian ministry is based on understanding the Spirit's function and presence in the ministry. She writes, "The Archbishop, Dr. Rowan Williams, has defined mission as 'finding out where the Holy Spirit is at work and joining in.' . . . and so we must learn to recognize what the Spirit of God is doing in the world before we can participate in mission."[122] True mission is possible through the Holy Spirit – the mission's author. Kim comments, "Increasingly the theology of *missio Dei* is interpreted as 'finding out where the Spirit is at work and joining in and it is acknowledged that the Holy Spirit is 'the chief agent of mission.'"[123]

Consequently, the Spirit, by his action, widens the perspective of mission. Kim writes, "The spirit blows where he wills (John 3:8). This encourages mission flexibility. The Spirit comes and goes and cannot be relied on or forced

---

120. Kim, 144.

121. Kim, "Missiology as Global Conversation," 45.

122. Kim, "Discerning the Spirit," 3.

123. Kirsteen Kim, "Mission Theology of the Church" *International Review of Mission*, Volume 99 Number / April 2010, 51–52.

to support the church's mission."¹²⁴ Kim approvingly quotes Moltmann, who believed that the work of the Spirit in the world is beyond the boundaries of Christian confession. This approach might best be known as "mission pneumatology."¹²⁵ Based on various biblical references to the Spirit, Kim identifies three different pneumatological studies in mission: (1) the "Pentecostal," which begins with the outpouring of the Holy Spirit on the day of Pentecost; (2) the "catholic," which starts with the work of the Holy Spirit in the life and ministry of Jesus Christ; and (3) the "orthodox," a perspective that goes back to the Spirit's role in creation as the hermeneutical key.¹²⁶ The mission of the Spirit, which started on the day of Pentecost, crossed the border of Israel: it went beyond God's chosen people, seeking the liberation of people without any discrimination. Just as with the disciples whom Jesus encountered on the road to Emmaus, we cannot always recognize God's revelation immediately. This point was made in some of the creation theology promoted at Canberra. All three perspectives of the Holy Spirit in mission assume that the Holy Spirit is at work in the world in a way that is not always explicitly linked to Christian confession. The effect of this, writes Kim, "was to broaden the scope of theology and mission and widen the source material, that is to support contextual methods against the classical."¹²⁷ Kim says that in this way, mission "is understood to be as holistic, life-giving and liberating as the movement of the Spirit, and also affirming of the work of the Spirit in other communities, cultures and even religions."¹²⁸ Kim quotes Bosch affirmatively: "In Bosch's work, mission is understood as the task of the church to continue the mission of Jesus Christ, which was initiated by the Spirit at Pentecost, and guided and empowered by the Holy Spirit through subsequent history."¹²⁹ The church that the Spirit animates is naturally a missionary movement.¹³⁰ It is essential to appreciate the reach of the holistic mission of the Spirit everywhere.

Kirsteen Kim argues for the importance of cultivating Christian theologies based on the Holy Spirit and recognizes the significance and possibility of

---

124. Kim, "Mission Theology," 53.
125. Kim, *Holy Spirit in the World*, 177.
126. Kim, "Discerning the Spirit," 4.
127. Kim, "Missiology as Global Conversation," 46.
128. Kim, "Mission's Changing Landscape," 263.
129. Kim, "Missiology as Global Conversation," 47.
130. Kim, "Mission Theology," 52.

doing so in the Indian context because of frequent spiritual experiences taking place among people. Kim suggests that there is an overlap between other religious people's spirituality and the work of the Holy Spirit. This recognition allows for reconciliation among all people. However, Kim recognized the need to distinguish between the Spirit and different spirits. She believed that the Spirit who works without any restriction is well able to reveal mysterious things to people. In addition, the Spirit serves as an agent of the Christian mission to bring holistic life to everyone without any discrimination based on religion.

5.2.5 Summary

Kim's theological contributions in relation to the spiritual experience of people could be summarized as follows:

An Agent of Equality: Kim observes that there should not be any obstacle to stop the Spirit to extend his work among people. In general ethnicity, race, gender, culture, and religion are common factors that distinguish people. But when it comes to spiritual experiences, the Spirit impartially helps people to experience God in the midst of diverse situations and reveals God's provision of equal opportunities for human beings. Kim confirms this with references to different biblical passages and the thoughts of various theologians. She says that the Holy Spirit's outpouring demolishes the distinctions between people based on ethnicity and gender. People begin to experience the Spirit inside and outside the church, beyond any church doctrines or traditions. Presenting the teachings of Karl Rahner and Paul Tillich, Kim also reveals the possibility of experiencing the Spirit in different human cultures. So, there is no cultural limitation in receiving spiritual experiences.

Similarly, Kim recognizes the work of the Spirit in different religions. Her writings points to the presence of the Spirit in religions such as Korean shamanism and Indian Hinduism and seek to overcome the limitations we sometimes impose on people's spiritual experiences. In doing this, Kim uses the creation theology of Christian theologians like Moltmann to demonstrate the Spirit's presence in all human beings without any discrimination. While the spiritual experiences people receive from the Spirit are culturally specific, the intention behind these experiences is the same – to convey God's message to his people.

Revelation of Mystery: People's mindsets and thought patterns are moulded by their cultural beliefs. Similarly, in spiritual experiences, a person's emotions, intuition, and intelligence are actively involved. Kim illustrates this in her explanation of Luke 24:13–32. On the way to Emmaus, it was only later – aided by their knowledge of the Scriptures and their personal relationship (and previous experience) with Jesus – that the disciples realized that Jesus was with them. This event reveals the role of human knowledge and faith in recognizing religious experience. Such insights will differ from person to person due to the diversity of their cultures and personal experiences. But wherever the Spirit is involved, whether in human culture or experience, God's revelation will also be evident. Different faiths and distinct traditional factors function as a medium to know God through spiritual experiences. However, Kim asserts that it is very difficult to the transcendent nature of the Spirit in our plural world. So, it is essential to discern the presence of the Spirit. For Kim, right discernment is only possible for people who have experienced the Spirit. She believed that Christian discernment of the Spirit is based on four aspects: the confession of Jesus as Lord (ecclesial), the fruit of the Spirit (ethical), the practice of the gifts of the Spirit (charismatic), and a consideration of the poor (liberation). Nobody should reject an experience of the Spirit that produces such results. Instead, they must admit that such experiences result from God's activity.

The Mission of Reconciliation: The Holy Spirit is the agent of a holistic mission that started with Jesus. At the time of Jesus's earthly ministry, the Spirit indwelt Jesus. Kim says that Jesus is, thus, both the receiver and the giver of the Spirit. Jesus's mission of uniting God and humankind was revealed through the active presence of the Spirit in his life. Moreover, the reconciling mission of Jesus continues after the resurrection – both inside and outside the church, through the work of the Spirit, the mission of the Spirit precedes and goes beyond Jesus's incarnation. The success of this mission is made possible through the inward changes in human lives that result in spiritual experiences. Real spiritual experience connects people with God and with one another. Thus the mission of the Spirit is establishing peace and justice. Based on the life of Jesus, Christians are asked to acknowledge and accept the work of the Spirit both inside and outside the church. The work of the Spirit in the human heart is God's real mission, and this mission functions as a mission of reconciliation through the experience of the Spirit.

Kim describes how people's experiences from the Spirit can reconcile people of different religious faiths. In the Indian context, Kim notes the work of the Spirit within Hinduism by explaining different Hindu terms and ideologies. She finds the "unifying nature" of the Spirit in the Hindu term *atman*, which refers to the human soul. The Hindu term *antaryamin* conveys the idea of the "indwelling nature" of the Spirit in all human beings. Another Hindu term, Shakti, describes "the creating power" of God as primal energy, the feminine power of creation. Kim also points out the Hindu ideology of "God as Spirit" and "all life is one with this Universal Spirit." Kim supports the teachings of Vandana Mataji, who represented Jesus Christ as a supreme guru to Hindus through his moral lessons. Because the good and the truth found in different religions are expressions of truth and goodness common to all humanity, they encourage uniformity and harmony among people of different faiths. So, experiencing the Spirit in the multireligious faiths practised in India can help to establish religious harmony.

5.3 Moltmann and Kim on Religious Experience: An Evaluation

5.3.1 Significance of Pneumatology

Both these Western theologians, Jurgen Moltmann and Kirsteen Kim, root their theological discussions in pneumatology. They find it more feasible to convey God's message to people through the work of the Spirit that takes place among them. Moltmann focuses on the work of the Spirit that results in the "transformation" of people, both in their personal and social lives, whereas Kim's focus is more on the "reconciliation" of people with God and with one another. Moltmann believed that this transformation through experiencing the Spirit empowers people to connect with their creator God and with their fellow beings. These theologians root their conclusions in parallel with the work of the Spirit in Jesus's life. The role of the Spirit in transforming people and establishing reconciliation is significant in theology.

5.3.2 Need for Transformation

For Moltmann, the life of Jesus in the power of the Spirit exemplifies how humans should behave. Kim points out that while the holistic mission of reconciliation was started by Jesus, the Spirit now functions as an agent of that same mission through people. The Spirit is an agent of a holistic mission that brings holistic transformations in human life and reconciliation between people. The transformation receives through the Spirit can touch every area of human life. This is because the real mission of the Spirit focuses on what happens in the human heart through the work of the Spirit. Thus, both theologians emphasize how spiritual experiences build a relationship between God and human beings. Moltmann's understanding of how theology should benefit people and society closely resembles Indian philosopher Vivekananda's anticipation of religious experience that leads to personal and social transformation.

5.3.3 Religious Experience and Hinduism

Compared with Moltmann's theology, Kim's explanations of the work of the Spirit seem to have a more direct connection with our studies. She explains the unlimited work of the Spirit in Hinduism by using different Hindu terms that connect with the Spirit. Kim believed that in the Indian context, the possibility of reconciliation between Hinduism and Christianity is shown most powerfully by connecting Hindu terms with Christian experience and giving value to these spiritual experiences among Hindus. Kim's explanation of the Spirit's nature in Hinduism as indwelling, unifying, and bringing harmony is more connected with the true spiritual experience of people than Moltmann's theology. Her theological concepts of the Spirit as the one who crosses boundaries, establishes the will of God, and acts as the mediator of God's revelation and the agent of God's mission expresses well the active work of the Spirit in this world. However, the contributions of both these theologians concerning the work of the Spirit, particularly outside the church, strengthened the relationships between different religious faiths. Their theologies challenge Christians to reconsider the activities of the Spirit that take place among other religious people, especially in an Indian context.

Describing spiritual activities in human lives, both theologians hold to similar theological concepts – they hope to form a "new community of hope" through transformation and reconciliation. Moltmann believed that peoples' spiritual experiences function as a driving force to engage in selfless activity on behalf of others. Similarly, Kim observes that the experiences people receive from the Spirit help them to reconstruct broken relationships with God and other people. Both theologians believed that spiritual experiences, by providing blessed hope, help people to start a new life. The people who become part of this new community will bear the fruit of the Spirit and become part of the kingdom of God.

5.3.4 General Revelation

Moltmann and Kim viewed spiritual experiences as one of the ways God communicates with people. Such experiences reveal God's intention to impart his attributes to people and to have fellowship with them. Kim believed that spiritual experiences are distinct opportunities that people receive from the Spirit to experience God and receive his messages. The Spirit's works are unpredictable and vary from person to person. Moltmann says that the unpredictable works of the Spirit evident in human creativity and culture lead humans to spiritual experiences. The biblical perspective of the Spirit's unbounded works, discussed by both Kim and Moltmann, offer the possibility of knowing God's will. But it is essential to have an open attitude towards the Spirit when considering the various religious experiences of people outside the church. The positive response of people towards the Spirit is essential to understand God's revelation through non-Christian religious experiences.

CHAPTER 6

A Pneumatological Understanding of Hindu Religious Experience

In the preceding chapters, we sought to construct a theology of the Spirit's presence in the Hindu experience and assess its relevance for Christian theology and mission. Beginning with both the biblical and the Hindu understandings of religious experiences, we then turned to the contributions of Christian theologians on this particular topic and found, in their writings, evidence of the Spirit's presence in the Hindu religious experience. Although theological attention has been paid to this topic in the context of India, an investigation of the presence of the Spirit in the Hindu religious experience provides new insight into our discussion. Similarly, the topic has proved relevant within the growing theological discussion on the Spirit's mission and role in different religious experiences.

Generally, religious experiences add beauty to their own religions and cultures through their unusual power and positive results. But equally important is the fact that through religious experiences and what they reveal, the Spirit of God challenges people ethically and theologically. God expects a response, and not just self-satisfaction, from people. In the preceding pages, we sought to understand Hindu religious experience theologically and not only in respect to their producing certain positive results: experiencing bliss, inner strength, moral nature, bizarre power, and mysterious knowledge – for religious experience always gives such remarkable results. We have also considered instances where God revealed himself to people even beyond the Christian faith – for example, to Abimelech through a dream (Gen 20:3–6), to King Neco and King Huram through revelation (2 Kings 23:29–30; 1 Kings

7:13), to Balaam through a vision (Num 22:34–41), to Augur and Lemuel through their spiritual insight (Prov 30:1; 31:1), to Cornelius through his piety and morality (Acts 10:3–6), and to the people of Athens through their religiosity (Acts 17:22–23). If a theology of the Spirit's presence in other cultures is to be biblically and theologically correct, the approach of Christian theology and mission towards the Hindu religious experience must be corrected.

In chapter 1, we learned that the increased interest in religious experience in Christian theology is one compelling reason for attempting a constructive theology of the Spirit's presence in the Indian context. Let us examine what a new focus on the Spirit's presence in the Hindu religious experience might mean for this increasingly vital theological topic.

6.1 Experience

Religious experience, the essence of religion and spirituality among people, remains mysterious in its source and unusual outcomes. This is because God and his dealings with people remain a mystery, even as they function as a medium of God's general revelation. Searching for reality is the true goal and purpose of human life and the central purpose of all religions. The spiritual experience given by the Spirit helps people to recognize the reality of the Creator. Thus, the invisible presence of the Spirit is nonetheless visible in religious experience as a triggering, guiding, and empowering force to bring people closer to God. The Spirit is present in all human life as the "breath/giver of life" (as the Nicene Creed recognizes), helping us to know reality. This presence of the Spirit in human life sometimes functions as our conscience, is evident in and through nature, and is seen in human history. As Howard expresses it, "Knowledge of God's existence and divine attributes are revealed externally in nature, while knowledge of God's perfect law is given internally, i.e. 'written on his heart.'"[1] According to Bruce Demarest and Gordon Lewis, we must recognize "the disclosure of God in nature, in providential history, and in the moral law within the heart, whereby all persons at all times and places gain a rudimentary understanding of the Creator and his moral demands."[2] These definitions lead to the idea of general revelation mediated

---

1. Howard, "General Revelation," 75.
2. Lewis and Demarest, *Integrative Theology*, 61.

through nature (creation), history (culture), and moral laws (conscience). Religious experience can become a form of general revelation, a "prevenient grace" that leads people towards the knowledge of Christ, who is the special revelation of God. God has experientially revealed himself in all (or at least many) religions, but this experience, as von Hugel recognizes, is found "at its deepest and purest" in Christ.[3] Yet, as the Christian theologian Samartha recognizes, God is a mystery, and his spiritual revelations remain a mystery to people. It is God's intention that humanity seek and find him within his mysterious revelations. The presence of the Spirit in the medium of religious experience seems to be a mystery that directs people to draw closer to God.

Even after the fall, God's spiritual engagement with people has not been lost for the Spirit's revealing presence with human beings is visible as inner knowledge. Ajith Fernando observes that this inner knowledge of God in human beings functions as part of the general revelation of God. He writes that there are three sources of truth outside the Bible: reminiscent knowledge, based on the original revelation of God; intuitional knowledge, which comes from the use of our natural instincts; and inferential knowledge, which comes from observing creation.[4] In theology, these types of knowledge is classified under the heading of *general revelation*. But for all three sources of knowledge to become a revelation, the enlivening presence of the Spirit must be received. This truth, derived from God, is available to all people. But as Fernando perhaps underemphasizes, the role of the Spirit is also necessary.[5] The biblical narration of the Spirit's function in human life as the breath of life and consciousness undoubtedly supports this idea. Andrew K. Gabriel comments that

> the Spirit dwells in all things is consistent with Paul, who wrote to the Ephesians that God is 'over all, and through all and in all' (Eph 4:6) and that God 'fills everything in every way' (Eph 1:23) . . . The Spirit dwells in all things as the Creator and sustainer of all things.[6]

---

3. Hugel, *Philosophy of Religion*, 39.

4. Ajith Fernando, *Sharing the Truth in Love: How to Relate to People of Other Faiths*. Baker Books, 2001, 28.

5. Fernando, *Sharing the Truth*, 74.

6. Gabriel, "Intensity of the Spirit," 370.

The expected outcomes of the Hindu religious experience: mysterious knowledge, truth, purity of mind, goodness, and union with the absolute, are the Spirit's contribution to human lives. Religious experience enables people to attain mysterious knowledge, to realign their actions, and to experience beauty. This revelation through religious experience exceeds any human intellectual knowledge. Lalruaktima asserts that such unlimited revelatory knowledge is impossible to gain through scientific investigation of the world.[7] Similarly, Diehl says that "revelation is the source of all true human knowledge."[8] We must distinguish human knowledge from the knowledge or revelation imparted by that outside force. In Hinduism, revelations of mysterious knowledge and an understanding of the Supreme Being are Vedantic ideologies achieved by Hindu rishis through religious experience. For Amos Yong, these philosophical and scriptural revelations are the outcomes of yogis – that is,

> the personal experience of the Spirit by the rishis [sages and holy persons of other traditions], inasmuch as it is in God's providence a first personal breakthrough of God to the nations, and in so far as it has been authentically recorded in their sacred scriptures, is a personal word of God addressed to them through intermediaries of his choice.[9]

In the case of India, Hindu religiosity fortifies the accumulation of mysterious knowledge through its wealth of spiritual revelations.

Due to the unfinished and limited nature of religious experience, it is not wise to be satisfied with the outcomes produced by such experiences. God's mystical revelation to people is always partial and, sometimes, even unpredictable. These religious experiences impart a limited knowledge of God and demand that human beings seek him further. As Michael Lacewing says, "So disagreements between religions don't show that religious experiences aren't veridical, only that they can tell us very little about the nature of the divine."[10] Nevertheless, Cooke considers the knowledge acquired through religious experience to be authentic and valid. He writes, "At the heart of the mystery

---

7. Lalruatkima, *Understanding Christian Faith*, 50–51.
8. Diehl, "Evangelicalism," 441–448.
9. Yong, *Beyond the Impasse*, 51.
10. Lacewing, "Argument from Religious Experience," 3.

of divine loving of humans is that a person enjoying this religious experience does not simply know about God, one knows God."[11] This suggests that religious experience is not merely meant for self-satisfaction or enjoyment but, rather, that people may recognize the source behind it. The essential reality here is not the religious experience but the source of that experience – the one who wants to communicate his message to us. When people begin to give priority to the experience, they unknowingly forget the essence of religious experience, which is its divine source. Religious experiences are God-given opportunities for people to identify God's Spirit and his will.

The Hindu philosopher Vivekananda believed that the spiritual discipline of yoga could help people obtain mystical experience and greater knowledge of the truth. This truth, in Hinduism, accommodates different meanings: knowing the ultimate Brahman, experiencing the divine bliss or *Satyananda*, and confronting the powerful being – Shiva or Virashaiva. Vivekananda believed that knowing the truth is an internal desire of all human beings and that nothing will satisfy us until we know the truth – we are reminded of Augustine's Christian assertion that our hearts are restless until they find rest in God.[12] The human affinity for knowing Reality, our insight into the existence of ultimate truth, and the satisfaction that comes through knowing the truth is nothing but the Spirit's work in human life. The Spirit leads us into the truth and helps us to know Reality. Simply claiming to know the truth in religious experience is insufficient; such experience should channel us to know the Truth – Christ, who said, "I am . . . the truth" (John 14:6 NIV). John 8:32 (NIV) says, "Then you will know the truth, and the truth will set you free." Here is the ultimate outcome of experiencing the truth, an outcome that the Hindu religion confuses because it searches for the truth only through the self-discipline of religious experience. The positive results found in religious experience do not mean that it makes a person perfect, as a Hindu craves. Vivekananda's anticipation of achieving mysterious knowledge, knowing truth, getting self-satisfaction, and achieving moral character through religious experience are not in themselves sufficient for a person to become perfect or to unite with the ultimate one; rather, they are an important first step towards coming closer to knowing the perfect God.

---

11. Cooke, *Power and the Spirit*, 187.
12. Augustine, *Confessions*, 1,1.5.

6.2 Culture

Culture and human creativity – the supporting factors of religious experience – embrace the mysterious presence of the Spirit and channels by which people may know the will of God. The work of the Spirit is present in all these cultural factors – traditional faiths, arts, religiosity, and moral principles – because they convey God's truth, beauty, and goodness. From a biblical perspective, God is the source of these transcendentals, and he is willing to pass these on to human beings. In the Old Testament, God imparted the Spirit of divine wisdom – *hokmah*, meaning "skill" – to Huram, who was a non-Israelite (see Chapter 3). Huram was able to do all the architectural works required by King Solomon in constructing the Jerusalem Temple. The cultural plurality that Huram represented was not a barrier for the Spirit to work. To give another example, Balaam was a non-Israelite who continually received God's messages from within his own culture and was able to teach King Balak about who God is and how God deals with his people. Again, Balaam's cultural background was not a barrier for him to hear God and know God's intention. But, sadly, the "spiritual insights" he received through revelatory events did not change Balaam himself.

In the New Testament, while Paul was sharing the gospel with the Athenians, he decisively used a traditional poem to reveal the spiritual truth that was applicable in that particular culture. It is the Spirit who imparted such knowledge in that culture so that people could know God. But when Paul revealed this truth to the Athenians, only a few were interested in knowing more and only a few responded to the revelation. In the case of the Gentile Cornelius, his dream became a channel of salvation for him and his whole household. Similarly, in Acts 10, we see how people's religiosity might lead them, through the Spirit, to achieve knowledge about God. The Spirit's broader revelation becomes an initial medium of salvation for some, but not for all. In fact, the Spirit functions as an agent of unity, and a guide to understand the truth in human life through various cultural events.

The presence of the Spirit in religious experiences has the power to enliven all human cultural systems because it functions as a medium leading people towards God. As we observed earlier, Chenchiah admired his past religious faith (Hinduism), which led him to recognize spiritual reality more easily. Thus, he praises the positive features of Hindu culture and represents it as the "spiritual mother" that helped him to know the truth. So, it is not surprising that Chenchiah made use of Indian religious traditions in constructing a better theology for India. He saw himself as similar to the apostle Paul, who observed certain realities in other religions and did not hesitate to accept and use these in his witness. But Paul was aware of the limitation of such knowledge, even as it played a significant role in directing people to know the truth. His message and instruction always sought to help people understand that Jesus alone is the way and the truth. Ajith Fernando comments, "But Paul showed, as he did in Athens, that the highest truths in these religions did not go far enough. Paul knew that the truth residing in other faiths would not bring eternal salvation. For that, Christ is the only way."[13] Bernard Cooke says,

> Religious faith is a distinctive way of knowing. While it takes account of verifiable evidence and is reinforced when such evidence exists, it is grounded in one's religious experience and in trusting acceptance of others' witness to their religious experience. Because of this second element, faith begins and develops within one or another community of believers.[14]

And for Paul, this was the community that believed in Jesus. The presence of the Spirit in human culture, tradition, creativity, skills, art, and architecture was one expression of God's universal revelation to all people. Ultimately, however, the full light of God's revelation in Jesus became necessary.

The Spirit, who motivates people to create unusual things, mysteriously attracts people towards the perfection of beauty. The limited human ability of artists and architects, who are part of human culture, may make a person open to trust the perfect God. But this requires being granted eyes to see and ears to hear. This is the work of the Spirit. As Parker suggests, there is a "beautifying agency of the Holy Spirit within the arts."[15] "Looking particularly within the arts, a consideration of the now-and-not-yet, eschatological dimension of the Spirit's work will . . . allow for consideration regarding the creation and mediation of understanding evoked from art, as well as for response affected through art."[16] The Spirit's work in human culture can guide people to see the ultimate glory of beauty. "In a sense the Spirit is drawing

---

13. Fernando, *Sharing the Truth*, 71.
14. Cooke, *Power and the Spirit*, 143.
15. Parker, "Holy Spirit in the Arts," 208.
16. Parker, 208.

the beauty of creation into union with divine beauty in the consummation at the eschaton. Pannenberg uses the metaphor of a force field within this union to speak of the Spirit's power pervading all creation."[17] Both the narrative of Scripture and Christian theological interpretation reveal that the Spirit opens people's eyes to God's beauty through their own arts and traditional religious faiths. And the same Spirit points us to the ultimate beauty – Jesus Christ. To know Jesus means knowing the perfect truth and beauty. Patrick Sherry says that "the Fathers glory is reflected in the Son, his perfect image, and diffused through the Holy Spirit" and "that the Spirit has the mission of communicating God's beauty to the world"[18] Contrary to what Hinduism teaches, the positive results of religious experience – though a result of the Spirit's presence – are not a sign of perfection, nor is the bliss of its religious experience perfect bliss. Rather, these spiritual experiences are indicators of knowing the provider of all good things.

6.3 Church

A biblical and theological understanding of religious experience suggests that the work of the Spirit cannot be limited to what takes place within the walls of the church. The Spirit of God has no barrier to moving beyond these walls to provide opportunities for people to recognize God. In the Old Testament, God's revelation includes divine messages to King Neco, a non-Israelite (2 Kings 23:29–30), and artistic skills that God gave to Huram, another Gentile, again illustrating the Spirit's intervention in people's lives without discrimination. The unrestricted work of the Spirit recorded in the Scripture becomes most fully manifest in the overflow of the Spirit in the book of Acts. The Indian theologian Samartha's explanation of the four marks of the Spirit – the mark of freedom, the mark of boundlessness, the one who builds new relationships, and the one who empowers new community – is consistent with what we have noted about the works of the Spirit outside the church.

The Spirit of God plays a significant role in the religious experience of many outside the church, creating the hope of a better future through building a relationship between God and humankind. People perceive the divine

---

17. Karkkainen, "Working of the Spirit," 208–209.
18. Sherry, *Spirit and Beauty*, 160.

commitment to peace and justice in their religious experiences, which enables them to exercise these same values in their own community. Thus, the Indian theologian Chenchiah argues that guiding people to love others and establish peace is the work of the Spirit. This brings hope to the hopeless. Jurgen Moltmann's "theology of hope" also argues for a new community that moves towards a new world through the power of the Spirit. Moreover, it is as a result of the Spirit's involvement in human life that the Kirsteen Kim's concept of "peace and reconciliation" and Moltmann's concept of "social justice" are realized.

Kim believed that the Spirit functions as a reconciler in human life, bringing unity between God and humankind, and this often repeated theological assertion seems similar to the Hindu concept of union with the Absolute. According to Vivekananda, in the Vedantic philosophy of Hinduism, the ultimate goal of the Hindu religious experience is a merging with the Absolute. Samartha's theological contribution helps us to understand how Hindu and Christian thought might connect at this point by relating the Hindu concept of *advaita* with the divine nature of the union. For him, this union does not mean merging with the absolute but adopting the divine nature within human life. This is possible not by any human effort but only with the help of the Spirit. "The Spirit is the principal unifying agent within creation and therefore a disregard for the Spirit may be seen in the breakdown of relationship."[19] The unity, justice, love, and equality that can be established in a community through experiencing the Spirit creates that ideal society that Vivekananda anticipated.

Understanding the presence of the Spirit in religious experience enables Christians to change their attitude towards their neighbours of other religious faiths. Since religious experiences are closely associated with the spirituality of all human beings, acknowledging an invisible and mysterious power at work behind these demonstrates a certain commonality in such experiences. This can be a meeting point for interfaith dialogue. Amos Yong views the Spirit's presence in religious experience as both the starting and ending point of dialogue.[20] Similarly, in Samartha's theology of dialogue, the insight received through spiritual experiences helps build new relationships with other

---

19. Dabney, "Nature of the Spirit," 216.
20. Yong, *Beyond the Impasse*, 100.

communities. Religious experiences – those spiritual interventions that happen in human life – can establish peace and harmony between people. Reconsidering people's traditional beliefs from the perspective of an experience of the Spirit can overcome the human misunderstanding that good things are absent in other traditional faiths and help Christians recognize that people of other faiths can also experience God. It can thus help Christians to accept their neighbours, even while not accepting all that their neighbour might believe. The presence of the Spirit in human life, without any partiality, should cause Christians to widen their hearts to accept the Spirit's presence in other communities. It should open us to see the culture of other religious faiths not as a threat to the church but as a resource through which to hear God speak.

In Christian missions, experiences of the Spirit function as a medium to convey God's revelation. The spiritual nature of these religious experiences and their engagement with human activities thus facilitates the work of evangelists in building a bridge between the gospel and people of other faiths. Such religious experience is characterized by vagueness in relation to its source and limitations in its results. It remains incomplete. Such "failings," however, can be considered an advantage to evangelists in articulating "God." This was so for the apostle Paul. As a connecting factor, religious experiences can play a significant role in missions due to the mysterious presence of the Spirit in such experiences. In his ministry, Paul used the spirituality of the Athenians as a means to share the gospel. Chenchiah's explanation of the Spirit as "cosmic energy" or Kim's understanding of the Spirit as an "agent of mission" may open the door to people reaching out to God. For Kim, this is the mission of the Spirit, functioning in every person through their faith, experience, culture, skill, conscience, and morality, yet without interfering in their self-determination. To understand God and his message in religious experience, it is essential to recognize people's positive response towards the work of the Spirit.

6.4 Tradition

Turning to the church's traditional understanding of religious experience can further augment our understanding of the importance of the Spirit in this present world. The increasing interest in spirituality in today's world reinforces Christianity's move towards embracing pneumatological theologies. According to Sandra M. Schneiders, "spirituality is a holistic discipline in that its inquiry into human spiritual experience is not limited to explorations of the explicitly religious, i.e. the so-called 'interior life.'"[21] It adopts the nature of an ecumenical, interreligious, and cross-cultural outlook. Kirsteen Kim rightly noted that the contemporary trend in the twenty-first century is for people to prioritize spirituality rather than philosophical thoughts. This led her to value pneumatological-based theologies in Christianity. Theologians like Chenchiah and Moltmann have also emphasized the need to construct theology that centres on the third person of the Trinity – the Holy Spirit. Perhaps this is because, as Millard J. Erickson says, the Holy Spirit is active in the lives of believers – just as he is active within the Trinity – and we can find broader implications of his work in the world.[22]

Moreover, the work of the Spirit in creating spiritual experiences for people is more prominent than that of any other member of the Trinity.[23] As Won Yong Ji wrote in 1895,

> Pneumatology in Christian theology, which deals with the place and work of the Third Person of the Trinity, the Holy Spirit, is one of the most widely discussed points in modern theological circles. Special attention has been given to the Holy Spirit during the third quarter of the twentieth century, and it peaked in the 70s, as evidenced in a flood of publications on this subject.[24]

And nothing has changed in the intervening years. The significance of experiences of the Spirit in theology has increased due to the cultural popularity of human spirituality.

The growing cultural phenomena of spirituality emphasize the relevance of considering human spiritual experience in Christian theology and the essentiality of knowing the truth within that religious experience. In contrast, in places like India, people prioritize such experiences. Schneiders writes,

---

21. Schneiders, "Spirituality in the Academy," 693.
22. Millard J. Erickson, *Christian Theology*. 2nd ed., Baker Academic, 1998, 878.
23. Erickson, *Christian Theology*, 846.
24. Won Yong Ji, "Work of the Holy Spirit," 204.

> Although theology is an important moment within the investigation of [all] religious experience (as we saw in the case of mysticism), it is precisely because spirituality is interested in the experience *as* experience, i.e. in its phenomenological wholeness, that it must utilize whatever approaches are relevant to the reality being studied.[25]

In India, different theologians began interpreting spiritual experience in their context years ago.

> Although this effort was made as early as the sixteenth century, with the pioneering efforts of Robert De Nobili (1577–1656),[26] the expression 'Indian Christian theology' refers to a distinct theological tradition that flowered in the 19th and the early 20th centuries with the aim of explaining the Gospel message in interaction with various philosophies, ideologies and sociopolitical realities of India.[27]

Robin Boyd says, "It was only in the 19th century that some sort of Christological formulations began to appear as a result of Hindu-Christian encounter."[28] At present, the human priority given to spirituality emphasizes the need to consider the Spirit's work in Indian Christian theology. Of particular relevance is Moltmann's theology of hope, based on a Trinitarian pneumatology that emphasizes Jesus's Spirit-filled actions. His theology, which emphasizes the engagement of spiritual life with action, points to a blessed hope. Similarly, his theology of Shekhinah emphasizes the presence of God's glory, which leads people to engage in moral activities. Such reflections can help Christian theology to connect with Indian spirituality.

Christian theologians' observations of the presence of the Spirit in other religious traditions increase the scope of pneumatological theologies in Christianity, allowing them to communicate their truth to other religions more easily. We should not deny the truth and goodness present in other

---

25. Schneiders, "Spirituality in the Academy," 692.

26. Robert De Nobili came to India as a Jesuit missionary in 1605. He adapted Hindu customs and practices; he also studied Sanskrit and Tamil and attempted to draw theological vocabularies from these languages. Stephan, *Christian Theology*, 92.

27. Manohar, "Spirit Christology," 171.

28. Boyd, *Introduction to Indian Christian Theology*, 17–18.

religious faiths. Keith Edward Johnson represents Amos Yong's understanding of the Spirit's presence in other religions: "The Holy Spirit is present and active among non-Christian religions and . . . Christians must learn to discern the Spirit's presence."[29] Yong comments, "The possible presence and activity of the Spirit in other traditions mean the possible existence of theological insights in other traditions that may positively impact Christian theology. To deny the latter possibility is to lapse into an extremely anemic pneumatology even on biblical grounds."[30] Theology should communicate the truth in a way that the public can understand. In India, the origin of Hinduism and its philosophical thoughts rested upon the spiritual experience of people, which they achieved through spiritual discipline. Their concept of experience (*anubhava*) being more important than reasoning (*tarka*) accentuates the need for Christians to construct pneumatological theologies. Such theologies can function as an appropriate entry point for Christians to explain the truth to Hindus.

Focusing upon the religious experiences of Hindus provides a platform to investigate the Spirit's (God's) presence and direction based on its positive outcomes or lack thereof. Spiritual experiences and moral principles are central in Indian Hindu thought, which emphasizes that the divine nature of a purified heart and an orientation of kindness towards our neighbours are God-given qualities. This reality is rooted within human lives as an inner knowledge, consciousness, and morality (Rom 2:27–29) and is given through the Spirit. As Parker says, the Holy Spirit is a mediator to sanctify the people to receive God's nature. He writes, "In sanctifying creation the Holy Spirit plays a mediator role in drawing creation into the divine life of the Godhead."[31] Good works overflow from our human relationship with God and should benefit others through our good relationships. Here is Moltmann's theological argument. His instructions give priority to those spiritual experiences that produce public benefits. In Moltmann's theology, the Spirit grants access to our neighbour. His is a "public theology." However, Moltmann, Kim, and other theologians also emphasized that experiencing the good and demonstrating the fruit of the Spirit based on the religious experience of

---

29. Johnson, "'Trinitarian' Theology," 160.
30. Yong, *Discerning the Spirit(s)*, 317.
31. Parker, "Holy Spirit in the Arts," 210.

non-Christian religions is not an end product; rather, true theology should lead people to take new steps towards knowing the truth of the source of all goodness – God.

6.5 Two Biblical Qualifiers

The biblically based theology of religious experience presented in this study has psychological, cultural, and spiritual dimensions. Whether demonic or divine, spiritual discipline and internal craving call for concerted work in the area of discernment if the Spirit's presence is to fulfil the role envisaged in the Christian theology of religions. This conviction is particularly true for India, where multiple faiths are practised and where there is, thus, the need to be discerning about the work of the Spirit. One criteria for recognizing the presence of the Spirit in religious experience is the positive results we see. If someone's religious experience produces good results, it cannot be rejected outright as not being the work of the Spirit. Numbers 10:32 (NIV) says, "Good things the LORD gives us." Charles DeCelles's exposition of Matthew 25:34–36 reminds us that "love directed to a neighbor is automatically directed to Christ, and from Christ to God."[32] Discerning the Spirit's work in other religions enables us to recognize God's impartial revelation to humanity.

By and large, religious experience is part of God's general revelation to us, but such revelation does not provide salvific knowledge of God. In the words of Daniel Howard, "Knowledge obtained from general revelation is not considered salvific in nature because it lacks salvation knowledge. Knowledge disclosed in general revelation is only about God as Creator and other 'general' divine attributes, not God as Redeemer and other salvific knowledge."[33] Howard says, "Although humans do not obtain salvific knowledge from general revelation, they nevertheless, have true and accurate knowledge of God's existence, his attributes, and moral law."[34] God does not leave anyone without the opportunity to know him, and this can include the distinct religious experiences of non-Christians. The presence of the Spirit is vividly seen everywhere in helping people to fulfil God's desire that people taste him

---

32. DeCelles, "Unbound," 42.
33. Howard, "General Revelation," 69.
34. Howard, 69.

and, ultimately, know more and more of him in Christ. As W. E. Hocking put it: "The concept of Christ is extended to include that unbound Spirit who finds and has stood at the door of every man, and who, in various guises, still appears to him who opens, both as an impersonal word and as a personal presence."[35]

A second qualification is essential. Not only does the Spirit's general presence need to be complete by the Spirit's leading a person to Christ, but the work of the Spirit in religious experience, assisting a person to be transformed into a new person, does not create a perfect or ideal person as Hinduism expects. Vivekananda's belief that one can become perfect without knowing the "perfect one" is misguided. Biblical and theological studies reject the possibility that a person may become perfect by self-effort. For two thousand years, Christian theologians have recognized that nobody can achieve these excellent qualities until the Spirit empowers them. It is the Spirit who provides hope that people may be transformed. Theologically, this is sometimes labelled "glorification" and must await human final transformation eschatologically. Glorification is not the state of becoming divine or perfect by our own effort but refers to receiving divine characteristics through internal transformation brought about by the Spirit. Chenchiah's theology of new people and new creation through the power of the Spirit supports this point. Jesus, who walked in the Spirit, is an example for human beings to follow. God-given religious experiences have the power to transform people into new creations.

Such "sanctification" will remain partial here and now, even as we look forward to our "glorification" one day. This transformation helps both to eliminate old practices that are wrong and superstitious beliefs and to start a new life in the new community – the church of God. The persistent occurrence of multiple religious experiences in human life does not make a person perfect. Rather, the Spirit's intervention in human life empowers us and transforms us into a new creation. Samartha believed that this new community is able to cut through all barriers of religion, culture, ideology, race, and language through the power of the Spirit. Becoming part of this new community is based upon the positive response of people towards the Spirit. Joining this community – which adopts peace, hope, and love – institutes a

---

35. Hocking, *Coming World Civilization*, 168–169.

new culture. Vivekananda's expectation of forming an "ideal man" and an "ideal society" is realized here.

6.6 Pneumatology of Religious Experience: Conclusion

This study has examined the theology of the Spirit's presence in the Hindu experience and its relevance to Christian theology and mission. The theological understanding of the work of the Spirit in Hindu religious experience – having considered experience, culture, church, tradition, and the Bible – has provided certain preliminary conclusions for a Christian theology particularly suited to India.

First, the religious experience can function as one of the media of God's general revelation; it is not just an experience of self-satisfaction or happiness with positive results based on various trigger factors. The possibility of conveying God's revelation through religious experience is fortified by the mysterious nature and power of religious experience, which parallels the mysterious presence of the Spirit in such experiences. The different media of God's general revelation – nature, culture, human creativity, morality, and religious experience with positive results – do not despise the presence of the Spirit but find their empowerment through the Spirit. The religious experiences connected with these sources find their origin in the work of the Spirit in them. S. J. Samartha's representation of God and his work as a mystery is supported by other theologians like Jurgen Moltmann and Kirsteen Kim. This mystery can compel people to seek and find out the author behind the mystery. Swami Vivekananda's understanding of human thirst for knowing the truth is the work of the mysterious presence of the Spirit in human life; the Spirit is the "breath of life," who provides "inner knowledge." Religious experience is not merely for self-satisfaction, bliss, or goodness but is meant to help adherents recognize its source. The expected outcomes of religious experience – a revelation of mysteries, knowledge, truth, purity of mind, goodness, and unification with the supreme God – do not yield perfect results but only partial fulfilment. Yet this religious experience is a form of general revelation, a "prevenient grace" that leads people to know Christ, who is the specific revelation of God.

Second, recognizing the Spirit's presence in the religious experience of different cultures challenges Christians who have a cautious and predominantly negative assumption about the work of the Spirit outside the church. Distinct cultural factors –such as art, skill, poetry, philosophy, moral principles, religiosity, spiritual insights, and religious faiths – do not exist merely to reveal cultural glory but to give direction from the Spirit to know God's will and his ways. As culture is plural in nature, the mysterious works of the Spirit in culture are also plural. Samartha believed that plurality is true to the nature of God, and he uses this concept to bring unity among people. He viewed the Spirit is an agent of unity, guiding people to know life's reality through religious experiences based on different cultural backgrounds. P. Chenchiah's consideration of his past religiosity (Hindu spiritual understandings) as his "spiritual mother" suggests that we should value other cultural faiths. Thus, both Samartha and Chenchiah help us to consider the work of the Spirit in other cultures and, in the process, give us a better theological approach to relating to non-Christian people. Our limited human ability in arts, skill, philosophy, and creativity, which are part of human culture, should help us to recognize a perfect God. But as we have seen, through a focus on Scripture and Christian theological interpretation, the Spirit ultimately opens people's eyes to know God's beauty through their own arts and traditional religious faiths. We must correct the misconception of Christians that God only deals with his own people.

Third, recognizing the Spirit's presence in non-Christian religious experience will help us to correct church doctrine and denominational restrictions, thus helping the church to more effectively fulfil the mission entrusted to us. As Chenchiah says, to respect the mysterious works of the Spirit in other religious faith, breaks all "calamitous factors" (dogmas, traditions, rituals, institutions, sacraments, priests and pastors), which sometimes removes God's glory from the churches.[36] Chenchiah's advice concerning including the Holy Spirit in our church's doctrine and philosophy can play a significant role in furthering the church's mission, particularly in multireligious nations like India. But it will also be an important corrective to those churches that are rooted in stringent doctrinal decrees. As religious experiences are recognized as being closely associated with human spirituality, spiritual relationships

---

36. Chenchiah, "Jesus and Non-Christian Faiths,"., 53.

can be built between people, which will open new ways to know the truth. Samartha's recommendations about being open and accepting towards the spiritual experiences of other religious people can allow for a meeting point for interfaith "dialogue." This will help Christians to better hear people outside the church. Acknowledging the presence of the Spirit in religious experience will change the church's attitude towards its neighbours. This can help to cultivate harmonious living between different religious communities. Such acceptance reduces the distance created by discrimination and builds closer relationships between people of different faiths, which will help the church to accomplish God's mission. This can become instrumental in the church accomplishing God's mission.

Fourth, recognizing the Spirit's presence in religious experience can help us develop a more holistic understanding of the Holy Spirit, which will lead us to construct a more robust and pneumatologically-based theology. In India, a theology of the Holy Spirit has been found to be more relevant because it gives priority to people's spiritual experience. Kim's observation about the contemporary trends of people who prioritize spirituality and believe that the spiritual experience has potential beyond individual fulfilment and temporal satisfaction points to the essential need to rethink spiritual lessons and approaches within Christendom. Her suggestion that "a pneumatology for the twenty-first century needs to begin from the experience of spirits below rather than from the assertion of one Spirit from above"[37] seems essential. Chenchiah's contribution of a pneumatological-based Christology, Moltmann's contributions of Trinitarian pneumatology, a theology of Shekhinah, and a theology of love, and Kim's theology of pneumatology all remind us that we can no longer ignore the Spirit. We must grow out of our infancy and begin investigating the full ramifications of the Spirit – both his person and his power. As Samartha believed, in Indian Christian theology, "*tarka* (logic) must be subordinated to *anubhava* (experience)," which points to the need to connect with the Eastern tradition of spirituality more than the Western-based reasoning in our theologies. This will answer the centuries-old problem that Indian churches have faced as they wrongly attempted to Westernize their culture. If the church emphasizes the work of the Spirit and demonstrates

---

37. Kirsteen Kim, "Post-Modern Mission A paradigm shift in David Bosch's theology of mission?" *International Review of Mission* Vol. LXXXIX No.353, 176.

evidence of a more colourful gospel, this will help to eliminate many criticisms of Hindu philosophers such as Mahatma Gandhi, S. Radhakrishnan, and Swami Vivekananda concerning the Westernized colour of Christianity.

The fulfilment of God's intention through religious experience is based on our varied human responses towards the guidance of the Spirit. The Bible shows that people like Abimelech, Cornelius, and the Athenians on Mars Hill who embraced an attitude of humbleness and obedience to the Spirit received the blessings of God. Indeed, the biblical account of Jesus's life serves as a model for how we should live submissively to the Spirit. Having said this, discernment is also essential in responding to spiritual experiences because of the presence of evil spirits in the world. Balaam lacked this discernment but Neco did not. We must heed Samartha's call to discern (*viveka*) the Spirit instead of seeking control, while noting Kim's criteria for discerning the Spirit as ecclesial, ethical, charismatic, and liberating. Here, the biblical teachings can help a person to discern the source of religious experience which people receives. Samartha's and Kim's theological contributions remind us of our biblical responsibility to grow in spiritual maturity and discern the Spirit's spiritual activities (Rom 8:4–5; 2 Cor 11:14; Gal 5:16; Eph 6:11–12; 2 Tim 2:25–26; Jude 19–21).

This study suggests that the proposed pneumatological approach to understanding Hindu religious tradition can also help us to understand other such religions present in the world. Since the unbounded work of the Spirit through creation, culture, tradition, and religious experience is a reality, a similar kind of constructive theology is essential for Christians wherever they want to engage with other religious faiths. The benefit of such an approach for understanding and communicating with our neighbouring faiths increases the relevance of pneumatology in understanding all religious experiences. Moreover, this study opens other avenues for Christian theology to explore as it considers how religious experience might best be allied to problematic areas such as salvation, other spirits, and discernment. Such an approach could also help lessen the disunity between religions because it is rooted in the conviction that all positive effects come from one Spirit through whom we can understand God's will and purpose.

Glossary of Hindi/Sanskrit Words

The anglicized spellings of Hindi and Sanskrit words that are frequently used by Vivekananda, Chenchiah, Samartha, and Kirsteen Kim are listed below, together with the meanings given to these terms in the context of theological discussion. These selected words are usually italicized in the text. The original spelling (italicization and capitalization) has been retained in quotations. Any dissimilarity in spelling that appears in quotations is noted here in brackets.

adi purusha	primordial being, primeval male, or Supreme Being (Shiva)
advaita	non-dualism, monism, oneness, philosophy of non-dualism
aham brahmasmi	I am Brahman
ahamkara	egotism
ananda	joy, bliss
antaryamin	inner working of the Spirit or the one who dwells or rules within
anubhava (*anubhavah*)	experience, intuition
ashramic	one living in an ashram
atman	soul, self, spirit
avatara	incarnation or descent (of a God to earth)
bhaktas	people who devoted to a particular god or goddess
bhakti	devotion, worship, love
Brahman	the Supreme Being of Vedantic philosophy, the universal Spirit, the impersonal Absolute
darshana	vision, glimpse or view
epics and *puranas*	ancient Hindu literary works

gerua	a garment that symbolizes spiritual authority
jivanmukta	liberation within this life
jnana	knowledge
kaivalya	separateness or detachment from the world (the ultimate goal of Raja-Yoga)
Mahasakti	the female divine force in Hinduism (Mahadevi, Durga, Kali)
mahasamadhi	high yogic state
marga	way, path to liberation
moksha (mukti)	liberation, freedom, salvation
nirvikalpasamadhi	the transcendent experience or last step (samadhi)
paramatman	supreme (best, first, greatest) spirit
prajapathi	lord of creation and protector
prana	breathe, life, energy
rebirth	the Hindu concept of obtaining new life after death
sadhana	a means of accomplishing something
samsara	the continuous cycle of life, death, and reincarnation
sanatana dharma	eternal religion
sat-cit-ananda	ultimate being, pure consciousness, and perfect bliss
sayujya	liberation of the soul
Shakti (sakti)	power, energy, force; the goddess, god's consort, female energy
tarka	logic
Veda	"The Vedas" – the body of sacred knowledge held to be the basis of true belief and practice among Hindus; the Hindu scriptures
Visvakarma	deity of all craftsmen and architects
viveka	the ability to discern, discernment, discrimination
yoga	union, harmony, oneness; a way of achieving union with god

Selected Bibliography

Primary Sources

Chenchiah, P. "The Christian Message in a Non-Christian World." In *Rethinking Christianity in India,* edited by G. V. Job, D. S. Amalorpavadass, A. N. Sudarisanam., et al., 32–41. Madras: Hogarth, 1938.

———. "Christianity and Hinduism" (Pamphlet 1928). Reprinted in *The Theology of Chenchiah: With Selections from His Writings,* edited by D. A. Thangasamy, 68–75. Bangalore: CISRS, 1966.

———. "Amara Vinuta – Praised of the Angels – Christmas." *The Pilgrim* 10, no. 4 (December 1951): 1–2.

———. "The Christian Asrama." In *Theology and Church in India.* Edited by V. Devasahayam. Christian Literature Society, 1966.

———. "The Church and the Indian Christian." In *Rethinking Christianity in India,* edited by G. V. Job, D. S. Amalorpavadass, A. N. Sudarisanam, 150–170. Madras: Hogarth, 1938.

———. "Correspondence: Letter and Reply, T. R. Venkatarama Sastr." *The Pilgrim* 10, no. 2 (June 1951): 34–36.

———. "Hindu and Christian Religious Magazines (January to April 1951)." *The Pilgrim* 10, no. 3 (September 1951): 32–34.

———. "In Memoriam – Late Sri Venturi Prabhakara Sastri" *The Pilgrim* 10, no. 4 (December 1951): 2–3.

———. "Jesus and Non-Christian Faiths." In *Rethinking Christianity in India,* edited by G. V. Job, D. S. Amalorpavadass, A. N. Sudarisanam., 83–94. Madras: Hogarth, 1938.

———. "In Memoriam: Prof. M. Hiriyanne" *The Pilgrim* 9, no. 4 (December 1950): 4.

———. "Our Theological Task VI: Review and Restatement." *The Guardian* 25, no. 6 (1947): 161–165.

———. "The Passing Away of the Maharishi." *The Pilgrim* 9, no. 2 (June 1950): 1–2.

———. "The Psychology of the Hindu Mind and the Presentation of the Christian Message." *The Pilgrim* 8, no. 1 (March 1949): 11–13.

———. "Puranas: Suggestions for Group Study." *The Pilgrim* 11, no. 1 (March 1952): 9–12.

———. "Religion in Contemporary India." In *Rethinking Christianity in India*, edited by G. V. Job et al., 27–44. Madras: Hogarth, 1938.

———. "Review: How to Present Christ to a Hindu (Das)." *The Pilgrim* 9, no. 4 (December 1950): 18–19.

———. "Review: Swami Sivananda's Lectures." *The Pilgrim* 11, no. 2 (June 1952): 16.

———. "Some Misconceptions about the Hindu Caste System." *The Pilgrim* 12, no. 2 (May 1953): 17–21.

———. "Who is Jesus?" In *The Theology of Chenchiah: With Selections from His Writings*, edited by D. A. Thangasamy, 142–157. Bangalore: CISRS, 1966.

———. "Yoga Defined." *The Guardian* (1944). Reprinted in *The Theology of Chenchiah: With Selections from His Writings*, edited by D. A. Thangasamy, 262–63. Bangalore: CISRS, 1966.

———. "Yoga of Holy Spirit." *The Guardian* (1944): 136–137. Reprinted in *The Theology of Chenchiah: With Selections from His Writings*, edited by D. A. Thangasamy, 106–110. Bangalore: CISRS, 1966.

Kim, Kirsteen. "Robin Boyd. Beyond Captivity: Explorations in Indian Christian History and Theology, reviewed by Kirsteen Kim." *Studies in World Christianity* 22, no. 2 (August 2016): 173–174.

———. "'Discerning Spirit' or 'Discerning the Spirits'?: Two Paradigms of Engaged Pneumatology Illustrated by the Works of T. Gorringe and A. Yong." *Communio Viatorum* 60, no. 1 (2018): 28–49.

———. "Discerning the Spirit: The First Act of Mission." *Norsk Tidsskrift for Misjonsvitenskap* 1 (2008): 3–21.

———. "Evangelii Gaudium and the Prospects for Ecumenical Mission." *International Review of Mission* 104, no. 2 (November 2015): 336–344.

———. "Globalization of Protestant Movements since the 1960s." *The Ecumenical Review* 63, no. 2 (July 2011): 136–147.

———. "Globalizing Theology: Belief and Practice in an Era of World Christianity." *International Bulletin of Missionary Research* 31, no. 3 (July 2007): 154.

———. "God of Life: Evangelism Today." *International Review of Mission* 103, no. 1 (April 2014): 87–92.

———. "Mission Theology of the Church" *International Review of Mission*, Volume 99 Number / April 2010, 51–52.

———. "Post-Modern Mission A paradigm shift in David Bosch's theology of mission?" *International Review of Mission* Vol. LXXXIX No.353, 172–179.

———. "Review: Encountering Modernity: Christianity in East Asia and Asian America, edited by Albert L. Park and David K. Yoo." *Journal of Korean Religions* 5, no. 2 (October 2014): 180–182.

———. "Review: Beyond Captivity: Explorations in Indian Christian History and Theology." Studies in World Christianity 22, no. 2 (August 2016): 173–174.

———. "Review: The Gospel among the Nations: A Documentary History of Inculturation." *Modern Believing* 54, no. 1 (January 2013): 77–79.

———. "The Holy Spirit in Mission in India: Indian Contribution to Contemporary Mission Pneumatology."*Oxford Centre for Mission Studies* (6 April 2004): 1–8.

———. *The Holy Spirit in the World: A Global Conversation*. New York: Orbis Books, 2007.

———. "Introducing the New Statement on Mission and Evangelism." *International Review of Mission* 101, no. 2 (November 2012): 316–321.

———. "Korean Discourse on Mission: The Spiritual Vision for the Nation of Rev. Kyung-Chik Han." *Missiology* 44, no. 1 (January 2016): 33–49.

———. "Korean Pentecostalism and Shamanism: Developing Theological Self-Understanding in a Land of Many Spirits." *PentecoStudies* 16, no. 1 (2017): 59–84.

———. "Missiology as Global Conversation of (Contextual) Theologies" *Mission Studies* 21, no. 1 (1 Jan. 2004): 39–53.

———. "Mission after the Arusha Conference on World Mission and Evangelism, 2018." *International Review of Mission* 107, no. 2 (December 2018): 413–427.

———. "Review: Mission from Conversion to Conversation." *Mission Studies* 32, no. 1 (2015): 153–154.

———. "Mission Pneumatology with Special Reference to the Indian Theologies of the Holy Spirit of Stanley Samartha, Vandana, and Samuel Rayan." PhD diss., The University of Birmingham, 2002.

———. "Mission Theology of the Church." *International Review of Mission* 99, no. 1 (April 2010): 39–55.

———. "Mission's Changing Landscape: Global Flows and Christian Movements." *International Review of Mission* 100, no. 2 (November 2011): 244–267.

———. "Review: Polycentric Missiology: Twenty-First-Century Mission from Everyone to Everywhere." *Themelios* 42, no. 2 (August 2017): 427–428.

———. "Post-Modern Mission: A Paradigm Shift in David Bosch's Theology of Mission?" *International Review of Mission* 89, no. 353 (April 2000): 172–179.

———. "The Potential of Pneumatology for Mission in Contemporary Europe." *International Review of Mission* 95, nos. 378–379 (July–October 2006): 334–340.

———. "The Reconciling Spirit: The Dove with Colour and Strength." *International Review of Mission* 94, no. 372 (January 2005): 20–29.

———. "Spirit and 'spirits' at the Canberra Assembly of the World Council of Churches of Churches, 1991." *Missiology* 32, no. 3 (July 2004): 349–365.

———. "Theology and Down Syndrome: Reimagining Disability in Late Modernity." *International Journal of Public Theology* 5, no. 2 (2011): 252–253.

———. "Review: The Unexpected Christian Century: The Reversal and Transformation of Global Christianity, 1900–2000." *International Review of Mission* 106, no. 2 (December 2017): 449–451.

Moltmann, Jurgen. "Christianity: A Religion of Joy." Presentation at *Yale Center for Faith & Culture*. 7–8 September 2012.

———. *The Church in the Power of the Spirit: A Contribution to Messianic Ecclesiology*. Translated by Margaret Kohl. London: SCM, 1977.

———. *The Coming of God: Christian Eschatology*. London: SCM, 1996.

———. *God for a Secular Society: The Public Relevance of Theology*. Translated by Margaret Kohl. London: SCM, 1999.

———. *History and the Triune God: Contributions to Trinitarian Theology*. Translated by John Bowden. London: SCM, 1991.

———. "Is 'Pluralistic Theology' Useful for the Dialogue of World Religions?" In *Christian Uniqueness Reconsidered: The Myth of a Pluralistic Theology of Religions*, edited by Gavin D'Costa. 131–144. New York: Orbis Books, 1990.

———. "Natural Theology." In *Experiences in Theology*, 67–74 Minneapolis: Fortress, 2000.

———. "The Mission of the Spirit: The Gospel of Life." In *Mission: An Invitation to God's Future*, edited by Timothy Yates, 118–139. Sheffield: Cliff College Press, 2000.

———. "The Spirit Gives Life: Spirituality and Vitality." In *All Together in One Place: Theological Papers from the Brighton Conference on World Evangelization*, edited by Harold D. Hunter and Peter D. Hocken, 249–267. Sheffield: Sheffield Academic, 1993.

———. *The Spirit of Life: A Universal Affirmation*. Translated by Margaret Kohl. Minneapolis: Fortress, 1992.

———. "Theological Proposals towards the Resolution of the Filioque Controversy." In *Spirit of God, Spirit of Christ: Ecumenical Reflections on the Filioque Controversy*, edited by Lukas Vischer, 164–173. Geneva: WCC, 1981.

———. *The Trinity and the Kingdom: The Doctrine of God*. Translated by Margaret Kohl. Minneapolis: Fortress 1981.

Samartha, S. J. "Basic Beliefs and Practices of Village Religion in South India." *Religion and Society* 8, no. 2 (1961): 7–20.

———. *Between Two Cultures: Ecumenical Ministry in a Pluralist World*. Geneva: WCC, 1996.

_____. "Commitment and Tolerance in a Pluralist Society." *NCC Review* 106, no. 2 (February 1986): 71–77.

_____. *Courage for Dialogue: Ecumenical Issues in Inter-Religious Relationships*. Geneva: WCC, 1981.

_____. "Dialogue as a Quest for New Relationships." *Journal of the Chair in Christianity* 1, no. 1 (November 1989): 46–60.

_____. "Dialogue: Significant Issues in the Continuing Debate." *The Ecumenical Review* 24, no. 3 (July 1972): 327–340.

_____. "Globalization and Its Cultural Consequences: A Theological Response." In *Ethical Issues in the Struggles for Justice: Quest for Pluriform Communities*, edited by Daniel Chetti and M. P. Joseph, 251–270. Tiruvalla: Christava Sahitya Samiti, 1998.

_____. "Guidelines on Dialogue." *The Ecumenical Review* 31, no. 2 (April 1979): 155–162.

_____. *The Hindu View of History: Classical and Modern*. Bangalore: CISRS, 1959.

_____. "The Holy Spirit and People of Other Faiths." *The Ecumenical Review* 42 (July–October 1990): 250–263.

_____. "The Holy Spirit and People of Various Faiths, Cultures, and Ideologies." Lecture given at the Oxford Institute of Methodist Studies, Lincoln College, Oxford, July 1973.

_____. "In Search of a Revised Christology: A Response to Paul Knitter." *Current Dialogue* 21 (December 1991): 32–35.

_____. "Indian Realities and the Wholeness of Christ." *Missiology* 10, no. 3 (July 1982): 301–317.

_____. *The Lordship of Jesus Christ and Religious Pluralism*. Madras: CLS, 1981.

_____. "Major Issues in the Hindu-Christian Dialogue in India Today." In *Inter-Religious Dialogue*, edited by Herbert J. Singh, 145–169. Bangalore: CISRS, 1967.

_____. *My Neighbour's Faith – and Mine*. Geneva: WCC, 1986.

_____. *One Christ – Many Religions*. New York: Orbis Books, 1991.

_____. *The Other Side of the River*. Madras: CLS, 1983.

_____. "Partners in Community: Some Reflections on Hindu-Christian Relations Today." *Occasional Bulletin of Missionary Research* 4, no. 2 (April 1980): 78–82.

_____. *The Pilgrim Christ: Sermons, Poems, Bible Studies*. Bangalore: Asian Trading Corporation, 1994.

_____. "The Promise of the Spirit." In *The Pilgrim Christ: Sermons, Poems, Bible Studies*, by S. J. Samartha, 70–79. Bangalore: Asian Trading Corporation, 1994.

_____. "Redeeming the Creation." In *The Pilgrim Christ: Sermons, Poems, Bible Studies*, by S. J. Samartha, 81–90. Bangalore: Asian Trading Corporation, 1994.

———. "Religion, Culture and Power." In *The Pilgrim Christ: Sermons, Poems, Bible Studies*, by S. J. Samartha, 91–101. Bangalore: Asian Trading Corporation, 1994.

———. "Theologies of Religion and Theologies of Liberation: A Search for Relationship." *Journal of Dharma* 21, no. 2 (April–June 1996): 188–197.

———. "Vision and Reality: Reflections on the Church of South India, 1947–1997." *Lexington Theological* 33 no. 1 (1998), 47–60.

———. Letter. Cf. Robert J. Schreiter, "Response to 'The Lordship of Jesus Christ and Religious Pluralism.'" In *The Lordship of Jesus Christ and Religious Pluralism*, by S. J. Samartha, 37–42.

Vivekananda, Swami. *Bhakti-Yoga: The Yoga of Love and Devotion*. Calcutta: Advaita Ashrama, 1964.

———. *Caste, Culture and Socialism*. Calcutta: Advaita Ashrama, 1947.

———. *The Complete Works of Swami Vivekananda*. 9 vols. Calcutta: Advaita Ashrama, 1997. www.ramakrishnavivekananda.info.

———. *The East and West in Defence of Hinduism*. Calcutta: Advaita Ashrama, 1968.

———. *Letters of Swami Vivekananda*. 4th ed. Calcutta: Advaita Ashrama, 1976.

———. *Life after Death*. Calcutta: Advaita Ashrama, 1968.

———. *Modern India*. Calcutta: Advaita Ashrama, 1971.

———. *My India: The India Eternal*. 1st ed. Calcutta: Ramakrishna Mission Institute of Culture. 1980.

———. *My Life and Mission*. Calcutta: Advaita Ashrama, 1971.

———. *Powers of the Mind*. Calcutta: Advaita Ashrama, 1970.

———. *Practical Vedanta and Other Lectures*. Calcutta: Advaita Ashrama, 2007.

———. *Raja Yoga: Conquering the Internal Nature*. Calcutta: Advaita Ashrama, 1986.

———. *Realisation and Its Methods*. Calcutta: Advaita Ashrama, 1971.

———. *Religion of Love*. Calcutta: Udbodhan Office, 1922.

———. *Salvation and Service*. Calcutta: Advaita Ashrama, 1998.

———. *The Science and Philosophy of Religion*. Calcutta:. Udbodhan Office, 1931

———. *The Science and Philosophy of Religion: A Comparative Study of Sankhya, Vedanta and Other Systems of Thought*. Calcutta: Udbodhan Office, 1908.

———. *Six Lessons on Raja Yoga*. Calcutta: Udbodhan Office, 1969.

———. *Speeches and Writings of Swami Vivekananda*. Madras: G. A. Natesan & Co. 1899.

———. "Swami Vivekananda 1863–1902." *Prospects* 33, no. 2 (June 2003): 231–245.

———. *Thoughts on Vedanta*. Calcutta: Udbodhan Office, 1964.

———. *Vedanta Philosophy Inspired Talks*. Calcutta: Udbodhan Office, 1909.

———. *Vedanta: Voice of Freedom*. Edited by Swami Chetanananda. St. Louis: Vedanta Society of St. Louis, 1991.
———. *Work and Its Secret*. Calcutta: Advaita Ashrama, 1968.

Secondary Sources: Books

Appasamy, A. J. *Christianity as Bhakti Marga: A Study of the Johannine Doctrine of Love*. Madras: Christian Literature Society, 1926.
Avis, Paul, ed. *Divine Revelation*. London: Darton, Longman & Todd, 1997.
Bhajanananda, Swami. *Harmony of Religions: From the Standpoint of Sri Ramakrishna and Swami Vivekananda*. Calcutta: Ramakrishna Mission Institute of Culture, 2008.
Boyd, Robin H. S. An Introduction to *Indian Christian Theology*. Delhi: ISPCK, 1989.
———. *Khristadvaita: A Theology for India*. Madras: CLS, 1977.
Brueggemann, Walter, and Tod Linafelt. *An Introduction to the Old Testament*. 2nd ed. Louisville: Westminster John Knox, 2003.
Chacko, Laji. *Introduction to Christian Theologies in India*. West Bengal: SCEPTRE, 2014.
Chakkarai, V. *Jesus the Avatar*. Madras: CLS, 1926.
Cooke, Bernard. *Power and the Spirit of God: Toward an Experience-Based Pneumatology*. New York: Oxford University Press, 2008.
Coward, Harold. *Sin and Salvation in the World Religions: A Short Introduction*. Oxford: Oneworld, 2003.
Dabney, D. Lyle. "The Nature of the Spirit: Creation as a Premonition of God." In *Starting with the Spirit,* edited by Stephen Pickard and Gordon Preece, 33–52. Adelaide: ATF, 2001.
Das Gupta, R. K. *Swami Vivekananda's Vedantic Socialism*. Calcutta: Ramakrishna Mission Institute of Culture, 1995.
Déchanet, J. M. *Christian Yoga*. London: Burns & Oates, 1964.
Deissmann, A. *The Religion of Jesus and the Faith of Paul*. London: Hodder & Stoughton, 1923.
Dunn, James D. G. *Jesus and the Spirit*: A study of the religious and charismatic experience of Jesus and the first Christians as reflected in the New Testament. Philadelphia: Westminster Press, 1975.
Erickson, Millard J. *Christian Theology*. Grand Rapids: Baker Books House, 1990.
Fernando, Ajith. *Sharing the Truth in Love: How to Relate to People of Other Faith*. Grand Rapids: Discovery House, 2001.
Fruchtenbaum, Arnold G. *The Book of Genesis*. San Antonio: Ariel Ministries, 2008.

Gambhirananda, Swami. *Holy Mother: Sri Sarada Devi.* Chennai: Sri Ramakrishna Math, 1955.

Gandhi, M. K. *The Essence of Hinduism.* Edited by V. B. Kher. Ahmedabad: Navajivan Publishing House, 1987.

Giri, Swami Nirmalananda. *Om Yoga: Its Theory and Practice.* Calcutta: Atma Jyoti Press, 2006.

Griffith-Dickson, Gwen. "Religious Experience." In *The Routledge Companion to Philosophy of Religion*, edited by Chad Meister and Paul Copan, 561–571. London: Routledge, 2007.

Hardy, Alister. *The Spiritual Nature of Man.* Oxford: Clarendon, 1979.

Hocking, W. E. *The Coming World Civilization.* New York: Harper, 1956.

Hugel, F. von. *Essays and Addresses on the Philosophy of Religion.* 2nd Ed. New York: Dutton, 1926.

Ignatius IV (Patriarch of Antioch). *The Resurrection and the Modern Man.* Translated by Stephen Bingham. New York: St. Vladimir's Seminary Press, 1985.

Jathanna, O. V. *The Decisiveness of the Christ-Event and the Universality of Christianity in a World of Religious Plurality.* Bern: Peter Lang, 1981.

Johnson, Elizabeth. *Quest for the Living God: Mapping Frontiers in the Theology of God.* New York: Continuum, 2007.

Johnson, Luke Timothy. *Scripture and Discernment: Decision Making in the Church.* Nashville: Abingdon, 1996.

Johnston, Robert K. *God's Wider Presence: Reconsidering General Revelation.* Grand Rapids: Baker Academic, 2014.

Joseph, P. V. *Indian Interpretation of the Holy Spirit.* Delhi: ISPCK, 2007.

Karkkainen, Veli-Matti, Kirsteen Kim, and Amos Yong, eds. *Interdisciplinary and Religio-Cultural Discourses on a Spirit-Filled World: Loosing the Spirits*, New York: Palgrave Macmillan, 2013.

Katz, Steven T. "Language, Epistemology, and Mysticism." In *Mysticism and Philosophical Analysis*, edited by Steven T. Katz. London: Sheldon, 1978.

Klootwijk, Eeuwout. *Commitment and Openness: The Interreligious Dialogue and Theology of Religions in the Work of Stanley J. Samartha.* Zoetermeer: Uitgeverij Boekencentrum, 1992.

Klostermaier, Klaus K. *A Survey of Hinduism.* Albany: State University of New York Press, 2007.

Lalruatkima. *Understanding Christian Faith.* Calcutta: SCEPTRE, 2013.

Lewis, G. R., and B. A. Demarest. *Integrative Theology: Spirit-Given Life: God's People Present and Future.* Vol. 3. Grand Rapids: Zondervan, 1987.

Lewis, H. D. "Worship and Idolatry." In *Contemporary British Philosophy*, edited by H. D. Lewis, 139–152. London: George Allen & Unwin, 1976.

Lokeswarananda, Swami. *Swami Vivekananda: The Friend of All*. Calcutta: Ramakrishna Mission Institute of Culture, 1991.

Maldonado, Guillermo. *The Glory of God: Experience a Supernatural Encounter with His Presence*. New Kensington: Whitaker House, 2012.

Mantzaridis, Georgios I. *The Deification of Man: St. Gregory Palamas and the Orthodox Tradition*. Translated by Liadain Sherrard. New York: St. Vladimir's Seminary Press, 1984.

Marbaniang, Domenic. *Theology of Revelation in the Bible and the Writings of 19th and 20th Century Theologians*. (n.p.: n.p) 2007.

Martin, C. B. *Religious Belief*. Ithaca: Cornell University Press, 1959.

Newbigin, Lesslie. *The Light Has Come: An Exposition of the Fourth Gospel*. Edinburgh: Handsel, 1982.

Otto, Rudolf. *The Idea of the Holy*. Translated by John W. Harvey. London: Oxford University Press, 1958.

Panikkar, Raimundo. *The Inter-religious Dialogue*. New York: Paulist Press, 1999.

Pinnock, Clark. H. *Flame of Love: A Theology of the Holy Spirit*. Downers Grove: InterVarsity Press, 1996.

———. *A Wideness in God's Mercy: The Finality of Jesus Christ in a World of Religions*. Grand Rapids: Zondervan, 1992.

Radhakrishnan, S. *An Idealistic View of Life*. London: George Allen & Unwin, 1932.

Rankin, Marianne. *An Introduction to Religious and Spiritual Experience*. London: Continuum, 2008.

Rogers, Gaikwad. "Reconceptualizing Religion, Dialogue, Theology and Mission in Pluralistic Society: The Contribution of S. J. Samartha." In *Interfaith Relations after One Hundred Years: Christian Mission among Other Faiths*, edited by Marina Ngursangzeli Behera, 147–164. Oxford: Regnum, 2011.

Sharma, Jyotirmaya. *A Restatement of Religion: Swami Vivekananda and the Making of Hindu Nationalism*. New Haven: Yale University Press, 2013.

Sherry, Patrick. *Spirit and Beauty: An Introduction to Theological Aesthetics*. London: SCM, 2002.

Slavicek, Louise, Chipley. *Mother Teresa: Caring for the World's Poor*. New York: Chelsea House, 2007.

Smart, Ninian. *The Religious Experience of Mankind*. 3rd ed. New York: Scribner's Sons, 1984.

Stephen, M. *A Christian Theology in the Indian Context*. Delhi: ISPCK, 2001.

Stephen, Abraham. *The Social Philosophy of Swami Vivekananda: Its Relevance to Modern India*. Delhi: ISPCK, 2005.

Sumithra, Sunand. *Christian Theologies from an Indian Perspective*. Bangalore: Theological Book Trust, 1990.

Tapasyananda, Swami. *The Philosophical and Religious Lectures of Swami Vivekananda*. Calcutta: Advaita Ashrama, 1999.

Tennent, Timothy C. *Building Christianity on Indian Foundations: The Legacy of Brahmabandhaba Upadhyay*. Delhi: ISPCK, 2000.

Thangasamy, D. A., ed. *The Theology of Chenchiah: With Selections from His Writings*. Bangalore: CISRS, 1966.

Thomas, M. M. *The Acknowledged Christ of the Indian Renaissance*. Bangalore: CISRS, 1970.

———. *Risking Christ for Christ's Sake*. Geneva: WCC, 1987.

Venkataraman, Babu Immanuel. "Acts." In *South Asia Bible Commentary*, edited by Brian Wintle, 1451–1509. India: Open Door Publications, 2015.

Yale, John, ed. *What Religion Is in the Words of Swami Vivekananda*. London: Phoenix House, 1963.

Yong, Amos. *Beyond the Impasse*. Grand Rapids: Baker, 2003.

———. *Discerning the Spirit(s): A Pentecostal-Charismatic Contribution to Christian Theology of Religions*. Sheffield: Sheffield Academic, 2000.

Articles

Appasamy, A. J. "Bhakti in the Bhagavad Gita." *The Pilgrim* 7, no. 3 (October 1947): 57–68.

Boyd, Robin H. S. "The Philosophical Context of Indian Christian Theology with Special Reference to P. Chenchiah." In *Indian Voices in Today's Theological Debate*, edited by Horst Burkle and Wolfgang M. W. Roth. Lucknow: Lucknow Publishing House with Delhi and Madras: ISPCK & CLS (1972): 47–69.

Charles, J. Daryl. "Engaging the (Neo) Pagan Mind: Paul's Encounter with Athenian Culture as a Model for Cultural Apologetics (Acts 17:16–34)." *Trinity Journal* 16 (1995): 47–62.

Crowe, Frederick E. "Son of God, Holy Spirit, and World Religions." In *Appropriating the Lonergan Idea*, edited by Michael Vertin, 324–343. Toronto: University of Toronto Press, 1996.

Das, R. C. "A Modern Apologetics for Hinduism." *The Pilgrim* 3, no. 1 (1943): 15–24.

DeCelles, Charles. "The Holy Spirit, Unbound In Her Saving Work." *In The Spirit of the Lord is Upon Me: The Holy Spirit in the Old and New Testaments*, edited by William J. Larkin Jr. and Jo Ann H. Larkin, 115–130. Grand Rapids: Eerdmans, 1996.

Diehl, David W. "Evangelicalism and General Revelation: An Unfinished Agenda." *Journal of the Evangelical Theological Society* 30 (1987), 441–455.

Gabriel, Andrew K. "The Intensity of the Spirit in a Spirit-Filled World: Spirit Baptism, Subsequence, and the Spirit of Creation." *Pneuma* 34 (2012): 365–382.

Jathanna, O. V. "Memorial Service for Dr. S. J. Samartha, St. Mark's Cathedral." *Indian Journal of Theology* 43, nos. 1 & 2 (2001): 84–86.

Jipp, Joshua W. "Paul's Areopagus Speech of Acts 17:16–34 as Both Critique and Propaganda." *Journal of Biblical Literature* 131, no. 3 (2012): 567–588.

Johnston, Robert K. "Discerning the Spirit in Culture." *Ex Auditu* 23 (2007): 52–69.

Karkkainen, Veli-Matti. "The Working of the Spirit of God in Creation and in the People of God: The Pneumatology of Wolfhart Pannenberg." *Pneuma* 26, no. 1 (2004): 17–35.

Mehltretter, Sara Ann. "Dorothy Day, Union Square Speech (6 November 1965)." *Voices of Democracy* 1 (2006): 165–186.

Oleska, Michael J. "The Holy Spirit's Action in Human Society: An Orthodox Perspective." In *The Holy Spirit and the Christian Life: Theological Perspectives*, edited by Veli-Matti Kärkkäinen, 105–124. Grand Rapids, MI: Eerdmans, 2008.

Oudtshoorn, Andre van. "Taking a New Look at General Revelation." *Australian eJournal of Theology* 21, no. 3 (December /2014): 1–18.

Reddy, P. Sreenivasulu. "A Critical Analysis of 'The Hindu View of Life' by Dr. Sarvepalli Radhakrishnan." *Online International Interdisciplinary Research Journal* 4, no. 2 (March–April 2014): 337–339.

Sooklal, Anil. "The Neo-Vedanta Philosophy of Swami Vivekananda." *Nidan* 5, (1993), 47–64.

Yitik, Ali Ihsan. "Swami Vivekananda's Idea of Religious Diversity and Harmony." *Journal of Religious Culture* 49 (2001): 47–61.

Yong, Amos. "The Turn to Pneumatology in Christian Theology of Religions: Conduit or Detour?" *Journal of Ecumenical Studies* 35, nos. 3–4 (Summer–Fall 1998): 417–432.

Won, Yong Ji. "The Work of the Holy Spirit and the Charismatic Movements, from Luther's Perspective." *Journal of Theological Studies,* vol. 15, no. 2 (2022): 145–163.

Others

Speeches and Writings of Swami Vivekananda: A Comprehensive Collection with Four Portraits. Madras: Natesan & Co., n.d.

Appasamy, A. J. "Christological Reconstruction and Ramanuja's Philosophy." *International Review of Mission* 42 (1952): 170–176.

Dahle, Lars. "Acts 17:16–34: An Apologetic Model Then and Now?" *Tyndale Bulletin* 53, no. 2 (2002): 313–316.

Daniel, J. T. K. "Understanding of the Work of the Holy Spirit in India." *Andover Newton Review* Serampore College, Hooghly.

Das, R. C. *Autobiographical Reflections*. Unpublished typescript of handwritten manuscript (1976): 118–128.

Dein, Simon. "Religious Experience: Perspectives and Research Paradigms." *World Cultural Psychiatry Research Review* 6, no. 1 (2011): 3–9.

Dhavamony, Mariasusai. "Indian Christian Theology." In *Theology of the Church and the World,* edited by Joseph A. Bracken and Stephen B. Bevans, 65–78. Maryknoll, NY: Orbis Books, 1997.

Dunham, Robert E. "Acts 17:16–34." *Interpretation* 60, no. 2 (April 2006): 202–204.

Hayes, Richard P. "Reflections on September 11, 1893." (10 August 2003), 1–8.

Howard, Daniel "A Critical Analysis of General Revelation." *Criswell Theological Review* 8, no. 1 (Fall 2010).

Immanuel. "Review: The Influence of Hinduism on Indian Christians." *The Pilgrim* 9, no. 4 (December 1950): 24–25.

James, William. The Varieties of Religious Experience: A Study in Human Nature. New York: Longmans, Green, and Co., 1902.

Johnson, Keith Edward. "A 'Trinitarian' Theology of Religions? An Augustinian Assessment of Several Recent Proposals." PhD diss., Duke University, 2007.

Jones, Constance A., and James D. Ryan. *Encyclopedia of Hinduism*. New York: Facts On File, 2007.

Jones, Lindsay, ed. *Encyclopedia of Religion*. 2nd ed. Detroit : Thomson/Gale, 2005.

Kalathil, C. J. "Review: The Development of the Gita Concept of God." *The Pilgrim* 10, no. 1 (March 1951): 23–25.

Knitter, Paul. "Stanley Samartha's One Christ – Many Religions – Plaudits and Problems." *Current Dialogue* 21 (December 1991): 28–29.

Lacewing, Michael. "The Argument from Religious Experience." *In Philosophy of Religion: A Guide and Anthology,* edited by Brian Davies, 452–460, London: Routledge: Taylor & Francis Group, 2017.

Manohar, Christina. *Spirit Christology An Indian Christian Perspective*. Delhi: ISPCK, 2009.

Manohar, Christina. "Spirit Christology: An Indian Christian Perspective." PhD diss., University of Gloucestershire, 2007.

Parker, Christian. "The Holy Spirit in the Arts: A Pneumatological Now-and-Not-Yet Approach to Beauty." *Colloquium* 46, no. 2 (2014): 207–223.

Popiolek, Piotr. "Evolution of Matter and Spirit, Rediscovering Slowacki's Mysticism and Teilhard de Chardin's Theology." In *Analecta Husserliana: The Yearbook of Phenomenological Research* Volume CXVII, edited by Anna-Teresa Tymieniecka, 169–181. Bridgewater: The World Phenomenology Institute, 2014.

Prabhananda, Swami. "Swami Vivekananda 1863–1903." *Prospects* 33, no. 2 (June 2003): 231–245.

Selected Bibliography

Prabhavananda, Swami. "Review: Vedic Religion and Philosophy." *The Pilgrim* 10, no. 1 (March 1951): 17–18.

Raj, Victor. "Text and Context of Indian Christian Theology." *Theology Today*, vol. 50, no. 3 (1998): 123–134.

Rajagukguk, Nimrot. "A Critical Analysis of Stanley J. Samartha's Concept of Christian Dialogue with People of Other Living Faiths, and its Relevance to the Indonesian Context." PhD diss., University of the Western Cape, February 2011.

Rodhe, David. "Review: Deliver Us from Evil: Studies on the Vedic Idea of Salvation." *The Pilgrim* 10, no. 1 (March 1951): 14–15.

Sagane, N. K. "Review: Ramana Maharishi: The Mystic Sage of Arunachalam." *The Pilgrim* 10, no. 1 (March 1951): 33–34.

Samartha, S. J. "This is Eternal Life." In *Understanding Salvation*, edited by John Doe, 123–145. New York: Oxford University Press, 2001.

Schneiders, Sandra M. "Spirituality in the Academy." *Theological Studies* 50 (1989): 676–697.

Schwarz, Hans. "Reflections on the Work of the Spirit outside the Church." *Niue Zeitschrift fur Systematische Theologie and Religions philosophie* 23, no. 1 (1981): 197–211.

WCC draft report. Quoted in *God's Wider Presence: Reconsidering General Revelation*, by Robert K. Johnston, 147–149. Grand Rapids: Baker Academic, 2014.

Langham Literature, with its publishing work, is a ministry of Langham Partnership.

Langham Partnership is a global fellowship working in pursuit of the vision God entrusted to its founder John Stott –

to facilitate the growth of the church in maturity and Christ-likeness through raising the standards of biblical preaching and teaching.

Our vision is to see churches in the Majority World equipped for mission and growing to maturity in Christ through the ministry of pastors and leaders who believe, teach and live by the word of God.

Our mission is to strengthen the ministry of the word of God through:
- nurturing national movements for biblical preaching
- fostering the creation and distribution of evangelical literature
- enhancing evangelical theological education

especially in countries where churches are under-resourced.

Our ministry

Langham Preaching partners with national leaders to nurture indigenous biblical preaching movements for pastors and lay preachers all around the world. With the support of a team of trainers from many countries, a multi-level programme of seminars provides practical training, and is followed by a programme for training local facilitators. Local preachers' groups and national and regional networks ensure continuity and ongoing development, seeking to build vigorous movements committed to Bible exposition.

Langham Literature provides Majority World preachers, scholars and seminary libraries with evangelical books and electronic resources through publishing and distribution, grants and discounts. The programme also fosters the creation of indigenous evangelical books in many languages, through writer's grants, strengthening local evangelical publishing houses, and investment in major regional literature projects, such as one volume Bible commentaries like the Africa Bible Commentary and the South Asia Bible Commentary.

Langham Scholars provides financial support for evangelical doctoral students from the Majority World so that, when they return home, they may train pastors and other Christian leaders with sound, biblical and theological teaching. This programme equips those who equip others. Langham Scholars also works in partnership with Majority World seminaries in strengthening evangelical theological education. A growing number of Langham Scholars study in high quality doctoral programmes in the Majority World itself. As well as teaching the next generation of pastors, graduated Langham Scholars exercise significant influence through their writing and leadership.

To learn more about Langham Partnership and the work we do visit langham.org

www.ingramcontent.com/pod-product-compliance
Lightning Source LLC
Chambersburg PA
CBHW070806230426

43665CB00017B/2501